William Prynne

## The Unbishoping of Timothy and Titus

and of the Angel of the Church of Ephesus - or, A brief elaborate discourse, proving

Timothy and the Angel to be no first, sole, or diocaesan bishop of Ephesus, nor

Titus of Crete

William Prynne

**The Unbishoping of Timothy and Titus**
and of the Angel of the Church of Ephesus - or, A brief elaborate discourse, proving Timothy
and the Angel to be no first, sole, or diocaesan bishop of Ephesus, nor Titus of Crete

ISBN/EAN: 9783337815400

Printed in Europe, USA, Canada, Australia, Japan

Cover: Foto ©Lupo / pixelio.de

More available books at **www.hansebooks.com**

# THE UNBISHOPING OF
# TIMOTHY AND TITUS,
### AND OF THE
## *Angel of the Church of* EPHESUS:
### OR,

A brief elaborate *Discourse*, proving *Timothy* and the ANGEL to be no first, sole, or Diocæsan Bishop of *Ephesus*, nor *Titus* of *Crete*; and that the power of Ordination, or *imposition of hands*, belongs *Jure Divino* to Presbyters, as well as to *Bishops*, and not to Bishops only, as Bishops; who by *Divine Institution* are evidenced to be one and the same with *Presbyters*, and *many over one City, Church*, not *one over many Cities or Churches.*

Wherein all Objections, Pretences to the contrary are fully answered; and the pretended *Superiority* of Bishops over other Ministers and Presbyters, and their sole *right of Ordination Jure Divino*, (now much contended for) are utterly subverted in a most perspicuous manner.

By WILLIAM PRYNNE Esquire, Bencher of *Lincolns Inne*; a Well-wisher to Gods truth, the *Kings* just Prerogative, the Peoples Liberties, and the Churches Peace.

Matth. 15. 13.
*Every plant which my heavenly Father hath not planted, shall be rooted out.*
Chrysostom. Opus imperfectum in Matth. Hom. 35.
*Quicunque desideraverit Primatum in terra, inveniet in Cælo confusionem; ut jam inter servos Christi, non sit de Primatu certamen.*

First Compiled, Printed in the year 1636. Reprinted for publike good and satisfaction, Anno 1660. And are to be sold by *Edward Thomas* at the *Adam* and *Eve* in *Little Britain*.

To the Right Reverend Fathers in God, *William* Lord Arch-bishop of *Canterbury*: And *Richard* Lord Arch-bishop of *York*, Primates and Metropolitans of all ENGLAND.

**M**Y *Lords*, I have sundry times heard both of you jointly and severally protesting even in open Court, not only in the \* *High Commission*, but in Dr. *Laytons*, and two other cases since, in the Starchamber (whether seriously or vauntingly only let the event determine;) *That if you could not prove your Episcopal Jurisdiction and function which you now claim and exercise over other Ministers, and your selves as you are Bishops, to be superior in power, dignity and degree to other Ministers*, Jure Divino (a Doctrine which (a) *Patrick* Adamson, *Arch-bishop of S. Andrews in Scotland, publickly recanted in the Synod of Fiffe, Anno* 1591. *as directly repugnant to, and having no foundation at all in the word of God,*) *You would forthwith cast away your Rochets off your backs, lay down your Bishopricks at his Majesties feet, and not continue Bishops one hour longer.* What your Lordships have so oft averted, and publikely promised before many witnesses, (I hope *bonâ fide*, because judicially in full

\* *In Master Thomas Brewers, Doctor Bastwicks, and sundry other cases since.*

a *An. Melvini Patricii Adamsoni Palinodia, printed Anno* 1630.

B           Court

## The Epistle Dedicatory.

Court upon good advise, not rashly on some sudden fit of choler,) I shall make bold, to challenge you to make good without more delay; either by giving a solid, satisfactory, speedy answer to this short *Treatise*, (consisting only of two *Questions*, which you may divide between you, and so speedily reply to, if your great (*b*) *secular occasions*, not *your praying*, and (*c*) *frequent preaching*, *which are truly Episcopal*, though you deem them over mean imployments for Archbishops, interrupt you not.) which manifests all that *Jus Divinum* which hitherto both or either your Lordships have pretended for your Episcopalities, to be but a meer absurd ridiculous fiction, having not the least shadow of Scripture to support it; or in case you either cannot or fail to give such an Answer to it in convenient time; by pulling off your Rochets, and resigning up your Archbishopricks (which without all question are but a meer humane and no divine Institution, as I have evidenced:) into his Majesties hands, (*d*) *from whom, you dare not deny, you onely and wholly received them, with all your Episcopal Jurisdiction and Authority thereunto annexed*, whereby you difference your selves from, or advance your selves above your Fellow-Ministers, as their supream Lords, unless you will split your selves against the hard rock of a Præmunire, and the Statutes of 26. *H*. 8. c. 1. 31. *H*. 8. c. 9. 10. 37. *H*.8. c. 17. 1 Ed. 6. c. 2. 1 *Eliz*. c. 1. 5. *Eliz*. c. 1. 8. *Eliz*. c. 1. which Acts as they will inform your Lordships, notwithstanding all your former vaunts and brags of divine right, *That the Archbishops, Bishops, Arch-deacons, and other Ecclesiasticall persons of this Realm,* HAVE NO MANNER OF JURISDICTION ECCLESIASTICAL, BUT BY, UNDER AND FROM THE KINGS ROYAL MAJESTY; *to whom by holy Scripture* ALL AUTHORITY AND POWER IS WHOLY GIVEN, *to hear and determine all manner of causes Ecclesiasticall, and to correct vice and sin whatsoever, and to all such persons as his * Majesty shall appoint thereunto: That all authority and Jurisdiction spiritual and temporal is derived and deducted from the Kings Majesty, as supream head of the Church and Realm of* England; *and so justly acknowledged by the Cleargy thereof:*

---

b *See Master Tyndals Obedience of a Christian man. And the holy Practise of Popish Prelates.*
c 1 Tim. 1, 2, 3.
2 Tim. 4. 1. to 5
Tit. 1. and 2.
1 Pet. 5. 2. 3.

d 31. H. 8. c. 9.
37. H. 8. c. 17.
1. E. 6. c. 1. and all the Bishops Patents for their consecration and Cong. desires.

* *Not Archbishops or Bishops, who can make no Chancellours, Vicar-generals Commissaries or Officials, unless the King by his special Patent give them power so to do in express words, as these Statutes evidence, and the Bishops Patents in Ed. the 6. Reign.*

*thereof*: *That all Courts Ecclesiasticall within the Realm were then* (and now ought to be, though they are not) *kept by no other power or authority either forreign or within the Realm, but by the authority of his most excellent Majesty only; and that by vertue of some special Commission or Letters Patents under his Majesties great Seal, and in his name and right alone: That all power of Visitation of the Ecclesiastical State and Persons* (much more then of our Universities exempt from Archiepiscopal and Episcopall Jurisdiction) *is united and annexed as a royal prerogative to the Kings Imperial Crown, and to be executed by none but by Patents under him: And that all your Citations, process, Excommunications, Probates of Wills, Commissions of Administration, &c. ought to be made only in his Majesties name, and sealed with his Seal, as they were in* * King Henry the eight, and King Edwards days, witness the Bishops Registers, Process and Probates of Wils in their two Reigns (and now are in your High Commission) *that so both the Courts and process might be* † *known to be his Majesties by leaving his Image, stile and superscription ingraven on them, and to be derived unto you, not by any divine right, but by his Princely grace alone, who hath as absolute an Ecclesiastical Jurisdiction, as any of his Royal Progenitors enjoyed, both by the Laws of God and* (a) *of the Realm*: So they will inforce your Lordships to acknowledge, (unless you will renounce your Allegiance to your most gracious Soveraign, whose meer grace hath advanced you to what you now are and enjoy) that all your Episcopal Jurisdiction, whereby you are distinguished from, or elevated above any ordinary Presbyters and Ministers, is not from any divine Charter or Commission from Christ, but * *onely in, by, from, and under his Majesty*; and so not *Jure Divino*, as you have thus frequently cracked and boasted to the world; so as you must either now forthwith renounce your Bishopricks according to your Protestations, or else be guilty of breach of promise; unless you can prove you enjoy them only by a divine right, and yet only in, by, from, and *are meer usurpers on his Majesties Crown and Ecclesiasticall Prerogative, in keeping Consistories, Visitations, and Exercising Episcopal Jurisdiction in their own names, without any Patent or Commission from the King.*

* See a Breviate of the Bishops intolerable Usurpations on the Kings Prerogative Royal Subjects liberties. Printed.
† Mat. 22. 20. 21. Sir John Davis his Irish Reports. p. 97. 98 a. 26. Hen. 8. c. 1. 37. H. 8. c. 17. 1 Ed. 6. c. 2. 1 Eliz. c. 1. 5. Eliz. c. 1. 8. Eliz. c. 1.

* In case they have any Charters or Commission under his Majesties Seal. which all of them now want, and so

## The Epistle Dedicatory.

under his Majesty, as *Supream head and Governour upon earth of the Church of England*, which is a contradiction.

If your Lordships, to maintain your divine pretended Episcopall Jurisdiction shall flie to (b) *Doctor John Pocklington* for ay'd, who (by † one of your *Domestick Chaplains* approbation) hath lately published in print, *That you by Gods mercy to our Church, are able lineally to set down your Succession in your Episcopall dignity, from St. Peters Chair at Rome, to S. Gregory, and from him, from our first Archbishop S. Augustine* (though we had some (d) *Archbishops before his coming*, if our Historians truly inform us) our *English Apostle* (as the *Papists would have him* ſt led ; though * *Bishop* Jewel, (f) Fox, and (g) others, renounce him) *downward to his Grave that now sits in his Chair, Primate and Metropolitan of all England*. I shall then desire your Lordships and this Doctor to prove, and resolve these questions.

First, Whether S. *Peter* was a real Bishop by Divine Institution?

Secondly, Whether he was ever a real Bishop of *Rome?* of which this *Doctor* is so impatient, that he breaks out into (h) these passionate words well worthy your Episcopall Censure: *Whereby their vanity may appear, that upon idle ghesses against all antiquity, make fools beleev:* that S. *Peter was* (k) *never at Rome; making the Succession of Bishops and truth of the Latine Churches, a: questionable as the Centurists orders.*

Thirdly, Whether *Peter* was * sole Bishop of *Rome*, or rather *Paul* also Bishop as well as he, yea both of them joint Bishops of *Rome* at the same time, and that by divine Institution *? If so, thence it will follow, that there ought to be † two Bishops of *Rome* (and so of *Canterbury*) at the same time, not one alone, or two several persons at least to constitute one Bishop.

Fourthly, Whether it will follow from *Peters* being Bishop of *Rome*, *Jure Divino*, that the Arch-bishops of *Canterbury*

---

b *Sunday no Sabbath*, p. 2. & 24.
† W. Bray.
d See Antiquit. Eccles. Brit. Godwins Conversion of Brittanie. Bishop Usher de Brittan: Ecclesiarum Primordiis. with others, who write of King Lucius, and Speedes History, book 6. p. 73. to 8:.
* *Defence of the Apolog. part* 5. c. 1. Divis. 1. *Reply to Harding.* Artic. 1. Divis. 14.
f *Acts and Monuments* vol. 2. p. 95. to 120.
g Speed. Hist. l. 6. c. 9.
h Page 42.
† See *Quest*. Object. 6. Answ. 2. and most of our learned writers who have affirmed, that Peter was never

at Rome, much less Bishop there, upon such grounds as this Doctor cannot answer k Epiphanins, Contr. Hæreses l. 1. Hæ: 27. Col. 88. 89. Eusebius Eccles. Hist. l. 3. c. 21. Iræneus L 3. c. 3, 4, 5. *write that both of them were Bishops of Rome at once, and not Peter the sole Bishop and Eusebius puts Paul in the first place before* Peter.

and

## The Epistle Dedicatory.

and *York* must necessarily be Archbishops *jure Divino*? since all Protestants deny his pretended Successors of *Rome* to be so?

Fifthly, Whether if this Doctrine be true, this Proposition can be denied; that your Lordships being lineally descended from the Church and Popes of *Rome* as Arch-bishops, are both the true and genuine sons and members of these two ghostly Parents? If you deny this inference, then you must renounce this divine Title to your Prelacies; if you subscribe unto it (as I presume you dare not) then all his Majesties subjects (who have in their (m) oaths of allegiance and supremacy, renounced all forraign Jurisdictions with the Bishops and Church of Rome abandoned by * several Acts of Parliament,) must renounce both you, and this your Episcopal Jurisdiction too, thus claimed: which since you can no ways substantially prove to be *Jure Divino*, I hope you will now lay down your Bishopricks, according to promise, (that his Majesty may enjoy their Temporalities) or else be thought never worthy faith or credit more in future time:

m 28 H 8.e. 10.1. El z.c.1.
* See Rastall, Tit. Rome. 3 Jac.c.4.

Neither may the seeming strangeness of the thing it self, deter you from it, this being no new thing amongst us, for Bishops not onely to refuse, but to resign and give over their Bishopricks. For which I shall present you with variety of presidents; It is recorded of * *Ammonius*, that when the Cleargy and people Elected him for their Bishop, and urged him to take a Bishoprick upon him, he fled away secretly and cut off his right ear, that the deformity of his body might be a Canonicall impediment to his election; and being yet deemed meet to be a Bishop by Tymotheus the Patriarke, though his Nose and his ears had been both cut off, by reason of his great learning and vertues; and the people drawing him against his will to accept that office, he replyed, that he would likewise cut off his tongue too, which pleased them, unless they would let him go & not make him a Bishop. † *Euagrius* the Philosopher, when he was constrained to accept a Bishoprick by Theophilus Alexandrinus, renounced his Ministry rather then he would accept it, such a dangerous office did he then repute it, and many good men else; who as *Nicephorus* records, refused anciently to accept thereof, though nothing so dangerous and pernicious an office then, as now. *Nicephorus* * *Blemides*, be-

* Socr.Scholast. l.4.c.18. in the greek 23. Niceph. Eccl. Hist. l.11.c.37. Petrus Blesensis Epist. 23.
† S crat. Eccl. Hist. l.4.c.18. Nieph.l.11.c, 37. c
* Niephori Gregoræ Hist. Rom.l.3.c.1.2. f. 9. Cent. Magd.13. Col. 982.

B 3 ing

## The Epistle Dedicatory.

*ing elected Patriarch of* Constantinople, *absolutely refused to accept it upon any terms:* (u) Werinbaldus *unanimously elected Bishop of* Spaires, *could by no means be induced to embrace it.* * Theophilus, *Archdeacon of* Adaina, *being chosen Bishop of that See, refused to receive it, and being forced both by the Ministers and people to take it against his Will, relinquished it shortly after though in an idle manner.* * Clement, *the first Pope of* Rome, *Pope* Cornelius, Ambrose, Augustine, Athanasius, Gregory Nazianzen *his father, Pope* Gregory *the first,* Alexander *Patriarch of* Jerusalem, Anatolius *Bishop of* Laodicea, Eustathius, *Bishop of* Antioch, Antiochus, Theophilus Alexandrinus, Dioscorus, Chrysanthus, *S.* Martin *Bishop of* Towers, *S.* Nicholas, Paulinus *of* Nola, Eusebius Pamphilus, Flavianus *of* Antioch, Marchus, *in ancient times were all inforced to accept of their Bishopricks full sore against their wills and judgements, by the overpressing importunity of other Bishops, Princes, Ministers and the people.* With others quoted to my hands by [a] Claudius Espencæus: [b] Euchericus *Bishop of* Lions, *and* Otto, *Bishop of* Bamburge, *were enforced in the same manner to be Bishops, very much against their liking*, as was [c] Cranmer *Arch-bishop of* Canterbury. [d] Ephræm Syrus, Nilammon, *and S.* Bernard, *all constantly refused divers great and wealthy Bishopricks, not onely offered to, but urged on them, with much importunity;* so [e] Adrian *refused the Archbishoprick of* Canterbury, though called to it, and urged to accept it: Bassianus *elected Bishop of the* Vangensi, [f] *furious* Memnon *whipped him before the Altar for three hours space, till he bedewed the Altar and new Testament with his blood, because he refused to accept that Episcopal charge and office.* [g] Bruno Signinas *rejected a Bishoprick offered to him*, saying. *A Bishoprick must be altogether forsaken of that man who would not be set at Christs left hand;* ( answerable whereunto is that [h] *of Pope* Marcellus *the* 2. *who smiting his hand upon the Table*, used these words: *I do not see how those that possess this high place can be saved.* [i] John Bugenhagius, *of late times repudiated the Bishoprick of* Csmine *in* Pomerland, *to which he was freely chosen.* From these and other Examples, most Bishops at their respective Ordinations though they greedily post and hunt after Bishopricks, and oft times purchase them

*by*

---

u Trithemius, Cent. Magd. 10. Col. 599.
* Cent. Magd. 6. Col. 644.

* Platina and others in their lives.

a Digref. lib. 3. in 1 Tim. c. 4. 5. 6. 7.
b Cent. Magd. 3. Col. 1335. Cent. 10. Col. 1541: see Cent. 13. Col. 1698.
c Fox Acts & Monuments, p. 1703.
d Espenceus Digref. in 1 Tim. l. 3. c. 4. 5, 6, 7.
e Godwins Catalo. p. 51.
f Cencur. Mag. 3. Col. 1043.
g Cent. 10. c. 10. in his life.
h Onuphrius and others in his life.
i Chytræus Chron. Saxoniz. l. 1. p. 10.

## The Epistle Dedicatory. 7

by Symoniacall contracts, more for their rich lordly Temporalities and Pallaces, then the Spiritual Offices which God requires at their hands; to wit in diligent, frequent preching of the Gospel, Administration of the Sacraments, fasting, almes and prayer, do yet for custome and fashion sake when they are to be ordained with an hypocritical modesty, and a doubled * *Nolo Nolo* to this Interogation, *Vis, Episcopary?* seem utterly to refuse the Office as dangerous to undertake, till pressed to accept it by a third demand, to which they gave their *Volo, Volo*.

* See Pontif. Romanum.

For Bishops renouncing their Bishopricks; you may find *Basilides* a Bishop in *Spain*, who about 230. years after Christ falling into heresie and blasphemy, and then into sicknes, confessed his sins, and voluntarily surrendred his Bishoprick out of conscience: *Episcopatum pro conscientia sua vulnere sponte deponens*, whereupon the people elected another in his place: So b *Gregory Nazienzen*, *Hierax*, *John* Bishop of *Antioch* out of *conscience, and for quietness sake*, renounced and repudiated their Bishopricks, betaking themselves to a more retired private life, wherein they might serve God better: To these I shall adde the memorable presidents of † *Arsenius*, *Germanus*, *Paulus Cyprius*, *Josephus*, *Becus*, *Gregorius Cyprius*, *Athanasius*, *John*, *Joannes Glicis*, *Antonius Studites*, *Cosmas* and *Theodosius*, all Patriarcks of *Constantinople*: as likewise of * *Gildenutus* Bishop of *Malden*, *Ulfranius* Bishop of *Senines* *Arnulph* Bishop of *Mets*, *Ado* Bishop of *Lyons*, *Victerbus* Bishop of *Ratisbon*, *Herigerus* Bishop of *Meniz*, *Michael* Bishop of *Ephesus*, *Adelbertus* Bishop of *Wirtenburg*. *Michael Opises* Patriarch of *Athens*, *Desiderius* Bishop of *Flaunders*, *Bruno* the third, Bishop of *Colen*; *Ulricus* the second Bishop of *Constance*, *Walther* Bishop of *Augusta*, *Gerbardus* Bishop *Herbipolis*, *Ulricus* Bishop of *Rhesia*, *Brincingus* Bishop of *Hildesheim*, *Conrade* the second Bishop of *Lubeck*. ⨥ *dum* Bishop of *Morini* in *Flaunders*, *Christianus* the second Bishop of *Marche*, *Sebetho* Bishop of *Augusta*. *Everhardus* Bishop of

a Cyprian Epist. 68. de Pemelii.
b Oratio ad 150. Episcopos Sonat. Ecclesiast. Hist. l. 5. c. 7. Vita ejus operibus prefixa
c Isidor. Pelusiots. l. 3. Epist. 223.
d Nicephaus. Eccl. Hist. l. 10. c. 11.
† Nic ph. Greg. Hist. Rom. l. 4. 2. 1 f. 12. 13. 14. l. 5. fol. .6. l. 6. f. 20, 21, 22. ¹4. l. 7. f. 29. l. 8. f. 31. Cent. Magd 8. Col 669.
672. Cent. 11. Col. 516. 518.
Cent. 12. Col. 1384.
Cent. 13. Col. 932. 983.

* *Vincentius* Spec. Hist. l. 24. c. 25. Cent. Magd. 7 Col. 5 2. 507. 508. Cent. 8. Col. 763. 786. Cent. 10. Col. 586. Cent. 11. Col. 515. 576. Cent. 82. Col. 1387. 1458. 1468. 1484. 1486. 1491. 1519. 1530. 1544. Cent. 13. Col. 1042. 1052. 1057. 1062. 1078. 1092. 1093. 1694. 1102. 1146.

*Rheemes,*

## The Epistle Dedicatory.

<sup>*</sup> *Omprius, Patina, others in his life.*

*l Cent. Magd.*
*5. col. 998.*
*1035. 1056.*
*Cent. 7. Col.*
*456. Cent. 8.*
*col. 807. cent.*
*10. col. 558.*
*cent. 11. col.*
*515. 546. 547.*
*cent. 12. col.*
*1447. 1458.*
*cent. 13. col.*
*1039. 1097.*
*1072.*
*Crankii Metropol.*

*Rhemes*, *Ulricus* Bishop of *Salsburg*, *Conradus* Bishop of *Hieldesheim*, *Conradus* Bishop of *Halberstat*, *Ludolphus* Bishop of the same See, *Gunterus* Bishop of *Magdeburge*? *Josias Odolphus*, Archbishop of *Vpsal* in *Swethland*. * Pope *Celestine* the fifth <sup>1</sup> *Athanasius* Bishop of the *Pareni*, *Eustathius* Bishop of *Pamphilia*, *Rusticus* Bishop of *Narbon*, *Remoclus* Bishop of *Utrech*, *Orgerus* Bishop of *Spires*, *Lambert* Bishop of *Florence*, *Lutulphus* Bishop of *Challars*, *Hugh* Bishop of *Towres*, *Burchardus* Bishop of *Wertzberge*, *Michael Ephesinus* Bishop of *Antioch*, *Desiderius* Bishop of the *Morini*, *Geoffry* Bishop of *Sylvanecta*, *Conrade* Bishop of *Batavia*, *Albertus Magnus* Bishop of *Ratisbone*, of ancient times: With *Lewis ab Eperstein*, *Bartholomew Suavenius*, and *John Frederick* Bishops of *Camene* in *Pomerland*, *Isaurus* Archbishop of *Riga*, *Baldaser* Bishop of *Suerin*, *Ericus*, *John* Duke of *Saxony*, and *Otto* Bishops of *Hildesheim*, *Hugh* the 47th. Bishop of *Constans*, *Frederick a Weda* and *Salentine* Archbishops of *Colen*, *Augustus* Bishop of *Meriburge*, *Jodocus* a Reke Bishop of *Derbet*, *Francis*, *Henry* and *Julius* Bishops of *Minda*, *Theodosius* a *Rheden* Bishop of *Lubeck*, *Christopher* Bishop of *Raceburge*, *Christopher* Bishop of *Breme*, of later times beyond the Seas, with sundry other Patriarcks, Archbishops and Bishops, *many of them by reason of age or sickness, others out of discontent, others out of a desire of peace, quietness, and ease from unnecessary cares, and troubles; others of them meerly out of conscience of the unlawfulness, danger, hurt, and sins accompanying the very office of Bishops as then it is, and yet is used;* have voluntarily renounced, resigned, relinquished, their Patriarkships, Archbishopricks, Bishopricks, and betook themselves to a more retired, religious, quiet, private, godly life, wherein they might serve God better, and shun those manifold occasions of evil and temptations, their Bishopricks would expose them unto; to the hazard of their Souls.

*If these many forraign examples, will no ways move your Lordships to give over your Bishopricks, as seeming over strange we have many pregnant Domestique presidents of like nature, which may perswade you to make good your promise, and induce you to an imitation of them.*

For

## The Epistle Dedicatory. 9

For I find that * *Robert Gemetlensis*, S. *Edmund Boniface*, *Symon Langham* and *Robert Kilwarby*, Archbishops of *Canterbury*; *Richard Beaveyes*, and *William de sancta Maria*, Bishops of *London*, *John Bokingham*, and *Philip Ripingdon*, Bishops of *Lincoln*, *Richard Pecke*, *Winefred* and *Roger de Wesekam*, Bishops of *Coventry* and *Lichfield*, *Hermane* Bishop of *Sherborn*, *Shaxtone*, Bishop of *Salisbury*, *William Warwest*, *John Voysy*, and *Miles Coverdale* (who being deprived in Queen *Maries* time, cared not to return to his Bishoprick in Queen *Elizabeths*, setling himself in *London*, and there leading a private life as an ordinary Minister) Bishops of *Exeter*; *John Carpenter* and Master *Hugh Latimer*, Bishops of *Wercester* (the later of whom † skipped for joy when he had cast off his Rochet, for that he was eased of so heavy a burthen, and blessed God that he had given him grace to make himself a *Quondam* Bishop; ) *Ralfe de Maydeston*, and *Thomas Spofford* Bishops of *Hereford*. *Putta Quickhelmus*, and *Haymo* Bishops of *Rochester*, ( the first of them becoming a Schoolmaster, spent the residue of his dayes in that kind of life, and could never abide to hear of returning to his Bishoprick; ) *Daniel* the six, and *Frithstane* the 23d. Bishops of *Winchester*, *Robert Sheborne* Bishop of *Chichester*, *Dubricius* Bishop of *Carleon*, *Sulghein*, Bishop of S. *Davids*, *John Hunden* Bishop of *Landaff*, *Cadueanus* Bishop of *Bangor*, *Geofry* and *Elguensis* Bishops of *S. Asaph*, *Colman*, S. *Cuthbert*, *Egelric* and *Nicholas de Furnham*, Bishops of *Lindesfarne* and *Durham*, (the later of whom first of all twise refused, and then at last resigned his Bishoprick out of conscience) *Paulinus de Leedes* (who peremptorily refused out of conscience to accept the Bishoprick of *Carlile*, though thereunto elected, and earnestly intreated by King *Henry* the second to accept the place, who offered him 300. Marks yearly revenue for the increase of his living there, as did *Sylvester de Everdon* refuse for a time to) *Walter Malclerk* Bishop of *Carlile* ; *Cedda*, *Cœna* alias *Albert*, *John*, *Athelwold*, *Thurstan*, *William Wickwane* Archbishops of *York*, who all voluntarily, (most out of *conscience, some out of choller, others for their ease, some for their age, others for other causes, best known to themselves) resigned these their respective Archbishopricks and Bishopricks, being so many domestick

* Godwins
Catalogue
of Bishops
of London.
1615. p. 70.
113: 118.
120. 188.
192. 219.
305. 306.
313. 314.
318. 313.
336. 353
397. 413.
414. 437.
538. 446.
447. 448.
456. 450.
477. 487.
504. 508.
532. 536.
543. 559.
564. 565.
567: 581.
585 596.
625. 631.
932. 635.
636. 654.
655. 675.
676.
† Fox Acts
and Monuments, p.
1578. and 4.
Sermons before King
Edward.
* As did Cœlarus, 2 Bishop
of Lichfield,
Mat.West. Æ.
656.

C pre

## The Epistle Dedicatory.

presidents to your Lordships (who have long since given over the main part of your Episcopal function, preaching,) now to do the like, according to your joint and several Promises, in case you cannot prove your Archiepiscopal and Episcopal Jurisdictions Jure Divino, and give a satisfactory Answer to these few pages, which I presume you can never do, since not onely <sup>t</sup> *Hierom*, <sup>u</sup> *Ambrose*, <sup>x</sup> *Chrysostom*, <sup>y</sup> *Augustine*, <sup>z</sup> *Sedulius, Remigius, Primasius, Theodoret, Haymo, Beda, Rabanus Maurus, Theophilact,* <sup>a</sup> *Isiodor Hispalensis,* <sup>b</sup> *Alcuvinus,* <sup>c</sup> *Oecumenius,* <sup>d</sup> *Gratian,* the
" Councils of *Carthage* 4 Can. 22. to 26. of *Aquisgran* c. 8. 10.
" 11. <sup>e</sup> *Juo Carntensis*, <sup>f</sup> *Peter Lombard*, <sup>g</sup> *Bruno* and <sup>h</sup> other an-
" cients, but even *Anselm* Archbishop of *Canterbury*, *Richard*
" Archbishop of *Ardmagh*, all the Archbishops, Bishops and
" Cleargy of *England* in 37. H. 8. in their Institution of a Chri-
" stian man, Chapter of Orders, subscribed with all their names,
" *Stokesly* Bishop of *London*, *Tonstall* Bishop of *Durham*, *Re-*
" *ginald Peacock*, Bishop of *Chichester*, *Bishop Hooper*, Bishop
" *Latimer*, Bishop *Jewel*, Bishop *Alley*, but even Archbishop
" *Whitgift* himself, and Bishop *Bridges*, to omit *Wickliff*, *Swin-*
" *derby*, *Walter Brute*, Sir *John Oldcastle*, Master *John Lambert*,
" Master *John Bradford*, and other our Martyrs, Master *Tho-*
" *mas Beacon*, Master *John Fox*, Mister *Alexander Nowel*, Doctor
" *Whitaker*, Doctor Humfry, Doctor *Willet*, Doctor *Ayray*,
" Doctor *Taylor*, Doctor *Ames*, Doctor *Raynolds*, Doctor
" *Fulke*, and others in * their authorized writings Printed here
" in *England*, *cum privilegio* and publick allowance; with the
" forecited Statutes of our Realm, and all the Bishops Patents in
" the Raign of King *Edward* the sixt, *in express terms,* conclude
" your Archiepiscopal, and Episcopal Jurisdiction too, over other
" Ministers, to be a meer humane invention long after the Apo-
" stles time, to prevent, (or *rather as the event hath ever since*
" *proved, to engender, foment, and occasion)* all schismes, factions,
" errors and disorders in the Church; when as <sup>k</sup> Christ himself,

<sup>t</sup> Epist. 2. 83. 85. in Tit. 1. Phil. 1. and 1. Tim. 3.
<sup>u</sup> In Eph. 4. and 1. Tim. 3.
<sup>x</sup> Hom. 1. in Phil. 1. Hom. 11. in 1 Tim. 3. Hom. 2. in Tit. 1.
<sup>y</sup> Ep. 19. 83. 85. Quaest. ex xtroq; mixtim. 100. 101.
<sup>z</sup> In Phil. 1. 1 Tit. 1. 5. 7. 1. Tim. c. 3. & 4. Acts 15. & 10. 17. 18
<sup>a</sup> Ori. l. 7. c. 12. l. 8. Eccl. Officiis. l. 2. c. 7.
<sup>b</sup> De divinis efficiis l. 2. c. 35. 36.
<sup>c</sup> In Acts 15 & 20. 1 Tim. 3. Phil. 1. 1 Tit. 1. 5. 7
<sup>d</sup> Distinct. 80. 93. Causa. 2. Qu. 7.

<sup>e</sup> Decretal. pars 5. c. 58. 59. 72. 107. 143. 144. <sup>f</sup> Sent. l. 4. Distinct. 14. <sup>g</sup> In Phil. 1. Tit. 1. & 1 Tim. 3. <sup>h</sup> Amalarius Fortunatus de Ecclef. Officiis, l. 2. c. 13. Basilius Magnus, in c. 3. Isa. Nazienzen. Orat. 9 13. 15. 21. 18. * Quoted by Gersomus Bucerus, the Petition to Queen Elizabeth. Master Parker, and Doctor Bastwicks Flagellum & Apologia. <sup>k</sup> Math. 20. 20. to 29. Marc. 10. 35. to 48. Luke 22. 23. to 28.

and

## The Epistle Dedicatory.

and ¹ his Apostles since, ordained a Parity, an equality both among his Apostles and Ministers, (whom all these assert to be one and the same with Bishops in order and degree, by divine right) and ever instituted many Bishops over every particular Church, but never any one Bishop or Minister over many, as the best means to preserve unity, and root out schisms, occasioned only by the pride, ambition, covetousness, power and Tyranny of domineering Prelates and Clergy-men.

Thus craving pardon for my boldness in pressing your Lordships like two honest plain dealing-men, to make good your words, that so we may once again become fellow-brethren, and walk hand in hand together like equals, without that infinite Lordly distance, which is now between, not only your Lordships and ordinary Ministers, but the chiefest Nobility, Judges, Justices and Gentry of this Realm, (now slighted, awed, vilified, oppressed by your Lordly power:) I take my leave and rest

*l* 1 Pet. 5. 1. to 6. Acts 14. 23. c. 20. 17. 28. Phil. 1. 1. Tit. 1. 5. 7. 1. Tim. 3. &c. c. 5. 17. c. 4. 14. Jam. 5. 14.
m *See Bishop Jewels Defence of the Apologie part. 2. c. 3. Divis. 5 an excellent place for this purpose.*

*Your Lordships faithful Monitor*

**W. P.**

# A Brief EXHORTATION

To the Arch-Bishops and Bishops of *England*, in respect of the present Pestilence. *Anno Dom.* 1636.

<small>
a *BishopWhites Title to his Treatise of the Sabbath day.*
b *Math.* 23.8,9, 10,11. c.20.25. 26.
*Jam.*3.1.
1 *Pet.*5.3.
c 1 *Jo.*2.15,16. 17.
*Jo.*17.14,15,16
*Mat.*6.14.
2 *Tim.*4.10.
*Si mundum prædicas contemnendum, contemne tu prius.* Bernard Serm. in Concil. Rhemensi.
</small>

MY LORDS, (for so you stile [a] *your selves*, and will be intituled by all men, notwithstanding the [b] *Lords own inhibition to the contrary,*) the Prophet *Isay.* c. 26.9. hath informed me, *That when Gods Judgments are on the Earth, the Inhabitants of the World will learn righteousness*: and who knows whither your Lordships, (as properly *inhabitants*, if not servants and lovers too, *of the World*, as any of whatever profession, *though you* [c] *should not be so*) may not now in this time of Pestilence, when Gods Judgments are every where so rife among us, *learn righteousness* as well as others, (if you think not your selves too wise to learn, and too old to be instructed) if any man will but take the pains to teach you.

Hearken therefore, I beseech you, as you tender either the preservation of your lives, in this time of mortality, or the salvation of your souls in the great day of Judgement, or the lives and souls of His Majesties Subjects, committed to your Charge, to a short Lecture (no ways overburthensome to your memories,) which I shall here read unto you for your good, if you

please

## The Epistle Dedicatory.

please either so to interpret it, or come with a sincere conscience for to hear it. It may be that in regard of your sacred Episcopal Order, you conceit your selves altogether *plague-free*, and as wholly exempt from *divine*, as you now strive to be from *temporal Jurisdiction*; (which makes you neither to dread the plague, which hath seized upon * *sundry Kings and laid them in the dust*,) nor as yet any way to endeavour by fasting and prayer, to prevent either it, or that famine likely to accompany it. But to instruct you how you are still but men (and so exposed to all those mortal sicknesses which continually assault the crazy fortresses of our *earthly Tabernacles*, *Non obstante* your Rochets, Miters, Crosiers, and all other your Episcopal harness,) give me leave in a word or two to acquaint you, That † *Pelagius the second* (though a Pope, and *Bishop of Rome*) notwithstanding his pontifical Robes, Exorcisms, Pompe, and Charms, *was both seized upon and devoured of this impartial disease*, An. Dom 591. as *Platina, Onuphrius, Anastasius, Stella, Fasciculus Temporum, Balæus, Luitprandius, Vstelius*, and others testifie in his life: which Plague (as (e) *Petrus Blesensis Archdeacon of Bath* records) *was sent by God as a just Judgment upon the Romans and Italians, for giving themselves to drinking, feasting*, DAUNCING, *sports and pastimes, even on Easter day and other following Holy days, after their participation of the blessed Sacrament of Christs body and blood* (many of them being consumed and dying of the Plague, in the very midst of their sports, mirth, ales and pastimes) and on this Pope himself, for not restraining them from this prophaneness: A president which should make your Lordships fear and tremble, this present *Plague* beginning here on Easter week last, as that Plague then did, no doubt for the self-same prophanation of Gods own day and Sacraments, with those abuses, sports, pastimes, sins, for which they then were plagued; which your Lordships have not only not restrained, but countenanced, patronized, yea propagated all you could, this Pope going not so far, that * *Cautinus* Bishop of *Avernium*, *Cato* his Successor in the same See, *Rupertus* Bishop of *Triers*, *Hermannus* Bishop of *Verdunum*, *Rainold* Bishop of *Colen*, *Conrade* Bishop of *Augusta*, *Walricus* Bishop of *Spiers*, *Ruggerus* Bishop of *Herbipolis*, and *Sigfridus* of the same, *Eberhardus* Bishop

* Theodos. second a. percur ar. dry Kings, *Kinredus* C. (whom Plat. in the life c. Pop: *Constantine* Reco. is to have been died ed of the Plague at *Rome*) with many others, Kings have died of the Plague.
d 2 *Cor.* 5.1.
† *Math. Westminster* An. 591 p. 231.
e *Sermo* 20. in *Letania Majori.*
1 *Cor.* 11.

* *Cent.Magd.6. Col.7. 31. Ibid. 137. Cent. 10. Col.575.Cent.11 Col.1454. Ibid. 1466.Ibid.1488 Ibid.1489.Cent 12. Col. 1492. and 1493. Col. 1512 1533.*

*shop of* Ratisbon, Gerion *Bishop of* Halberstat; *all dyed of the plague.* * *In the great Plague that happened in the Emperour* Frederick Barbarossa *his army in* Italy, *many German Prelates and some German Princes which came with him, died of the Pestilence,* neither their confecration, nor their function being any antidote against this disease. In the great *Councill of Basil: Anno* 1431. (to name no more forraign examples) Lodovicus *Patriarch of* Aquileia, *the Bishops of* Ebron, Lubeck, Constance, *and others, died of the Plague;* Æneas Silvius *himself (afterwards Pope) being there stricken with this disease, whereof he lay three days together at the point of death, all men despairing of his life, but yet by Gods help he escaped.*

If any of your Lordships should think these forraign Presidents prove not, that any English Prelates are obnoxious to the self-same disease; to rectify this mistake, I shall present you with some domestick examples, worthy your most serious confideration. ᵍ *Anno Dom.* 664. *on the* 26. *day of* October, Cedadda *the second Bishop of* Litchfield, *with all the Monkes of his Monasterie at* Lestinghen, *were taken away with the Plague.* The very next year following (h) *Anno* 665. Tuda, *or* Juba *the fourth Bishop of* Durham *dyed of the Pestilence.* Wigardus *Arch-Bishop of* Canterbury *Elect. the same year, with most of his Followers died at* Rome *of the Plague.* (i) *Anno* 1258. Fulco Basset *the* 45. *Bishop of* London, *was smitten to death with the same fatal disease.* (k) Michael Northbrooke *his Successor the* 57. *Bishop of* London, *Anno* 1361. *perished of the Plague; and the same year,* Reginald Brian *Bishop of* St. Davids, *being translated to* Ely, *deceased of the Plague before his translation could be perfected.* * Thomas Bradwarden *Arch-Bishop of* Canterbury, *anno* 1348. *dyed of the same disease.* And to cite no * more in so plain a case. (l) *Anno* 1500. Thomas Langhton *Bishop of* Winchester, *then Arch-Bishop of* Canterbury *elect but not enstalled, and* Thomas Rotheram *Arch-Bishop of* York, *were both in the self same year swept away together with this pestilential disease.*

These several Presidents, with those of (a) Pope Lucius *the* second, *and* Pope Celestine *the* second, *both taken away by the Plague within the compass of two years.* The Bishops of Parma, Rhegium,

* *Grimstons Imperial History p.* 490.

f *Fox Acts and Monuments, p.* 652.

g Mat. Westm. Godwins Catalogue of English Bishops *pag.* 183.
h Godwin Antiq.Ecclef.Brit. p. 13.
Godw. p. 53. 629.
i Godwin ibid. p. 195.
k Godwin ibid. p. 198. 414. * See Grafton. p. 123
l Godwin ibid. p. 164.244.617. Antiquit Ecclef.Brit.p. 345.

a Stella Platina, Fasciculus temporum Centur. Mag. 12. Col. 1407.

## The Epistle Dedicatory. 15

*b* Rhegium, *and* Millain. Anno 1085. (*c*) Daniel *the* 13. *Bishop of* Prague. Anno 1116. *the Bishop of* Marselles, *and all his Church, anno* 1348. *who all dyed of the Pestilence,* to omit others, may be a good Memento and Monition to your Lordships (being Bishops and Arch-bishops) to put you in mind, both of your mortality in general (which most fear you seldom seriously consider of, being so over-much taken up with * *secular imployments, not compatible with your spiritual functions,*) and that you, though Bishops, are subject to this disease and stroke of God as well as others, or these your Predecessors: and therefore should now at length, after so many weeks delay, endeavour to appease Gods wrath, and cease this Plague begun among us, (which every day spreads it self more and more) by publick fastings, prayer, preaching and humiliation, *the chief remedy,* not only (*m*) *prescribed in Scripture by God himself,* but likewise *by the whole Church and State of* England *in the two last great plagues both in* 1. *Jacobi, and in the first year of our present Soveraignes raigne, as the several Books of Common prayer and order of fasting, then published by these noble Princes special commands,* yet testifie on record *: both of these books joyntly confessing and bewayling, that among other sins occasioning these two dreadful man-eating Pests,* this was not the least; *That the* † SABBATH DAY *was not kept holy, but prophaned; and therefore no wonder that these plagues break in upon us.*

*b Bertoldus Constantinensis ad Leromanum appendix. Anno* 1085. *p.* 357.
*c Georgius Pontanus. Bohemia pi.e. l.* 3. *p.* 34.
*d Alberti Argentinensis Chron. Anno* 1348. *p.* 147.

* *Nemo potest duobus Dominis servire, Deo & Mammonae. Si te curiae, & maximè saccarii labyrinthis immerseris, magna spiritualis exercitii dispendia paticris. Quid tibi Christus te ad* 

*ad Fiscales redditus ut, vel horula brevi curam posthabeas animarum? Nunquid* 
*Telonium elegit? Matthaeus semel inde sumptus, denuo ad ipsum non rediit. Non fis ergo in turba corum qui secularia spiritualibus anteponunt, glutientes, Camelum, licem liquantes,* &c. *Petrus Blesensis De Instit. Episc. Tractatus. m* Num. 6. 15. 6. Ioel 1. 14. 15. 16. c. 2, 12. 13. 14. Is. 22. 12. 13. 14. Zeph. 2. 1. 2. † 1 Iac. stiles it.

And may not your Lordships and the whole Kingdome justly fear, that this very sin of *Sabbath breaking,* and prophaning Gods own sacred day by SPORTS, WAKES, MAY-GAMES, DAUNCING, drunkenness, chambring, wantonness, idleness, travelling, unnecessary labour, and the like, *which drew on these two former plagues upon us,* hath been one main cause of this present Pest; which begins thus freshly

16    *The Epistle Dedicatory.*

† So the Book of the time and place of prayer, and against disobedience and wilfull rebellion pa t. 3. a *Sunday no Sabbath*, p.6. 20. 21. a *Hist. of the Sabbath* part. 2. c. 8.

b *Of the Time and Place of Prayer.* See *Sunday a Sabbath.*

c *Bishop* White, *Doctor* Heylin, *Doctor* Pocklington, *Doctor* Primrose, *Christopher Dow,* Edmund Reeve and others.

† Sect. 38. n.1. p.111. Digres. 46. Sect. 43. n. 6. p. 165 166. * *In quartum Præceptum.*

‡ *In Ioan.* c. 7. * *Institution of a Christian man,* and a *Necessary Erudition,* &c. Exposition on the fourth Commandment.

to destroy us? It being most apparent to our shame (and I fear to all our smart) that the Lords-day Sabbath (*for so our own* † *Homilies stiled it before the troubles of Frankfort,* 1544. *When Doctor Heylyn, or Doctor Poclington and Doctor Boundes Books, Anno* 1595. † *fables that the Lords day was first anabaptized a Sabbath day, and Christned with this name by some Jewish God-father, to overthrow the Liturgie and Discipline of the Church of* England; who yet gave it this Title long before these ignorant Doctors dream, both in (b) her *Homilies* and approved writers works,] hath of late been more generally, publikely, audaciously prophaned in most places of the Realm by the fore-named Pastimes, abuses and disorders, then before those two sweeping plagues, not only in point of practise, which is ill; but even in Point of Doctrine, which is worse; many late *authorized* c *Histories, Treatises, Discourses of the Sabbath,* not fearing publikely *to maintain the Lawfulness of dauncing, morrises, may-games, dedication-Feasts, Pastimes, Sports and ordinary labour even on Gods own day, as the Doctrine of the Church of* England: when as acute *Master* John Sprint, *in his Proposition for the Christian Sabbath day, Printed by License,* London, 1607. p.4 (newly reprinted) and learned *Doctor* John White *in his* † *way to the true Church five times Printed by Authority* (yea *set forth and defended by Doctor* Francis White, *now Bishop of* Ely) expresly brand it, *not only as a Popish and Heathenish practise; but likewise as a point of Popish Religion, which directly tends to the maintenance of open sin and liberty of life, and expresly allows most palpable wickedness, directly tending to the desolation of publike government and private honesty;* being that which hath made the *Papists the most notorious Sabbath breakers that live,* * Zanchius and † Musculus *also branding this very Doctrine of liberty they now teach and the practise of it, as Popish,* and all the *Bishops, Clergy, King, Lords, Commons, and Parliament of* England *in King* Henry *the eighth his Raign, condemning it in* * *two severall Books, as meerly Jewish;* to check the dotage of those *Novil Doctors,* who now stile *the strict Sanctification of the Lords day by abstinence from dauncing, sports, and pastimes, Judaizing;* when as that they plead for, is truly such.

This gross prophanation therefore of the Lords day both in

Doctrine

Doctrine and practise, y aggravated with the late suspending, silencing, excommunicating, pursevanting, vexing, persecuting, depriving, crushing of many learned, painful, godly, conscionable Ministers, both against all the Rules of Canon Law, Common Law, Statute Law, conscience, reason, piety, charity, justice, and the Presidents of all former ages, meerly for refusing out of conscience upon their Episcopal Mandates, to have any hand or finger in acting or proclaiming any thing which might animate their people to this pestiferous sin. ( punished within these three years with many memorable † particular judgments of God, immediately executed from Heaven; ) hath no doubt so far provoked our most gracious God, that now he can hold z off his hands no longer from smiting us, with his dreadful Judgments, which some of us have already felt, and most of us now fear: who questionless will never take off his Pests and Judgements, from us, till your Lordships shall take off your most unjust Suspensions and censures from those who have thus suffered in his quarrel, and all of us repented of this our crying sin of prophaning Gods own sacred day, both in point of Doctrine and practise: An abhomination never more rife in any, then this our present age, by reason of your Lordships patronizing, propagating and defending it, in such a publick, shameless, violent manner, as no former age can ever paralell, to Gods dishonour, your own eternal infamy, and the fitting of your selves, and this whole Kingdom for those publick judgements, not only of a late cold extraordinary winter, and two excessive dry Summers, which threaten a famine of bread to recompence that *a Famine of Gods word*, which you have lately caused, to omit all other miseries which we suffer,) but likewise of that plague which is now dispersed: In the pulling down whereof, as your Lordships have had, no doubt, a deeper hand then others, so you have great cause to fear, you shall feel the irresistable mortiferous stroke thereof, as much, or more then others. The Plague, you well know, *is Gods own Arrow*, Psal. 91. 5. *who ordaineth his Arrows against the Persecutors*. P. 1. 7. 13. And are not some at least of your Lordships such? *It is Gods own hand,* 2 Sam. 24. 14. 15. Jer. 21. 6. *Now Gods hand shall find out all his enemies, his right hand shall find out those*

y 2 Chron. 36. 15. 16. 17.  
1 Thes. 1. 14. 15. 16.

† See a divine Tragedy Lately acted.

z Jer. 20. 9.

a Amos 8. 11.

D          that

*that hate him*, Pſal 21, 8. And are not many of your Lordſhips in that number ? It is, *Gods own brandiſhed ſword*, Pſal. 8 6. And whom doth God *wound and ſlay therewith but the † head of his Enemies, and the hairy ſcalp of thoſe who go on ſtill in their treſpaſſes*? And are not too many of your Lordſhips ſuch; who even now in the very midſt of Gods judgements, proceed on ſtill in your malicious, violent, implacable hatred, enmities, perſecutions againſt Gods faithful Miniſters, Saints, and the very power of holineſs, in your Lordly Pomp, ambition, avarice, pride, envy, arrogance, cruelty, oppreſſions, injuſtice, luxury, ſecularity, ſuppreſſion of preaching, prayer, faſting, Communion of Saints, and whatever favours of piety ? in prophaning of Gods own ſacred day, both in your Doctrine and practiſe; which is ſeldom worſe ſolemniz'd, or more prophaned, as † Mr. *Bucer* long ſince obſerved, *Quàm in ipſis Epiſcoporum aulis, then in Biſhops own Pallaces*, where neither Lord, nor Chaplain, nor ſervants, make any great conſcience of prophning it ſundry ways, to give the better example of piety and holineſs unto others. How then (being heavy laden with theſe many ſins, and having the prayers, cries, clamors, tears, ſighes groans, of all Gods children againſt you, if not of the whole Kingdom too; the daily imprecations of many diſtreſſed Miniſters, people, (whom you have moſt injuriouſly and inhumanely handled without any lawfull cauſe,) can you but fear Gods vengeance and expect his plagues, to ſweep ſuch Clods of ſin and miſchief, ſuch Peſts and Prodigies as many of you are, clean away; ᵈ *Be Wiſe now therefore*, O ye Kings, (for ſuch are you now become by giving abſolute Lawes, and preſcribing what Ceremonies, Articles, Rites, Oaths, Novelties you pleaſe, even in your own names and rights alone, unto His Majeſties people, and executing all Lordly, Kingly Soveraignty and Dominion over * *mens bodies and eſtates as well as ſouls*, *contrary to our Lawes, and our Saviours expreſs Inhibition*, Math. 20 25. 26.) *be learned O ye Iudges of the earth:* (for ſuch are you now in many temporal Courts, as well as Eccleſiaſtical, and would be gladly ſuch in more, in ſteed of being *preaching Biſhops* in your *Pulpits*, and Paſtors of mens ſouls:) *Serve the Lord in fear* (for that is your duty, not to be Lords your ſelves, or reverence

† Pſal. 68.21.
Deut. 32.41.

† In Pſ. 92.

d Pſ. 2. 9. 11. 12.

* *Animabus Prelatus es, non corporibus commune eſt nihil Prælato, cum Pilato, Petrus Bleſenſis. Tract. de Inſtitut. Epiſcopi,* Joanni Wigornienſi Epiſc. dicatus.

## The Epistle Dedicatory.

renced and served with fear, as Lords are wont to be: ) *and rejoyce unto him,* (not with Organes, Choristers, Pipes and Daunces, but) *with trembling: kiss the son* (whom you have hitherto buffeted † *persecuted in his faithful Ministers and Servants*) *least he be angry, and ye perish in the way, even now when his wrath is kindled but a little,* and his plagues but newly kindled; lest if ye refuse to turn from all your former sins and wickednesses, he begin at *last to bruise you with this his rod of iron, and dash you in pieces like a Potters vessel,* * *and there be none to deliver you from this his raging fury.* Remember I beseech you that of the Prophet *Nahum*, ᵍ *God is jealous, and the Lord revengeth, the Lord revengeth, and is furious; the Lord will take vengeance on his adversaries, and he reserveth wrath for his enemies.* And though he hath for a long time (h) *suffered you with much patience* (as he doth other vessels of Wrath *fitted to destruction,*) to spoyle, oppress and deal treacherously with his people; yet consider now, that the times are drawing near, wherein you may be recompenced with the like usage, as the Prophet *Isaiah* threatens. † *Wo to thee that spoylist, and thou that wast not spoyled, and dealest treacherously, and they dealt not treacherously with thee: When thou shalt cease to spoil thou shalt be spoyled; and when thou shalt make an end to deal treacherously, they shall deal treacherously with thee* Wherefore my Lords (k) *break off your sins* and sinful proceedings by sincere and timely repentance, and of *Lyons, Bears,* † *Wolves Thieves, Robbers,* (which many Bishops have degenerated into) become * *Lambs and Shepheards to Gods people*; and now at last, (m) *as the Elect of God, holy and beloved, put on bowels of mercies kindness, humbleness of mind, meekness, long suffering forbearing and forgiving all those against whom you have any quarrel, even as Christ forgave you, so also do ye. And above all things, put on Charity, which is the bond of perfectness, and let the peace of God rule in your hearts, to which you are also called in one body; and let the word of God dwell richly in you, in all Wisedom, &c.* And if you will divert this Past either from you selves or others; then presently † *begin to turn to the Lord With all your hearts, with fasting weeping, and with mourning sanctify a fast, call a solemn assembly, gather the Elders,* &c.

*Acts 9.4.5.

* Psal. 7. 12

g Nahum 1. 2.
b Rom. 9. 22.
† Isai. 33. 1.
*Væ his qui prædilent hominibus, nisi iis prædicat Deus. Petrus Blesensis, de Instit. Episcopi Tractat.*
k Dan. 4. 27.
* Acts 20. 22.
Joh. 10. 1. 20.
*Frequens est inter episcopos aliquem invenire, qui primum suæ promotionis annum deducet sine iniquitate; cumque in sua novitate sit factus agnus, vertatur aliquo tempore in Leonem. Petrus Blesensis, Epist. 7. &.*
l Isai. 1. 27.
m Col. 3. 12. 13.
† Joel. 2. 12. 13. 14. 15. 14. 15. 16.

D 2

*The Epistle Dedicatory.*

(and not by proxy but in proper person, if ever you will either be reputed the Priests or Ministers of the Lord,) *Weep between the Porch and the Altar, and say, Spare thy people O Lord, & give not thine heritage to reproach. Alas for the day of the Lord is at hand, and as a destruction from the Almighty shall it come, and who shall escape it?* And that your fast may be acceptable, be ware that it be not * *a fast for strife and debate, to smite with the fist of wickedness, or to make your voice to be heard on high; beware least it be only a hanging down of your heads like a bull rush, and afflicting of your souls onely for a day: But let it be that true fast, which God hath chosen, to loose the bands of wickedness, to let the oppressed go free, to undo the heavy burthens* (which you have lately laid on Ministers and people) *and to break of every yoak;* (wherewith you like Lordly † Barons have clogged the Consciences, yea bodies, of Gods servants, and brought them into a miserable bondage and captivity under you, as if they were your vassals, not Brethren:) *to break your bread to the hungry, to bring the poor that are cast out,* (yea the poor Ministers and Christians you have most unchristianly cast out of their livings, houses and Gods house it self, and thrown into your nasty prisons, where they must still be detained when others are set free) *to your houses,* (yea to their own houses, livings, and Gods house again,) *to cloath the naked, to draw out your soul to the hungry, to satisfie the afflicted soul; to turn away your feet from doing your pleasure on Gods holy day; to call the Sabbath a delight, the holy of the Lord honourable; to honour God alone therein, not doing your own ways, nor finding your own pleasure, not speaking your own words.*

* Isa. 58. 4. 14.

† *Quidam Episcopi Regum munificentias & eleemosinas antiquorum, abusi e Baronias & Regalia vocant. Et in occasionem turpissimæ servitutis & seipsos Barones appellant, vereor ne de illis queruletur Dominus, & dicet. Ipsi regnaverunt & non ex me. Principes exstiterunt & ego non cognovi. scias te assumpsisse Pastoris officium non Baronis. Certe Ioseph in Ægypto Patrem suum & fratres instruxit, ne dicerent Pharaoni, viri Pastores sumus: Maluit eos profiteri Pastoris officium, quam Principis aut Baronis.* Petrus Blesensis *Tractat. De Instit. Episcopi.*

o Zeph. 2. 3.

p Jer. 5. 9.

If thus you now fast and do (o) *peradventure you may be spared in the day of the Lords great wrath, and God will make our health to spring forth speedily:* But if you forbear to do it, and proceed on as you have done, be sure (p) *that God will visit you for these things, and that his soul shall be avenged on such a*

*Nation*

Nation as you are, He will no doubt (q) bring evil upon you, which you shall not be able to escap, in this year both of yours and his visitation: in which as you have most strangely vsed others, thrusting many of Gods best and painfullest Ministers from their Ministry in sundry places, upon meer new fancies and Articles of your own, against all law and justice; so God the Supream Visor, will in his justice visit you, in one kinde or other, with his most righteous Judgments, and cut you off with his plagues, as he hath done your forecited predecessors, or with some other signal Judgments of like nature. This you have cause to fear, and seriously to expect, unless you forthwith become * *New Creatures*: Loe I have in few words admonished you; If you amend, there may be hope of mercy, if you continue what ye are, contemn all admonitious, † *striving still as you have done, against God, his truth and people, you shall be ashamed, confounded and perish you shall become as nothing, and as a thing of nought*: For God hath spoken it, and he (ſ) *will make it good*. (t) *The Transgressors shall be destroyed together, the end of the wicked shall be cut off. For yet a little while, and the wicked shall not be, thou shalt diligently consider their place, and it shall not be found*. (u) *Consider what I have written, and the Lord give you understanding in all things*.

q Jer. 11.11.23

* 2 Cor. 5

† Isa. 41.11.12

ſ Numb. 23.10

t Psa. 37.10.38

u 2 Tim. 2.7.

Farewell.

## W. P.

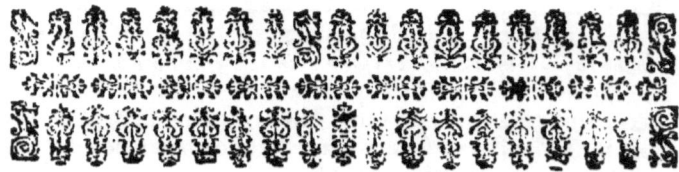

# To the Reader.

**C**Hristian Reader, what that Oracle of Wisedome hath registred; *Proverb.* 13. 10. *Onely by Pride cometh contention;* was never more really verified in any one particular, then in the Prelates: whose ambitious windy tumor, and overswelling pride, as in all former ages, so in this, hath (a) *filled the whole Christian world with warres, civil dissentions, and the Church it self, with endless schismes, controversies, contentions, which else would never had existence.* The pretended primacy of the great Pontifical Bishop of *Rome*, what tumults, battles, warres, treasons, rebellions, murders, martyrdomes, hath it ingendred on the one hand; what disputes, books of controversie, and paper-battles, on the other? What innumerable Schismes, Treatises (which the undoubted parity of Ministers and Bishops *Jure Divino* had prevented) have the Prelates pretended superiority by divine institution, over Presbyters and their fellow Ministers, produced in all ages, Churches, especially in our own; (from the first glimmerings of the Gospel in *John Wiclifes* dayes till now, more or less disquieted with this unhappy controversie?) which being raked up in ashes for a space, by reason of our Bishops waving of their divine right, which not

<small>a *See Platina & Anastasius de vitis Pontificum. Theotericus à Niem, Zabarel, & Joannis Marius de Schismate. Master Tyndals obedience of a Christian man; and practise of Popish Prelates. Doctor John White his Defence of the way, chapter the sixth, the fifth Homily against Disobedience and wilful rebellion. Fox Acts and Monuments throughout. Catalogus Testium Veritatis.*</small>

onely

*The Epistle Dedicatory.*

onely Arch Bishop (b) *Anselme*, (c) *Richardus Armachanus*, and (d) Bishop *Peacock* of old, but likewise (e) Bishop *Tonstal*, Bishop *Stokesly*, (f) Bishop *Hooper*, (g) Bishop *Jewell*, (h) Bishop *Alley*, (i) Bishop *Pilkington*, yea (Arch Bishop *Whitgift* himself, and (l) Bishop *Bridges*, our two late most learned Professors of Divinity, Doctor *John Reynolds* in his Letter to Sir *Francis Knowls* for *Oxford*; and Doctor * *William Whitaker* Regius Professor of Divinity for *Cambridge*, to omit all others, have since them publikely disclaimed; (confessing Bishops and Presbyters, Jure Divino to be all one, equal, and the same; *and the difference that is between them to be onely by custome, humane institution and the grant of Princes, not by divine right*; and the Statutes of 37. H. 8 c. 17. 1. E. 6 c 2. 1. & 2. *Mariæ c*. 8. & 1 *Elizab. c*. 1 have for ever judicially in full Parliament resolved again,t;) yet our present ambitious Prelates studying to surmount their predecessors, not onely in worldly pomp and power, derived from their indulgent Soveraign, but likewise in spiritual Jurisdiction, claimed from God himself, (though many of them have neither time nor care to preach, pray, or do him any Episcopal Service, being wholly taken up with secular offices, and affairs, and † *an oble to serve God for serving his incompatible enemies, Mammon, and the world,*) have lately blown abroad the coals, and resuscitated the violent flames of this contention afresh, by a new ambitious claim of all their Episcopal Soveraignity and Jurisdiction, *Jure Divino*, not only in their Sermons and Books, but even *in the High Commission Court it selfe*, in the late censure of Doctor *Bastwick*, for a Book written *onely against the Pope and Italian Bishops*, without any reflection upon them, as all men then conceived, and therefore wondred at; till their magnifying of the *Church of* (m) *Rome as a true Church in that Censure of his, and some late licensed Pamphlets*, their Antichristian Papal proceedings against Gods truth, Ministers, Ordinances, and the late authorizing of Doctor *Pocklingtons*

b Com. in Phil. 1. 1. in Tit. 1. 5. 7. in 1 Tim. 3. & 4.
c De Quest. Armenorum.
l. 11. c. r 108.
d Biæus Cent. 8. c. 19.
e Fox Acts Monuments, p. 572. 973.
f On the eighth Commandoment.
g Defence of the Apologie, part. 2. c 3. Divis. 1. 5. pag. 85. 99. 100. 101. & 9. Divis. 1 .p. 196. 262.
h Poor mans Library, part. 1. f. 95. 9.
i Exposition on Aggeus, vers. 1. & 2.
k Against Cartwright. p 38.
l Of the Princes Supremacy, p. 359.
* Contra Duraum, l. 6. sect. 1. Controu.
4 D. Ecclesiæ Regimine qu. 1. cap. 1. sect. 1. 2. cap. 2.

sect. 16. qu. 4. c. 3. sect. 25. 26. 27. 28. 29. 30. 31.  D. N. tis Eccl. Six. qu. 5. 1. l. p. 5-9.
Contr. 2. Concil. qu. 3. c. 2. p. 585. 587.  † Matth. 6. 24. Luc. 16. 13.  1 John 2. 15. 16.  m See Chownæus Collect. Theol. And Stelford's 5 Treatises.

*Sunday*

*n* Pag. 2.43.44. *Sunday no Sabbath*, by the Archbishop of Canterburies own Chaplain, Master Bray; which expresly avers, *That our Archbishops and Bishops can, and do lineally derive their pedegree and Succession from* Peter *and the Popes of* Rome; *hath since instructed the ignorant people, that* Popes, Italian *and English Bishops, are in truth* * *all members of the same body, Whelps of the same litter, branches of the same tree, and some of our present Prelates, the Pope o' Romes own lineally discended sons* ; so as they could not be sensible of, and highly offended, if not actually lashed, wounded with their fathers scourge; *Flagellum Pontificis & Episcoporum Latialium*, being a whip for them, as well as for the Italian Prelates.

* See Henry Stilbridge his Exhortatory Epistle. William Wraughton his Hunting of the Romish Fox.

Roderick Mors his *Complaint*, c. 23. Master Tyndals *his obedience of a Christian man, and Practise of Popish Prelates*. Fox *Acts and Monuments*, part 414. 514. 516. 518. Master Whethenhall his *Discourse of the Corruptions now in question with*, others.

Now because in that late Censure of theirs, they all founded the divine right of their Episcopal Super-intendency and Dominion over their Fellow-Presbyters, only on the Examples of *Timothy* and *Titus*, (whom they then new consecrated Diocælan Bishops over *Ephesus* and *Crete*, almost 1600 years after their decease, though *Christ* and *Paul* himself had never done it in their life times;) and on a supposed divine Monopoly of conferring *Orders* and imposing hands, appropriated (as they hold) by God himself, to Diocæfan Bishops, distinct in Jurisdiction power and degree from Ministers and Presbyters: I have therefore here for the future quieting of this much agitated Controversie, confined my discourse within the lists of such questions, (not formerly fully debated in the English tongue by any that I have met with) by the discussion whereof, I have (I suppose) so shaken these rotten pillars, and undermined these (*o*) *sandy foundations* of their high-towring, over-swelling Hierarchy, as that I have left them no divine prop or ground-work to support it longer; so as it must now certainly (for any stay is left it in the Scripture) come tumbling down headlong to the very ground, (and me thinks I hear the fall of it already sounding in my ears) unless with speed they wholly quit these false foundations, and bottom their Prelacy and Jurisdiction

*o* Mat. 7. 26. 27.

*The Epistle Dedicatory.*

riſdiction only on his *Majeſties Princely favor*, as Supream *Head* and *Governour* on earth of the Church of *England*, (not God or Chriſts divine inſtitution) which becauſe they have ſo lately judicially diſclaimed in open Court, and even at this preſent execute all *Acts of Epiſcopal juriſdiction* by their own inherent power, without any ſpecial Commiſſions from his Majeſty under his great Seal, keeping their Courts, viſitations, and making out all their Citations, Proceſs, Excommunications, probate of wills, Letters of Adminiſtration, &c. in their own names, and under their own Epiſcopal Seals as if they were abſolute Popes and Monarcks, contrary to the Statutes of 25. H. 8 c 19 26. H 8 c.1. 37. 1 Edw.6.c 2. 1. E iz c.8. Eliz.c.1. their *Oaths of Supremacy*, and their *High-Commiſſion* it ſelf, which might teach them another Leſſon (being it confines them to do all things by his Majeſties ſpecial Commiſſion, in his Name and under his Seal alone, when they are all joined together, much more therefore when they are divided in their ſeveral Dioces) and becauſe they have contrary to all theſe Acts and their Oaths, * *blotted out Cæſars Image and ſuperſcription, his Arms and royal Title out of their Courts, Proceſs, all their Eccleſiaſtical proceedings, and inſerted only their own in lieu thereof, that ſo they may appear to all the World to be no longer his but their own, and he (if he ſhould chance to chalenge and reſume them as his own) might not henceforth own or claim them to be his*, they have little reaſon now to attempt again, and his Majeſty far leſs reaſon to ſuffer; and ſo having neither God nor the King, divine nor humane Right to ſupport them, they muſt (as the proverb is, *between two ſtools the arſe goes to the ground*) row at laſt in the midſt of their uſurped greatneſs, ſpeedily fall flat unto the ground, and this their fall q prove very great, becauſe they now of late are grown ſo, * *not being content with the office of a Biſhop, but they muſt be alſo Kings, temporal Lords and chief ſtate officers, againſt Chriſts expreſs command, and Gods own Law, to ſway both Church and State at pleaſure, that ſo they may ingroſs into their ſacred hands the ſole rule and government of the world, having great poſſeſſions; and being great Lords alſo as they are Prelates, and yet doing little or nothing therefore in point of preaching feeding, and inſtructing the people committed to their ſpiritual charge, but only playing the part of a Biſhop, as a Chriſtmas game-player*

*See the Stat.
c. 3. H. 8. Stat 2.
c. 16. c. 2. c. 5.
26. H 8 c. 1. 14.
& 31. H. 8 c. 9.
37. H. 8. c. 1. E.
6. c. 2. & c. 1. E-
liz.c. 1. 5 H 3.
c. 19. 20. 27. H 3.
c. 15. 26. H.8 c. 7.
10. 30. H 8.c.20.
14. 34. H 8.c.22.
24. 26. 23. H 8.c.
9. 35. & 3. H.8.c.
17. 19. 33. H.8. c.
1. 3.*

* *See Sir* Iohn Davis his Iriſh Reports.f. 7 98 an excellent paſſage to this purpoſe.

q *Mat. 7:27.*

* *Doctor* Barnes Articles, Arti. 8. p. 211.
*Maſter* Tyndols P & ſe of Popiſh Prelates, P. 34. 348 &c. and obedience of a Chriſtian Man. 37. H. 8. c. 17

E

## The Epistle Dedicatory.

doth of a King, and as a Poppet, which springeth up and down, and cryeth Peep, Peep, and goeth his way, as * Doctor Barns writes wittily of the Bishops of his age. Which swelling greatness and ambition of theirs, as it will make their downfall the greater, so the speedier, it being a sure prognostick of their approaching ruin, as the greatness of any unnatural swelling in the body is of its present ensuing rupture; u Pride ever going before destruction, and a lofty spirit before a fall, and they usually dogging them at the heels; because * God himself resisteth the proud, but then most of all when they are at the highest; according to that of the Psalmist, † Thou puttest away all the wicked of the earth like dross, which as soon as ever it hath gotten up to the top of the pot, and elevated it self above the pure mettle, is then scummed off and cast away.

If these my unworthy Labours shall through Gods blessing on them, and thy prayers concurrence with them, contribute any assistance towards our Lordly Prelates *necessary Reformation*, or in case of obstinate perseverance in their Exorbitances' and Usurpations to their deserved speedy downfall (so far as they are opposite to piety, humility, unity, the propagation of the Gospel, and practicall power of holiness) for the ease, relief or comfort of Gods poor people, (* *who are now every where most wrongfully, without, yea † against all Law and reason oppressed, and cast out of their benefices, freeholds, possessions, imprisoned, fined, excommunicated, silenced, suspended, vilified, crushed and troden under feet by their intolerable tyranny, might and unbounded extravagant power*,) I shall neither repent me of the pening, nor thou thy self of the reading of it. Wherefore here humbly prostrating it to thy impartiall Censure, and commending it to the blessing of God, who to shew the infiniteness of his wisdom and power, doth oft times (z) *chuse the foolish things of the world, to confound the things that are mighty, and base things of the world, and things that are despised, yea and things that are not, to bring to nought things that are, that no flesh should glory in his presence*. I shall take my leave of thee till some further occasion.

Farewell, *And pray for me in my undemerited Bonds*, W. P.

*Marginal notes:*

* What the Keyes of the Church be. pag. 256.
u Prov. 16. 18.
* 1. Pet. 5. 5.
† Psa. 119. 119.
* see Thomas Beacon his Supplication, Vol. 3. of his Works in folio fol. 21. to 15. A most excellent passage to this purpose suitable to our times.
† Magna Chart. c. 29. The Petition of Right. 3. Caroli, and other Statutes in Rastall Accusation.
z 1 Cor. 1. 27. 28. 29.

## An *Appendix* touching the *Occasions* and *Ends* of Re-Printing this *Treatise*, to prevent all mis-constructions.

*Kind Reader,*

THE *Occasions* inducing me to *Re-print* this *Treatise*, (which I compiled above 24 years since, whiles imprisoned in the Tower, by the causeless malice of some swaying *Prelates*) were three;

First, The boldness of a *Popish Preist*, (under the disguise of a *Sectary*) in Re-printing a pernicious *Pamphlet*, entituled, *Erastus Junior* ; *London*, 1660. sitting this Parliament, with his name prefixed to it, (Printed without a name some few moneths before) wherein he endeavors to prove ; *The Ministers* of the *Church of England*, whether *Episcopal* or *Presbyterian*, to be *no Ministers* ; and their *Ordination* no *Legal Ordination*, and thence infers : *Our Church to be no Church, Our Sacraments to be no Sacraments* ; because our *Ministers are no lawful ordained Ministers*.

Secondly, The *Extravagancies* of some of our *reviving English Bishops* and *Episcopal Clery-men*, who shaking hands with the *Council of Trent,* *Bellarmine,* *Jansenius, Erastus Junior* and our *Romish Adversaries*, even after their late years suppression and tribulation under the Cross, (which should have *crucified the world to them, and them unto the world,* and made them more *moderate and mild* to their *fellow-Ministers*, then yet they shew themselves) disown all *Ordinations* made by *Presbyters*, dureing our long-lasting troubles, pronouncing them *NUL* and *VOID*; and refusing to admit *Ministers ordained by Presbyters* to *Benefices* or *Fellowships*, unless they will *renounce their Orders*, and receive a *REORDINATION BY BISHOPS*: Whereby they *UN-CHURCH* all Presbyterian Protestant Churches both

a Sessio. 23. de Sacramento Ordinis cap.4. Surius Tomes. 4. p. 965.
b De Clericis. l. 3. q. 2.
c Alexipharmacum & Spongia
d Gal. 6. 14.
Eph. 4. 31. 32.
e Bishop Lauds Conference with Fisher, p. 175. 176. Bishop Mountagne. Originum Ecclef Tom. 1. pars posterior, p. 464. Canterburies Doom, at p. 389. to 335.

*The Epistle to the Reader.*

<small>f See Mr. Rutherfords *Due Rights of Presbytery* ch.8.sect. 8.</small>

at home and abroad, and *NUL* both their *Ministry* and *Sacraments*; when as they grant *Ordinations* made by *Popish Bishops and Priests*, even in *Rome* and *Spain* it self to be *lawfull*, valid, and all Sacraments administred by *them to be good, & not to be repeated*; never *RE ORDAINING* or *RE BAPTISING* any *Mass-Priests* or *Jesuits* who turn *Protestants*, but freely admitting them to exercise their Ministry without questioning their *Popish Ordination*: Which *present Errour* and *Exorbitancy* of theirs, tending highly to the *scandal, dishonour, subversion* of most Protestant *Churches*, and dissatisfaction of all such who have received the *Lords Supper, Baptism*, or *Orders* from Presbyterian *Ministers* not ordained by *Diocæsan* Bishops, pretending themselves Superior to *Presbyters*, and claiming the *sole power of Ordination*, not by Ecclesiastical *Constitution*, or the *Kings Concession*, but by *DIVINE RIGHT*, principally grounded on the *imaginary Episcopacies of Timothy, Titus*, and *Angel of the Church* of *Ephesus*, I long since refuted in this *Treatise* in such an irrefragable manner, that none of our *Bishops*, or their *Chaplains*, ever yet replyed thereto in above 24 years space: whereupon I deemed it very seasonable to reprint it now, for publick peace and satisfaction.

<small>g *Aug*.15 and 17. 1660.</small>

Thirdly, the [g] late unseasonable Motions of some *Members* in the *Commons House* it self, *That all Ministers ordained by Presbyters during our late Troubles should be put from their Livings & Ministry, unless they were re-ordained by Bishops, within one moneth*; since all *Serjeants at Law* made in those times, were recalled and made *Serjeants* by *New Writs* from the *King*: they putting no difference between *Ordination*, (a divine Ordinance conferred by *Presbyters* on others in all ages, Churches, by a *Divine Right* warranted by Scripture) & the call of *Serjeants at Law*, a meer humane institution peculiar to *England*, an inseparable branch of the [†] *Kings Prerogative*, the fountain of all Honour, as well Civil as Military.

<small>† *Fortescue de laudibus legum Angl.* c.50. *Dyer* f.72. *Cowels Interpreter* Tit. *Sergeant Crooks* 1 Rep. rf. 1. 2. 3. 4. 12. 67. 71. 84. 197. 567. 584. &c.</small>

As these were the only Occasions, so the sole ends I aimed at in republishing this *Discourse*, are

1. The Vindication of the *infallible Truths of God*; the *Divine Rights of Presbyters* and the *common people*; and of our *Kings just Prerogative* in and over all persons and causes Ecclesiastical

*siastical*, as well as civil, from the *Errors, impostures, Usurpations*, of *ambitious self seeking* \* *Popes and Prelates*.    \* 1 El'z. c. 1.

2. The prevention of all future Controversies in our Church 37. H. 8. c. 17. touching the *superiority of Bishops over Presbyters, their new Monopoly of conferring Orders, and exercising all sorts of Ecclesiastical Jurisdiction over Ministers and people*, in their Visitacons, Courts, and imposing oaths upon them, in their *own names Rights, and under their own Seals* alone, by pretext of *A DIVINE RIGHT*, without any *Commission* from our Kings, contrary to the *Statutes* of 26 H 8. c. 1. 37. H 8 c. 17. 1 E. 6. c. 2. 1 *Eliz* c. 1. 5. *Eliz* c. 1. The Petition of Right, 3. *Caroli*, and 17, *Carcii*, Ch. 11.

3. The reclaiming of our *Bishops and Prelatical Clergy* at this present from reviving their Pristine *Excesses, Errors*, innovations, pressures, which occasioned our late Troubles, and their own Overthrow, when they reputed themselves most secure and *best established* & may probably ingender new *Distractions* h *Ps.30.6.7.* if persisted in, more fatal to them then the former, out of which they are but newly delivered by His Majesties most Happy Restoration to His Crown, through the *Prayers* and Loyal *Endeavours* of many of those *Presbyterians* whom they now over much *maligne, oppress and discontent*.    i *Polychronium l.4.c.6. John*

4. To reconcile and unite (as much as may be) the *Episcopal Frith his Answer to Sir* and *Presbyterian Clergy*, by discovering and moderating both *Thomas Mores* their *Excesses, Extremities*, and Usurpations of k *Bishops over Preface.* Presbyters (occasioned by l *Bishops* great temporal Possessions, k *Mat. 26. 45.* and secular imployments, diverting them from *constant preaching*, Rom. 14. 43. which *Christ* himself and his *Apostles*, together with m St Luk. 19. 47. Ambrose, Chrysostom, (o) Augustine, (p) Cyril of *Jerusalem*, l c. 5. 42. c. 17. Aidan of old, and q Bishop *Hooper*, Bishop *Ridley* Bishop *Jewel* of later times, practised once or twice *EVERY* 17.c.19 9. H.5. *DAY* of the week without intermission; being the r principal 3. 3.1 Tim. 4. 2. 1.

m *De Sacramenti. l. 4. c. 1. l. 5. c. 1.* n *Homil. 3. 5 17. 9. 13. 22. in Genes.* o *Tract. 9. 16. 20. 21. 23. v. 29 35. 37. Joan.* p *Catech. Oratio 7. & 14 Catech. Mistag. 14. Socrates Ecclef. Hist. l. 7. c. 2.* q *Beda Ecclef. Hist. l. 3. c. 5. 6. &c.*
r *Fox Acts and Monuments, p. 1316. 1559. 1456. 1696.* s *His life before his works.* t *Mat. 28. 9 Mar. 16. 15. 16. 1 Cor. 1. 17. 18. c. 9. 14. 10. 20. Acts 20. 28. 30. 36. Rom. 10. 8. 15. c. 16. 5 Col. 1. 23. 28. Phil. 1. 15. 16. Eph. 3. 8. 1 Tim. 3. 17. c. 4. 13. 14. 15. 16. c. 31. 2. Tit. 1. 3. 9. 2 Tim. 4. 1. 2.*

## The Epistle to the Reader.

part of their *Episcopal Office*, now most neg ected by them:) and reducing them to that moderate primitive power and allay, which his Majesties Father King *CHARLES* of glorious memory, reduced them to in his *Treaty* with both Houses in the *Isle of Wight*[u], wherein (by his last paper but one) he abolished all but the *Apostolical Bishops*, invested only with a Negative voice and power in point of Ordination, diuesting them of their Temporalities for 99. years; That so like the *primitive Bishops*, they might henceforth govern our *Churches*, not by their own sole *arbitrary Injunctions, wills, pleasures*, but by [x] the *COMMON COUNSEL* and *ADVISE OF THEIR PRESBYTERS*, according to such Laws as shall be made in Parliament for that purpose; this being most consonant to Antiquity and tending best to Christian unity.

For my own part, I sincerely profess, that after many years diligent search, disquisition, perusal of most ancient and modern *Tractates of Church Government*, by the learnedst Advocates for *Popes, Bishops, Presbyterians, Independents,* and *Congregational Sectaries* of all kinds, I cou'd [*] never yet satisfie my judgment or conscience, that *Jesus Christ or his Apostles* had positively, plainly and peremptorily, prescribed or erected any such superiority of Bishops in power, or jurisdiction, or degree above other Ministers and Presbyters, as Popes and Bishops have long contended for; nor yet any such unalterable universal forms of Church Government, and Discipline to be observed in all Churches, places, ages, as some over-rigid Presbyterians, Independents, Anabaptists and other Sectaries have fancied and prescribed, to the prejudice of the supream Authority of Christian Kings and Magistrates in and over Ecclesiastical persons & causes: For, *the Gospel* (by Christs express command) b:ing to be[y] preached to all *Nations* and peop'e throughout *the whole world*, and that successively till all the Elect of God shal be gathered into the *Militant*, & translated to the *Church triumphant* at the end of *the world*: And most *Nations in the world* [z] differing from each other in their *Manners, Customs, Lawes, Rites* and *Civil forms* of Government (though (a) of *divine institution*, as much as *Ecclesiastical Government*, in the general) and the secular Laws, Governors and Governments of most Nations through

---

Marginal notes:

u. See my Speech, p. 66. 67. 68.

x Heirem. in Epist ad T t. Gerlomus Bochorus. De Gubernatione Ecclef. Davidis Blandelli *Apologia pro sententia Hieronymi*, Amstelodami 1646. Bishop Ushers model of Episcopacy.

*See my 12 serious Questions touching Church Government, London, 1644.

y Mat. 28. 19. 20. Mar. 16. 15. 16. Col. 1. 6. 23 Rom. 10. 18. c. 25. 26. Eph. 3. 3. to 10. c. 4. 11. 12. 13.

z Boemus de Moribus Gentium Alexander ab Alexandro Gen. Dierum. Purchas *Pilgrimage & Pilgrim.*

a Rom. 13. 1. 2. 3. Col. 1. 16. 17. Tit. 3. 1. 1 Tim. 2. 1. 2. 3.

*The Epistle to the Reader.*

through tract of time, wars, usurpations, divine dispensations and inevitable Necessities, differing much in several ages from what they formerly were; it was altogether *impossible* and *impracticable* to prescribe, establish any particular set form of Church Government & Governours in and under the Gospel, which should or cou'd be universally received, practised, submitted to by all Churches, Countries, Nations and Christians throughout the world, in all succeeding ages, the Government and Governours of the Church in several ages, places, being as Variable for the most part as the civil Governours and Government, as Ecclesiastical [b] *Historians, Councils, Canons,* and late years experience evidence beyond contradiction. Upon which consideration, as I have ever readily conformed to that Church Government which the King and Parliament have established, so far forth as it was warranted by our Laws, never opposing our Bishops *Ecclesiastical Jurisdiction,* so far as it was justly claimed and exercised by *Regall* and *Legall Authority*; but only its illegal Innovations, Exorbitances, and pretended *Divine sanction,* as distinct from & paramount *Presbytery*; So I shal now earnestly intreat, (and ô that I might perswade) all Bishops, Prelates, Presbyters, Independents and Sects whatsoever, to lay aside all unnecessary contests about *Precedency, Church government, superfluous Ceremonies* and *Formalities:* [*] *To study to walk worthy of that Christian Vocation, wherewith they are called with all lowliness and meekness, with long-suffering, forbearing one another in love, endeavouring to keep the unity of the spirit in the bond of peace; they being but one body, having but one spirit, one hope of their calling, one Lord, one Faith, one Baptism, one God and Father of all, who is above all, and through all, and in them all: To seek, pursue* [†] *follow peace with all men, and holiness without which no man shall see the Lord.* And patiently to expect, and cheerfully to submit to that *Model* of Church government, (with just liberty to truly tender consciences in points not fundamental & consistent with publick peace) which we all hope will ere long be setled by His Majesties pious endeavours, and *Royal Authority* (according to the Ministers and Commons House *Addresses* to His Majesty in pursuance of his own Royal Letters and Declaration from *Breda*) with the Advice of moderate,

[b] *See Centur. Magdeb c.6.7. 9. and 10. throughout Surius, Binius, and Crab, in their Tomes of Councils.*

[*] *Eph.4.1.2. with 3 8.*

[†] *Hebr. 12.14.*

derate, learned and pious Divines of all formerly diffenting parties, and both Houfes of Parliament, for the future *tranquility*
and *prosperity* both of our Churches and *Kingdoms*. Over which
God long preferve, and profper his *Majefties* moft *gracious and
pious* Raign, till he fhall exchange his *temporal* Crown for an
*Eternal*; and his *earthly* Kingdom for an *Heavenly*. b *And
let all the people thereunto fay* Amen: Amen:

a Pfal. 106. 40.

Lincoln's Inne,

August 20. 1660.         William Prynne.

# APOSTSCRIPT.

WHereas our *Bishops* and *Vicars General* ( as I am credibly informed) refuse to admit any Ministers ordained by Presbyters to Benefices, unlesse they will be reordained by Bishops, even since the Parliaments late adjournment; I shall desire them to take notice, that this their practise is expresly against the statute of 13 *Eliz.* ch. 12. intituled, *An Act to reform certain disorders touching Ministers of the church* ; which admits such ordinations to be valid, and to make them capable to be presented and admitted to benefices, as the prologue evidenceth. *That the Churches of the Queens Majesties Dominions may be served with Pastors of sound Religion, Be it Enacted by this present Parliament, that every person under the degree of a Bishop,* which doth or shall pretend to be a Priest or Minister of Gods holy Word and Sacraments, by reason of any other form of Institution, Consecration or Ordering, then the Forms set forth by Parliament, *in the time of the late King of worthy memory King* Edward *the sixth,* or now used in the Reign of our most Gracious Soveraign Lady; *shall in the presence of the Bishop or Guardian of the Spiritualties of some one Diocesse where* he hath or shall have Ecclesiastical living *declare his assent and subscribe to all the Articles of Religion* ; which ONLY *concern the confession of the Christian Faith, and the doctrine of the Sacraments* ( not Church-Government or Ceremonies ) *contained in a Book imprinted, entituled, Articles, &c. under pain of being* ipso facto *deprived.* No subsequent clause of that Act prescribing *Ordination by Bishops* to make Ministers capable of Benefices.

Besides, I desire all Bishops and their Advocates to take notice, that neither the Statute of 5 & 6 *Edw.* 6. c. 1. nor the Statute of 8 *Eliz.* c. 1. *prescribing the form and manner of making and consecrating Archbishops, Bishops, Priests and Deacons,* do null, make void, *in point of law or divinity,* any other form of Ordination of Ministers, Deacons, or consecration of Archbishops and Bishops by Presbyters, or others, than what is prescribed in these Acts & Book of Ordination, by any Negative Clauses; And the later of these Statutes, as it recites, That *divers Questions had lately grown upon the making and consecrating of Archbishops and Bishops within this Realm. Whether the same were, and be duly and orderly made according to the Law, or not*; *Whereupon it was thought convenient by the Act, partly to touch such Authorities as do allow and approve the making and consecrating of such Archbishops and Bishops, to be duly and orderly done, according to the laws of this Realm* (which it declares at large to be only by Act of Parliament, and the *Kings Prerogative Ecclesiastical and Spiritual over the Ecclesiastical state of this Realm*: not by any divine Right or Canonical Sanctions.) So upon this account it only enacts in the affirmative, *That such order and form for the consecrating of Archbishops and Bishops, and for the making of Priests, Deacons and Ministers, as was set forth in the time of the late King* Edward *the 6. and authorized by Parliament in the 5, and 6 year of the said late King, shall stand and be in full force and effect, and shall from henceforth be used and observed in all places within this Realm, and other the Queens Majesties Dominions and Countries*; *And that all Persons which have been, or shall be made, ordered or consecrated Archbishops, Bishops, Priests, Ministers of Gods holy Word or Sacraments, after the form and order prescribed in the said order and form how Archbishops, Bishops, Priests, Deacons and Ministers should be consecrated, made and ordered,* be in very deed, and also by authority hereof, declared and enacted to be, and shall be Archbishops, Bishops, Priests, Ministers and Deacons, and rightly made, ordered and consecrated, any Statute, Law, Canon, *or other thing to the contrary notwithstanding.* Without any negative Clause, either nulling (in point of Law or Divinity) or prohibiting any other form of ordaining Priests, Ministers, or Deacons, by Presbyters alone, either in our own or other Reformed Churches, beyond the Seas; or nulling any Ordinations made by Popish Bishops and Priests, after the *Roman Pontifical*, and Popish manner, in the reign of *Queen Mary*, in *England* or beyond the Seas, though *rejected by our English Bishops and Archbishops in *Edward* the 6 and Queen *Elizabeths* reign, yet they admitted such Ordinations to be good, *without*

*Antiq. Eccles. Brit. p. 430, to h3 9.*

*pressing them to be re-ordained*; And, which is most observable, *Cardinal Pool himself*, by authority from the *Pope*, and the *Popish Bishops*, and Parliament of 1 and 2. *Phil.* and *Mary*, ch 8. did not only confirm all *new Bishopricks, Divisions of Bishopricks, Cathedrals, Churches, Sales of Church-lands and goods, Marriages, Institutions to Benefices, and other Promotions, Ecclesiastical Dispensations, and judicial Proceedings before Ordinaries, Bishops, and Delegates*, during the pretended Schisme of *England*, from the Church of *Rome*, from the 20. year of King *Henry* the 8. to this very Parliament, but likewise ratified **all Orders and Benefices conferred on them** by Protestant Bishops, Ministers and Presbyters, without any *Re-ordination*: witnesse this Clause in *Cardinal Pooles* dispensation, *Ac omnes Ecclesiasticas seculares, seu quorumvis ordinum regulares personas quæ aliquas impetrationes, dispensationes, concessiones, gratias & indulta* tam **Ordines quam Beneficia Ecclesiastica**, *seu alias Spirituales materias prætensa auctoritate supremitatis Ecclesiæ Anglicanæ*, **Licet Nulliter**, *& de facto obtinuerunt, & ad cor reverse Ecclesiæ unitati restitutæ fuerint*, **in suis Ordinibus et Beneficiis** *per nos ipsos, seu à nobis ad id deputatos misericorditer recipiemus, prout jam multæ receptæ fuerint, secumque super his oportunè in Domino* **dispensabimus**. And therefore it seems monstrous and unreasonable to me, That our Bishops now after all our late wars and troubles (occasioned by their former Extravagances, and Excesses) should still be so obstinate and perverse, as for our Churches present and future peace, not to permit or dispense with *Presbyterian Ordinations, and Ministers made by Presbyters of our own Church and Religion*, or other *Reformed Churches*, during our late Schisms and *Troubles*, when the Pope himself, this Cardinal, and Popish Prelates in Queen *Maries* reign, were so indulgent in this kind; & sundry English Scholars who *fled beyond the Seas to preserve their lives, liberties and religion during her bloudy reign, where they received *Ordination* **from Presbyters** in many Protestant Churches of *Germany* and *Geneva*, were not only allowed and presented to Benefices as lawfull Ministers by our Bishops in *Qu. Eliz.* reign upon their return into *England*, without any reordination; but one or two of them made *Bishops*, without any previous Episcopal ordination, and Archbp. *Parker* himself consecrated by 3 *Bishops* & a *Presbyter*. And since

* *Balæus Scriptorum Brit Cent.* 9. p. 721, to 743. *Antiq. Eccles* Brit p 420, to 439. *Fox Acts and Monuments vol.* 3.

the Confessions of the Reformed Churches of *Helvetia, Bohemia, France, Belgia, Auspurge, Wirtenberge* and *Suevia*, all aver Ordination by *Presbyters* to be *just and lawful, without Bishops,* and *Bishops* and *Presbyters* by Gods law to be both one and the same in Order and Jurisdiction, as you may read at large in the *Harmony of Confessions,* Section 11.

In fine, I shall desire our Bishops to consider, that their own Ordaining of *Ministers by themselves in their privat chambers, without Presbyters & other Ministers, or out of their Diocess, or on any day, & in any Church,* is more illegal, irregular and uncanonical, then any *Ordinations* made by *Presbyters during the wars;* by the *Roman Pontifical,* the *Councils* of *Carthage, Trent,* the Book of *Ordination* it self, & their own applauded *Canons,* anno 1603. Canon 31, to 36. As for their Reordination of *Ministers ;* as they can finde no president or warrant for it in Scripture, or solid Antiquity; so the first and only antient president of it I have observed in *England* in former ages, was derived from *Rome,* and brought thence by *Theodor* Archbishop of *Canterbury,* who being sent into *England* by Pope *Vitalian* Anno 670. and ordaining Bishops in all fitting places, reprehended *Ceadda that he was not rightly consecrated (being made both a Priest and Bishop too only by the Abbot of *Hy* and his Monks, who were only Presbyters and no Bishops:) he answered him with a most humble voice, saying, If you know that I have not rightly taken upon me my Bishoprick, I willingly depart from my Office; for I never thought my self to be worthy of it, but for obedience sake, being commanded to undergo it, I consented though unworthy. Whereupon Theodor *hearing the humility of his answer,* replyed, *That he ought not to lay down his Bishoprick,* sed ipse ordinationem ejus denuo Catholica Ratione consummavit. Which amounted rather to a *confirmation,* then a *reconsecration;* & was no *reordination* of him as a *Presbyter,* but only a R:consecration of him after the *Roman mode,* as a Bishop; and so no president to justifie the *reordination* of Presbyterian Ministers by our Bishops now, who may as warrantably *rebaptize* all children baptized by them, as *reordain* them Ministers, for which they have neither Scripture, Canon, Statute, much less reason or discretion in such a time as this, which may instruct them that, *Immodicis brevis est ætas & rara senectus.*

* *Now daily & unduly practised*

* Beda Eccles. Hist. l. 4. c. 1, 2.

Quæst.

## QUESTION I.

## VVhether Timothy was ever a Diocæsan Bishop, or first, or sole Bishop of Ephesus?

IF the multitude, or common received opinion might take place, or our * Prelates be the Judges of this Controversie, they would presently conclude affirmatively without dispute; that *Timothy* was a Diocæsan Bishop; yea, the first and sole Bishop of the *Ephesians*. But if the Scripture, or verity may be umpire, it will evidently appear, that *Timothy* was no Bishop (I mean no such Bishop as *Jure divino*, or *humano*, is different from an ordinary Presbyter in dignity and degree) much less Bishop, or first or sole Bishop of *Ephesus*, as is generally conceived; which I shall clearly evidence and make good by these ensuing Scriptures and reasons.

*Bp. Dounham, Bp. White, Bp. Hall, and others.*

That *Timothy* was no Bishop in this sence, is apparent.

1. First, because S. *Paul* and *Luke*, who were best acquainted with him, and make frequent mention of him, never stile him a Bishop, neither is he termed a Bishop in any text of Scripture. S. *Paul* in his Epistles to him, calls him, *his own Son in the faith*, 1 Tim. 1. 2. *A good MINISTER* (not a Bishop) *of Jesu Christ*, 1 Tim. 4. 6. *His dearly belo-*

*That Timothy was no Bishop.*

*ved Son*, 2 Tim. 1, 2. *A good Soldier of Jesus Christ*, 2 Tim. 2. 3. *A workman that needeth not to be ashamed, rightly dividing the word*, 2 Tim. 2. 15. In his other Epistles, he termes him, *Our Brother Timothy*, Col. 1.1. 1 Thess. 1. 1. 1 Thess. 3. 2. 6. Phil. 2. 19. Hebr. 13. 23. *His fellow-workman*, Rom. 16.21. *His Brother and beloved Sonne*, 1 Cor. 4. 17. 2 Cor. 1. 19. Col. 1. 1. *A workman of the Lord*, 1 Cor. 16. 10. *A servant of Jesus Christ*, Phil. 1. 1. but never a Bishop. S. *Luke* termes him *Pauls Companion, Minister, attendant, and fellow-worker only*, Acts 16. 1, 2, 3. c. 17. 14, 15, c. 18. 5. c. 19. 22. c. 20. 4. never so much as intimating him to be a Bishop. The Scripture therefore never phrasing him a Bishop, nor giving him that Title, among all his other Epithites; it is an infallible argument, that he was in truth no Bishop, (such as our Bishops fancy him) but rather *an Evangelist*, as he is expresly stiled, 2 Tim. 4, 5. *Doe the works of an Evangelist.*

2. *Secondly*, Because he was S. *Pauls* Associate, Copartner, Brother and fellow-helper in his Apostolicall function, whence he often stiles him, *his Brother, his fellow-worker; and conjoyns him with him in the Prologues, the inscriptions and salutations of most of his Epistles, written in both their names*, witness 2 Cor. 1. 1. c. 4. 17. 2 Cor. 1. 1, 19. Col. 1. 1. 1 Thess. 1, 1. c. 3. 2. 2 Thess. 1. 1. Phil. 1. 1. c. 2, 19. Rom. 16. 21. Heb. 13. 23. *Timothy* therefore being a Copartner with S. *Paul* in his Apostleship, or Apostolicall function, (superior in degree to the Episcopal office, as our *Antagonists* plead and grant) as is apparent by *Ephes.* 4. 11. 1 Cor. 12. 18. and the general consent of all men; it is not probable that he would devest himselfe of his Apostolicall Jurisdiction, to become an inferior Bishop, or relinquish a superior to take up an inferior degree. Who ever saw of late any Archbishop or Bishop denuding himselfe of his Archiepiscopal or Episcopal preeminency, to be made a poor Country Vicar or Curate? And can we then conjecture, that *Timothy* would relinquish his Apostleship for an *Ephesian* Bishoprick; or else, hold it by way of *Commendam* with his Apostleship? (\**Commendaes* being not of such antiquity, and a meer late Popish innovation) or descend from an * *Evangelistship* to a Bishoprick?

3. *Thirdly*,

\* *Hobarts Reports*, p. 140, to 160.

\* See *Gersomus Bucerus de Gubernatione Ecclesie*, p. 512, 513, usque 518.

3. *Thirdly*, becaufe *Timothy* was ever either accompanying S. *Paul* in his Travels or bonds, as his fellow-helper, minifter, and affiftant; or elfe, fent by him from one Church to another, as his Meffenger, Delegate, or Collegue, to eftablifh, comfort, and inftruct them; being never long refident in any one fixed place, or Church, as all Bifhops were b We read Acts 16. 1, ufque 12. *That Timothy came firft of all to Paul when he was at Derbe and Liftra ; Paul then taking him to go forth with him; and that they went both together through the Churches of Phrygia, Galatia, Afia, Myfia, and at laft came to Philippi, where he abode with Paul; and from thence wrote and carried the firft Epiftle of Paul to the Corinthians,* as the * Poftfcript manifefts. In which Epiftle *Paul* writes thus unto them, 1 Cor. 16. 10. *Now if Timotheus come, fee that he may be with you without fear; for he worketh the work of the Lord, as I alfo do.* And c. 4..17. *For this caufe have I fent unto you Timotheus, who is my beloved Son and faithfull in the Lord, who fhall bring you into remembrance of my wayes which be in Chrift, as I teach every where in every Church.* By which it is apparent, that *Timothy* was fent by *Paul* from *Philippi* to *Corinth* (with, or after this Epiftle) to inftruct them; Where he continuing a while, repaired again to *Paul* to *Philippi*; & there joyned with *Paul* in the fecond Epiftle to the *Corinthians*, written in both their names; 2 Cor. 1. 1. informing them in the 19 verfe, *That the Sonne of God Jefus Chrift, who was preached among them by us, even by me, Sylvanus and Timotheus, was not yea and nay, but in him was yea.* By which it is evident, that *Timothy* had before this fecond Epiftle written, preached Jefus Chrift among the *Corinthians* by Pauls appointment. After which *Paul removing from Philippi, Timothy accompanied him to Theffalonica and Berea, where he abode, till Paul came to Athens; from whence he fent a command to Timothy to Berea, to come to him with all fpeed to Athens, where he ftayed for him,* Acts 17. 13, 14, 15, 16. Which he did accordingly, joyning with *Paul* in the firft and fecond Epiftles to the *Theffalonians*, written from *Athens, in both their names,* 1 Theff. 1. 1. 2 Theff. 1: 1. Yea whiles Paul ftayed at Athens, *he fent Timothy from thence to the Theffalonians, to eftablifh and comfort them concerning their faith;*

b See Cent. Mag. l.2. c.10. Col. 625, 626.

* If Poftfcripts be of Credit or the Bifhops make them.

faith; that they should not be moved by their afflictions: where he continuing for a space, came from them again to Paul at Athens, bringing him good tydings of their faith and charity, 1 Thess. 3. 1, to 7. After this, he removed with Paul to Corinth: from thence being sent into Macedonia he came again to Paul unto Corinth, Acts 18. 5. from whence Paul writing his Epistle to the Romans, remembers the salutation of Timotheus his Work-fellow to the Romans, among others, Rom. 16. 21. After this Paul removing to Ephesus, sent Timotheus and Erastus (two of those who there ministred unto him) into Macedonia; himself staying in Asia for a season, Acts 19. 20. From whence Paul afterwards passed into Macedonia and Greece, and then returning into Asia, Timotheus and others accompanied him; and going before tarried for him at Troas, Acts 20. 4, 5. Whither Paul sent for the Elders and Bishops of the Church of Ephesus, giving them a strict and severe charge, to take heed to themselves, and to all the flock over which the holy Ghost had made them BISHOPS, to feed the Church of God which he had purchased with his own blood, Act. 20. 17, 28, &c. A task fitter for Timothy to enjoyn them, had he been their Diocæsan, then Paul; and a charge more meet for Timothy to receive, then they, had he then been cheif Bishop of the See of Ephesus: who being so near Ephesus, should have accompanied these Elders and Bishops of his Church to Ephesus, when Paul dismissed them, rather then have left his flock at random after so strict a charge to feed them. But yet though these Elders went back to their Cures from Miletus, Timothy did not so, for from thence he accompanied Paul to Ierusalem, Act. 21. 15, 16, 17. & from thence to Rome. For the Epistle to the Colossans written from Rome) is penned in both their names, Col. 1. 1. and the Epistle to the Hebrews, (as the Postscript and others testifie) was written to the Hebrews from Italy, by Timothy; where Timothy was for a while imprisoned, and then set at liberty, Heb. 13. 23. After which Paul writes his Epistle to the Philippians from Rome, where he was in bonds; at which time Timothy was present with him joyning in this Epistle, Phil. 1. 1. wherein he informs the Philippians, that he trusted to send Timotheus shortly unto them, that he also might be of good comfort, when he should know their estate, Philip. 2. 19. whither

*If Timotheus were then Bishop of Ephesus, why did Paul thus send him from his Cure, & Bishops See?*

ther *Timothy* being sent by him, as is most probable, *Paul* wrote his *second Epistle to him*, at *his second appearing before Nero*, charging him to doe his diligence to come shortly to him before winter, 2 Tim. 4. 9. 21. he being then not at *Ephesus*, but at *Troas* or *Philippi*; as is apparent by 2 Tim. 4. 12, 13. and Philip 2. 19. *Timothy* therefore thus ever accompanying *Paul* in his Travels and Bonds, and travelling from one Church to another by his appointment and mission, never keeping any fixed residence in any one place, much lesse at *Ephesus*, could not be a Bishop or Presbyter of any particular Church; the Apostles instituting no non-resident Bishops or Elders, but such only *as were to reside with these flocks, over which the Holy Ghost had made them Bishops, or Overseers, to watch over and feed them with the bread of life, and to goe in and out before them both in life and doctrine*, as Acts 14. 23. c. 20. 28, 29. c. 21. 17, 18. 1 Pet. 5. 1, 2, 3. Col. 4. 17. Rom. 12. 6, 7, 8. 1 Tim. 5. 17. 2 Tim. 4. 3. Tit. 1. 5, 6, 7, 8. 1 Thess. 5. 12, 13. Heb. 13 17. John 10. 3, 4, 5, 14, 16, 27, 28. Ezeck. 34. 2, to 25. Jer. 23 3, 4. c. 3 15. Isay 56. 10, 11. c. 40. 11. Zech. 11. 17. infallibly evidence.

4. Fourthly, Because *Paul*, who best knew *Timothies* condition, expresly terms him, *A Minister of God* (not a Bishop) 1 Thess. 3. 2. informing him, *that if he did put the Brethren in minde of those things he enjoyned him, he should shew himself a good Minister* (not a Bishop) *of Jesus Christ*, 1 Tim. 4. 6. Therefore certainly he was no Bishop, but a Minister, when this Epistle was written to him, unlesse it be granted, *that every Minister is a Bishop, as Paul himself doth phrase them*, Act. 20. 28. Tit. 1. 5, 7. Phil. 1. 1. 1 Tim. 3. 1, 2, 3. Which the Opposites dare not grant, though an undoubted truth.

5. Because when *Paul* wrote his first Epistle to *Timothy*, he was then very young in years, 1 Tim. 4. 12. and but \*newly entred into the Ministry: whence he charged him, *to give attendance to reading, to exhortation, to doctrine, to meditate upon these things, and to give himself wholly to them, that his profiting might appear unto all men*, 1 Tim. 4. 13. 15. Instructing him in this Epistle, how and what way to preach, and how to demean himself in his Ministry into which he

\* See 1 Tim. 3. 14, 15.

was

was then but freshly entred, as most Expositors on this Epistle accord; and the 1 Tim. 1. 3. compared with Acts 16. 1, 2, 3, 4, 9, 10. c. 18, 19, 20, 21, c. 20. 1. to 13. clearly demonstrate. *Timothy* therefore being but in young years, and newly entred into the Ministry, when this first Epistle was written to him, was questionless not then instituted sole Bishop of *Ephesus* by *Paul*, who in this very Epistle to him, 1 Tim. 3. 6. among other qualifications of a Bishop enumerates this, *That he must not be a Novice* (as Timothy then was) *lest being lifted up with pride, he should fall into the condemnation of the Devil*: and so should have contradicted his own instructions to *Timothy, that a Bishop must be no Novice*, in creating him a Bishop; (which questionlesse he would not do) being but then a Novice.

6. Because *Paul* in the 1 Tim. 5. 1. chargeth *Timothy, Not to rebuke an Elder, but to intreat him as a Father.* If *Timothy* then was not to reproove Elders as a Father over them, *but to intreat Elders, as his Fathers*, he was certainly no Lord Bishop or Superintendent over Elders, but they rather Superiours unto him, being to entreat them only as spiritual Father; whereas Lord Bishops and their Chauncellors too, in our dayes, esteem the very best and gravest Ministers under them, not as their Fathers, but as underlings, Vicars, or Curates to them; not entreating them as Fathers, but rating, reviling, and domineering over them as if they were their Curs, Vassalls, and they their Lords and Masters paramount.

7. Because *Timothy was to account those Elders that ruled well, especially those who laboured in the word and doctrine, worthy of double honor*, 1 Tim. 5. 17. He therefore being to render double honor to those Elders that ruled well and laboured in the word and doctrine; and not to receive double honor from them; could be no Bishop, Father, o Lord paramount over them, Mal. 1. 6. Mat. 15. 4. Rom. 13. 7. 1 Tim. 6. 1. Honor ever coming for the most part, from the inferior to the superior.

8. Because *Paul* exhorts *Timothy, not to neglect the gift that was in him, which was given him by prophecy, with the laying on

*of the hands of the Presbytery*, 1 Tim. 4. 14. Now that gift which was given him by the laying on of the hands of the Presbytery, was not his Episcopal function, (unlesse the opposites grant that he was consecrated Bishop of *Ephesus* by the Presbyters of *Ephesus*:) but his Ministerial only: being therefore exhorted to exercise his Ministerial function only, *and to shew himself a good Minister of Jesus Christ*, 1 Tim. 4. 6, 14. not to exercise any Episcopal authority; he was questionlesse then no Bishop, but a Minister when this Epistle was compiled.

9. Because though *Timothy*, in the Postscript of the second Epistle to him, be falsely stiled, *the first Bishop of the Ephesians*, as I shall hereafter manifest, yet in the body and Postscript of the first Epistle, he is named *Timothy* only, without any mention of his *Ephesian* Bishoprick; he was therefore no Bishop either of *Ephesus* or any other place, when *Paul* sent his first Epistle to him; for otherwise he would have been stiled the first Bishop of *Ephesus* in the Postscript of the first Epistle, as well as of the second, as is probable, by the makers of these Postscripts.

10. It would not stand with the Pomp and State of a Bishop, (especially in our dayes) *to be commanded or posted up and down, from place to place, in such manner as Timothy was by Paul*, 1 Cor. 4. 7. Act. 17. 14, 15. 1 Thess. 1. 3. 1, to 7. Act. 19. 22. Phil. 3. 19. 2 Tim. 4. 9, 21. muchlesse, *to Minister to Paul, as Timothy did*, Act. 19. 22. but least of all, to *carry Pauls Cloak, his Books, and Parchments after him, which Timothy is enjoyned to bring from Troas to Rome*, 2 Tim. 4. 13. An office which our proud Prelates would scorne to execute, though *Paul* himself should command them, as being incompatible with their Episcopal dignity: *Timothy* therefore being so much at *Pauls* beck, as to be his *Messenger*, his *Minister*, his *Cloak-carrier*, and *Book-bearer* (even when some say he was the great Monarchical Prelate of all *Ephesus* and *Asia*) was certainly no Bishop, at leastwise no such Lordly Bishop as those of this age are.

2. *Secondly*. As all these several reasons evidence *Timothy* to be no Bishop, so in the next place, I shall manifest him

*That Timothy was not Bishop of Ephesus.*

to

to be no Bishop at all of *Ephesus*, at leastwise not the first, or sole Diocæsan Bishop of that City, and so by consequence, no Bishop at all, if not of *Ephesus*; since no other Bishoprick is assigned to him. The infallible verity whereof I shall thus demonstrate.

1. *First*, there is not one syllable in Scripture (wherein the Titles, Offices, actions of *Timothy* are frequently mentioned) which either directly, or by way of necessary consequence, imply *Timothy*, to be either a Bishop, or Bishop of *Ephesus*; which *Paul* in his Epistles to *Ephesus*, and *Timothy*, and St. *Luke* in the Acts, would never have pretermitted, had *Timothy* been Bishop of that famous City.

2. The Scripture makes no mention of *Timothies* being at *Ephesus*, or of his Preaching there, save only *that Paul besought* ( not commanded or ordered ) *him to abide still at Ephesus, whiles he went into Macedonia, that he might charge some, that they teach no other Doctrine; neither give heed to fables, and endlesse genealogies, which minister questions rather than edifying*, 1 Tim. 1. 3,4 *and to give attendance to reading, to exhortation, to doctrine, till he came thither himself,*( *which was but a short time after* ) 1 Tim. 4. 13, 14, 15. *Paul* therefore not instituting *Timothy* any Diocæsan Bishop of *Ephesus*, but only *beseeching* ( which was voluntary, not commanding) him, *to abide there,* ( * *till his own return from Macedonia,* ) *both to instruct the people, and to further himself in his own Studies*; not to reside there during life; it is an unanswerable argument, that he did not constitute him Bishop of *Ephesus*, as some vainly hence infer: contrary to the 1 Tim. 3. 14, 15.

* 1 Tim. 3. 14. c. 4. 13. *Gersomus, Bucerus, De Gubernatione Ecclesiæ:* p. 502. *usque* 507.

3. When *Timothy* was thus desired to abide at *Ephesus* by *Paul*, he was ‖ but newly entred into the Ministery, as appears by the 1 Tim. 1. 3 c. 3. 15. compared with, Act. 16. 1, 3, 9, 10, 11, 12. and by the 1 Tim. 4. 6, 10, 12, 13, 14. Now it is not probable that *Paul* would constitute *Timothy* a Diocæsan Bishop of all *Ephesus*, yea the very first Bishop of that famous See, being but a youth, so soon as he had ordained him to be a Minister; *and before he knew how to behave himself, in the House and Church of God*, which then ( it seems ) he did not, 1 Tim. 3. 15.

‖ *Vide Chytræum Onomast. in Timotheum, & Gersomum Bucerum: Dissertat. De Guber. Ecclesiæ.* p. 506, *to* 37.

4. *Assoon*

4. *Assoon as Paul returned again from Macedonia to Ephesus, he sent Timothy into Achaia, himself staying at Ephesus in Asia for a season,* Acts 19. 22, to 40. *and from thence he returned into Macedonia, and through it into Asia, accompanied with Timotheus, and others:* Acts 20. 1, to 7. after which we never read that *Timothy* writ, came or returned to *Ephesus.* Now if *Timothy* had been Bishop of *Ephesus,* it is not probable that *Paul* upon his return from Macedonia, *would have sent him from Ephesus into Macedonia, to Corinth, Philippi, and other Churches there*; as he did Acts 19. 22. c. 20. 4, 5. 1 Cor. 14. 17. 2 Cor. 1. 19. Phil. 2. 19. 1 Thess. 3. 1, 2, 6. or that *Timothy* would have gone from his own Episcopal See, into another Bishops Diocess, and never returned to his own Cure of *Ephesus,* (which for ought we read he never did after his first departure thence) *contrary to Pauls own direction to the Bishops of Ephesus,* Acts 20. 28.

5. We read, *that Paul sent Timothy into Macedonia,* Acts 19. 22. *to preach the Gospel to the Church of God there; that he sent him to the Church of Corinth to bring them in remembrance of his wayes which were in Christ, as he taught every where in every Church, and to work the work of the Lord,* 1 Cor. 4. 17. c. 16. 10. *and that he accordingly preached Jesus Christ the Sonne of God among them,* 2 Cor. 1. 19. That *he likewise sent him to the Church of Thessalonica, to establish and comfort them, concerning their faith,* 1 Thess. 3. 1, 2, 3, 4. *and after that to Philippi from Rome, that he might know the State of the Philippians, he having no man like minded, who would so naturally care for their state as Timothy,* Phil. 2. 19, 20. But we never read that *Paul* sent him to *Ephesus* either to comfort, exhort, confirm, instruct them, or to know their State after his first departure thence; which he would questionlesse have done, had he been their Bishop, rather than thus have imployed him to other Churches. *Timothy* therefore was rather Bishop of these Cities and Churches than of *Ephesus.*

6. As *Timothy* was sent by *Paul* to the Churches of *Corinth, Philippi,* and *Thessalonica,* so he joyns with *Paul* in his Epistles written to those Churches, directed to him in both their names: witnesse 2 Cor. 1. 1. Phil. 1. 1. 1 Thess. 1. 1. 2 Thess.

D                1. 1. in

in which Epistles *Paul makes frequent mention of Timothy:* witnesse 1 Cor. 4. 17. c. 16. 10. Phil. 2. 19. 1 Thess. 3. 2, 6. Moreover *he joyns with Paul in writing to the Colossians,* Col. 1. 1. and *Paul in his Epistle to the Romans,* c. 16. 21. *remembers his salutation by name to the Church and Saints of Rome,* and in his *Epistle to the Hebrews written by Timothy as his Scribe, he makes mention of his delivery out of prison by name,* Hebr. 13. 23.

\* *Note well.* \*But in the Epistle to the Ephesians, *written from Rome,* long after *Timothy* was supposed to be made first Bishop *of Ephesus, Timothy* (which is most observable) neither joyns with *Paul* in the inditement or salutation, neither doth *Paul* so much as once name or mention him throughout that Epistle, as he doth in all the other Epistles to the Churches whither he sent him, and in every of his Epistles else to any Church, except in his Epistle to the *Galathians.* *Timothy* therefore doubtlesse was not Bishop of *Ephesus* at this season; else he would have vouchsafed to have joyned with *Paul* in his Epistle to the *Ephesians,* as well as in his Epistles to other Churches; or *Paul* being his special Friend and applauder, would have made some honourable mention and recommendation of him to the Church of *Ephesus,* (his own peculiar Diocesse as some affirm,) as he doth in his Epistles to most other Churches, where he was never Bishop. An unanswerable argument in my opinion, that *Timothy* was never Bishop of *Ephesus,* since there is no news at all either from, or of, or to, or concerning him in *Pauls* Epistle to the *Ephesians,* of whom he is surmised, to be the first, sole and genuine Bishop, by our Prelates and others.

7. If *Timothy* were Bishop of *Ephesus* when *Paul* writ his first Epistle to him, why then did *Paul himself excommunicate Hymenus and Philetus, and deliver them unto Satan,* and not write to *Timothy* to excommunicate these Hereticks, and play the Bishop in his own Diocesse, 1 Tim. 1. 20 ? yea why did *Paul himself,* not *Timothy lay hands upon the Disciples there ordained, after such time as he was Bishop there,* Acts 19. 1, 6, ? Was it because *Timothy* was a negligent, or impotent Bishop, unwilling or unable to excommunicate Hereticks, or ordain Ministers? or in truth, because he was no Bishop then and there?

## The Un-bishoping of Timothy and Titus.

there? Not the first of these, since *Timothy* was neither negligent, nor impotent in his function: therefore the latter, he being then no Bishop, nor yet exercising his Episcopal Jurisdiction there.

8. Had *Timothy* been Bishop of *Ephesus*, when *Paul* wrote his first Epistle to him, no doubt *Paul when he sent for the Elders of the Church of Ephesus to Miletus to take his final farewell of them, and made a solemn speech unto them,* charging them, *To take heed unto themselves and to the flock over the which the Holy Ghost had made* THEM BISHOPS, *to feed the Church of God, which he had purchased with his own blood, &c.* Act. 20. 17. to 38. would have made some special mention of *Timothy*, and directed his speech more particularly to him by name, as being the Prime Bishop of that Church, to whom this charge did principally appertain. But *Paul* in that speech of his makes no particular mention at all of *Timothy*, neither doth he any part of his speech to him, he being none of the Elders of Ephesus sent for to Miletus, or any of that number whom the Holy Ghost had made Bishops of that flock and Church: he coming along with Paul out of Macedonia into Asia to Troas and Miletus, Acts 20. 3, 4, 5, &c. and so none of the number of Elders sent for and called from *Ephesus* to *Miletus*, to whom this speech of *Paul* was applyed. Therefore questionlesse he was not then Bishop, much lesse sole Bishop of *Ephesus*, as some groundlesly affirm, against this unanswerable text.

9. *Paul* himself, as he sent *Timothy to Philippi, Troas*, and other Churches, *to instruct, confirm, comfort, and inquire of their estates,* so he expresly writes to Timothy, 2 Tim. 4. 12. *that he had sent Tychicus unto Ephesus, for the selfsame purpose.* Which *Tychicus as* he did write the Epistle of Paul to the Ephesians from Rome, so Paul in that very Epistle of his to the Ephesians, c. 6. v. 21, 22. acquaints them, *That Tychicus a beloved brother and faithfull Minister in the Lord, should make known to them all things: whom* (saith he) *I have sent unto you for the same purpose, that ye might know our affairs, and that he might comfort your hearts.* So that if there were any particular Diocæsan Bishop of *Ephesus* instituted by *Paul*, this

*Tychicus*

*Tychicus* (whom *Dorotheus* makes one of the 70 Disciples and Bishop of *Chalcedon* in *Bithinia*) was more like to be the man, than *Timothy*, as these two Scriptures evidence.

10. *Paul* himself makes mention of *Elders in the Church of Ephesus* RULING WELL, *and labouring in the word and doctrine, and so worthy of double honor*, 1 Tim. 5. 17. Which *Elders* he expresly stiles, *Bishops of Ephesus*, Acts 20, 27, 28. These therefore *being instituted Bishops of Ephesus even by the Holy Ghost himself, and ruling, feeding, taking the care, and oversight of that Church by his appointment*, Acts 20. 27, 28. questionlesse Timothy at the selfsame season could not be Bishop there.

*That Timothy was neither the sole, nor the first Bishop of Ephesus.*

3. Thirdly, As *Timothy* was neither a Bishop, nor Bishop of *Ephesus*; so much lesse was he the first, or sole Bishop there, as the Postscript of the second Epistle to him, in some late Copies, terms him. Not the first Bishop of *Ephesus*: For, *as that Church was first planted by S. Paul, who continued there for a season*, Acts 18, 19, 20. & 19. 1, to 41. c. 20. 17, to 38. 1 Cor. 15. 32. c. 16. 8. 2 Tim. 1. 18. *and after that resided at Ephesus for two years and three moneths space together, disputing daily in the School of one Tyrannus, so that all they who were in Asia heard the Gospel*, Acts 19. 8, 9, 10. during which time of *Pauls* residence there (*in all* 3. *Years*) Acts 20. 31. there needed no Bishop to govern and sway this Church, neither is it probable that any Diocesan Bishop was there constituted: So *the two first that Paul left behind him at Ephesus at his first coming thither, to instruct that Church, were Priscilla and Aquila*, Acts 18. 18, 19. during *whose abode there, while Paul went from thence to Antioch, and over all the Countrie of Galatia and Phrygia, in order strengthning all the Disciples; a certain Jew, named Apollos, born at Alexandria, an eloquent man and mighty in the Scriptures came to Ephesus; Who being instructed in the way of the Lord, and fervent in the spirit, spake and taught diligently the things of the Lord; and began to speak boldly in the Lord: whom when Aquila and Priscilla had heard, they took him unto them, and expounded to him the way of God more perfectly*, Acts 18. 22, to 27. So that *Aquila whom Paul left first at Ephesus before Timothy*,

*The Un-bishoping of* Timothy *and* Titus.

and Apollos *who thus preached there,* may with greater reason be stiled, the first Bishops of Ephesus, than Timothy, whom Paul intreated *to stay there only at his last going into Macedonia,* Acts 20. 1. as * *most accord.* Besides, we read, that Paul at his second comming to Ephesus, before Timothy was constituted Bishop thereof, *finding certain Disciples there, about twelve in number, who were only baptised into the baptism of John, and had not received the Holy Ghost since they believed, baptised them in the name of the Lord Jesus, and when he had laid his hands upon them, the Holy Ghost came on them, and they spake with tongues, and prophecied,* Acts 19.1, to 18. *Which* 12. abiding at Ephesus, as is most probable, by Acts 20. 17, 28, 29. to rule and instruct the Lords flock in that City, may more properly be termed, the first Bishops of the *Ephesians,* then Timothy, who as he was not the first, *so much lesse was he the sole Bishop of that See;* as is *infallibly evident* by Acts 20. 4, 5, 15, 17, 18, 28, 29. Where we read, *that Paul returning through Macedonia into Asia, to go to Jerusalem, to the Feast of Pentecost, there accompanied him Gaius of Derbe, and Timotheus;* with others: (where Timothy *is reckoned to be of Derbe,* not Ephesus) *All these going before to Troas accompanied Paul to Miletus; who from thence sent to Ephesus, and called to him the Elders of that Church to Miletus. And when they were come thither, he said unto them, Ye know from the first day that I came into Asia, after what manner I have been with you at all seasons, &c. Take heed therefore unto your selves, and to all the flock over which the Holy Ghost hath made YOU BISHOPS* ( so the * Greek, yea the Latine and ancient English translations truly render it ) *to feed the Church of Christ, which he hath purchased with his own blood, &c.* From whence it is apparent:

* Bucerus De Gubern. Eccles. p. 504. usque 510 Cent. Magd. l. l. 2 c. 10. Col. 626.

* Ἐν ᾧ ὑμᾶς τὸ πνεῦμα τὸ ἅγιον ἔθετο ἐπισκόπους. In quo vos Spiritus Sanctus posuit EPISCOPOS.

*First,* That the Church of Ephesus at that time, *had not one but many Bishops, and that by the very institution of the Holy Ghost:* (as the Church of Philippi likewise then had, Phil. 1. 1. ) Therefore Timothy could not be sole Bishop there, by Pauls institution, in opposition to the Holy Ghost.

*Secondly,* That these Bishops *knew from the first day that* Paul

*Paul came into Asia, after what manner he had been with them at all seasons*: and therefore, in all likelyhood, were appointed Bishops of *Ephesus* at the very first planting of that Church, before *Timothy* was setled Bishop: so that he was not the first Bishop there; but these rather, before, or as soon as he.

*Thirdly*, That *Timothy* was neither an Elder, nor Bishop of that Church at this time when *Paul* took his farewell of it; *he coming with Paul out of Macedonia to Miletus, and being none of the Elders and Bishops sent for, from Ephesus, to whom alone Paul directed his speech*: who had he then been sole or prime Bishop of that See, *Paul* would not have stiled the Elders which he sent for, *Bishops of that flock*, at leastwise he would have made some special mention of *Timothy* in this speech of his, and given him some particular instructions for the instructing and governing of that Church: Or at least have honoured *Timothy* so far, as to have made him give this Episcopal charge and instruction to the Elders and Bishops of his own proper Church and Diocesse, or to have enjoyned them in special manner to reverence, honor and yield him all Canonical obedience as their supreme Diocæsan. All which *Paul* utterly neglects, or forgets to do; or particularly to charge *Timothy* to take heed to, or feed this flock, he being oft a Non-resident from it, as I have proved. Yea, *making such haste to be at Hierusalem by the feast of Pentecost*, v. 16. that he could not spare time to goe to *Ephesus*, he needed not to have sent for the Elders of *Ephesus* to *Miletus* to give them these instructions, since *Timothy* their Bishop was then present with him, to whom he might and would no doubt have imparted them, without further trouble, had he then in truth been Bishop, or sole Bishop of that Church. But this sending for these Elders in this haste, and stiling them *Bishops of that flock*, and that by the *Holy Ghosts* own institution, &c. without any mention at all of *Timothy*, who was none of the Elders sent for from *Ephesus*, is an infallible evidence, that he was neither Bishop, nor first or sole Bishop of that City.

*Fourthly, When Paul exhorted Timothy to abide at Ephesus, there were*

## The Un-bishoping of Timothy and Titus. 15

were then in that City Elders, who did both rule well, and labour in the word and doctrine, and so were worthy double-honor, 1 Tim. 5. 1. 17. 19. Now these very Elders, as *Paul* himself affirms, were made BISHOPS of the Church of *Ephesus* by the Holy Ghost, Acts 20. 17, 28. Therefore *Timothy* could not be *the first, the sole Bishop of the Ephesians, as the false Postscript of the second Epistle to him,* stiles him. Moreover, it was the Apostles manner in those times to place * many Bishops and Elders in every Church, not to constitute one Monarchical Bishop over many: witnesse Acts 11. 30. ch. 14. 23. ch. 15. 2, 4, 6, 22, 13. ch. 16. 4. ch. 20. 17, 28. ch. 21, 18. ch. 22. 5. Phil. 1. 1. 1 Tim. 5. 17. 1 Pet. 5. 1, 2, 3. Tit. 1. 5, 7. James 5. 14. Hebr. 13. 17. Acts 13. 1, 2. 1 Cor. 14. 29, 30, 31, 32. 1 Thess. 5. 12. 15. Rom. 16. 3, 9, 12. Col. 1 7. c. 4. 9, 12, 27. which testifie, that there were many Bishops and Elders both at *Jerusalem, Corinth, Philippi, Rome, Thessalonica, Colosse, Ephesus,* yea in all other Churches in Crete and elsewhere, at one time, by which the Church of God was taught and joyntly governed, as by a Common Council of Bishops and Elders, as g *Irenæus,* h *Ignatius, Cyprian* Epist. 6. 12. 28. 46. i *Ambrose,* k *Hierom,* and l other antients testifie. Hence m *Epiphanius* and *Eusebius* testifie, that *Paul* and *Peter* were joynt Bishops of *Rome* at the same time; and n *Tertullian* writing of the Church-governors in his age, saith; *Præsidentnt probati Seniores, &c.* that approved Elders ( not one Diocæsan Bishop) were Presidents over every several Christian Congregation; and in his Book *de Corona Militis,* he affirms the same, The rather because it was the usual course in the Primitive times, long after the Apostles to have divers Bishops in and over one and the same Church, not one over many Churches. Thus we read that o *Alexander* and *Narcissus* were both Bishops of *Jerusalem* at the same time; *Paulinus* and *Miletus* both Bishops of *Antioch* together; *Theodosius* and *Agapetus* were both Bishops of *Synada* at the same season. r *Valerius* and *Augustine* were both joynt Bishops of *Hippo* together, by the unanimous consent of the Clergy and people; and when as *Augustine*, was loath to be joyned a Bishop with *Valerius,* alleging it to be contrary to the
Custom

* See *Gersomus Bucerus. De Gubern. Eccles.* p. 302, 303, 304

g *Contra hæres.* l. 4. c. 43, 44. and l. 3. c. 2.
h *Epist.* 5, 6, 7, 8.
i *Com. in Phil.* 1. 1. 1 T. t. 1. 5, 7.
k *In Eph. f* 4.
l *Sedulius in Tit* 1. 5
m *Contra Hæres.* l. 1 Hæres. 27. Col 88, 89. *Eccles. Hist l.* 3. c. 31.
n. *Apologia contra Gentes* c. 39.
o *Euseb. Eccles. hist. l.* 6. c. 8, 10. in the Greek. 7. and 9 in the English.
p *Socrates Eccles. hist.* l. 5. c. 5.
q *Socrates* l. 7. c. 3.
r *Possidonius in vita Augustini* c. 8 *Cent. Magd.* 4. Col. 67 g. 58 a.

Custom of the Church, to have two Bishops in one City, they replied, *Non hoc esse inusitatum*, that this was no unusual thing, confirming this both by example of the *African*, and other forein Churches; Whereupon he was satisfied. In the *a* Church of *Rome*, we know there have been sometimes two, sometimes three, and once four Popes and Bishops at one time, Some adhering to the one, some to the other, but all of them conferring Orders, making Cardinalls, and exercising Papal jurisdiction. In the *b* Churches of *Constantinople*, *Alexandria*, *Jerusalem*, *Antioch*, and *Affrick*, during the *Arrian*, *Macedonian*, *Novatian* Heresies, and Schism of the *Donatists*, there were successively two or three Bishops together in them, and other Cities at once; the one orthodox, the other heretical and schismatical. Yea the first *Council of Nice*, Canon 7. admits the *Novatian Bishops* which conformed themselves to the Church and renounced their Errors, to enjoy the tile and dignity of Bishops, and to be associated with the *Orthodox Bishops*, if they thought fit. And *c* St. *Augustine* would have the *Donatists Bishops*, (where there was a *Donatist Bishop* and a *Catholick*,) if the *Donatists* returned unto the unity of the Church, that they should be received into the fellowship of the Bishops office, with the Catholick Bishops; if the people would suffer it; *Poterit quippe unusquisque nostrum honoris sibi socio copulato vicissim sedere eminentius, &c. utroque alterum cum honore mutuo præveniente. Nec novum aliquid est, &c.* As he there defines; Therefore this was then reputed no novaltie. *Platina d* records of *Rhotaris* King of the *Lombards*, who declined to the *Arrians*, that in all the Cities of his Kingdom, he permitted there should be two Bishops of equal power, the one a Catholick, the other an *Arian*; and that he placed two such Bishops in every City. *e Danæus* proves out of *Epiphanius*, That antiently in most Cities there were two or three Bishops. *f Nicephorus* writes, That the Scythians near *Ister*, have many and great Cities, all of them subject to one Bishop; But among other people we know, there are Bishops not only in every City, but also in every Village: especially among the *Arabians* in *Phrygia*, and

---

*a Platina, Balæus, Luitprandius, Albo de vitis Pontificum Theodorious a Niem. Zabarel & Marius de Scismate.*

*b Eusebius, Socrates, Nicephorus Tripartita Historia passim, Cent. Mag. 4, 5, 6, 7. c. 10. Augustinus contra Donatum.*

*c De Gestis cum Emerito Donatist. Tom. 7. pars 1. p. 781, 782. See M. Cartwrights answer to the Rhemish Testament, on Phil. 1. page 499.*

*d In vita Joannis 4. & Martini 7.*

*e In Augustinum de hæresibus, hær. 53. f Ecclesiast hist. l. 11. c 34. p. 758.*

## The Un-bishoping of Timothy and Titus.

and in *Cyprus* among the *Novatians* and *Montanists*; And *E-piphanius* writing of the Heresie of the *Meletians*; saith, *That in antient times, this was peculiar to Alexandria, that it had but one Bishop*, whereas OTHER CITIES HAD TWO. Yea, no longer since then the *a Council of Lat.* under *Innocent* the 3. there were divers Bishops in one City and Diocesse, where there were divers Nations of different Languages and Customs: Which though this Council disallowes where there is no necessity, yet it approves & permits where there is a necessity. Nay, *b* those Episcopal Canons, Constitutions, Decretalls, which prohibit, *that there should be many Bishops in one City*, or that there should be Bishops in Castels, Villages, small Towns and Parishes, *least the dignity of Bishops should become common and contemtible*; Manifest, that before these Canons & Constitutions, (made by *Bishops themselves*) there were many Bishops in one City and Diocesse; and a Bishop in every little Castle, Town and Country Village: To come nearer home, the Statute of 26 H. 8. c. 14. ordaining, *that there shall be many suffragan Bishops exercising Episcopal jurisdiction in one and the same Diocesse of England*; with the Statutes of 31 H. 8. c. 9. 33 H. 8. c. 31. 34 H. 8. c. 1. which erected divers new Bishopricks in *England*, and divided one Diocesse into many, both intimate and prove as much. Why then there may not now be divers Bishops in one City, one Church, as well as there were in the Apostles times, in the Primitive Church, and former ages, or as well as there are now divers Archbishops and Bishops in one Kingdom; divers Ministers in one Cathedral and Parish Church, I cannot yet conceive; unlesse Bishops will now make themselves such absolute Lordly Monarks and Kings, *as cannot admit of any c equals or corrivals with them*, and be more ambitious, proud, vain-glorious, covetous, unsociable, than the Bishops in the Apostles and Primitive times, whose successors they pretend themselves to be in words, though they disclaim them utterly in their Manners, Lordlinesse, Pomp, and supercilious Deportment, which they will not lay down for the peace and unity of the Church of Christ.

Since therefore the Apostles themselves ordained many

*a Concil. lat cap 9. Surius Tom 3. p 740.*

*b Surius Tom. 1 p. 210, 222, 226, 343, 459, 165, 414, 467. 799. Tom. 3. 740, 537.*

*\*David Blundellus, Apologia pro Sententia Hieronymi, sect. 3. p. 178, 179.*

*c Nec quenquam jam ferre potest Cæsarve priorē, Pompeiusve parem. Lucan l. 1.*

E El-

Elders and Bishops in every City and in *Ephesus* too, it is neither possible, nor probable that *Timothy* alone should be constituted sole Bishop of *Ephesus*.

Finally it is recorded by d *Irenæus*, e *Eusebius*, f *Nicephorus*, g *Metaphrastes*, h *Hierom*, i *Chytræus*, k *Baronius*, * and many others quoted to my hand by *Gersomus Bucerus: Dissertatio De Gubernatione Ecclesiæ* p. 520, to 526. That St. *John* the beloved Apostle, after the Council held at *Hierusalem Act.* 15. resorted to *Ephesus*, residing, governing, and instructing that Church (which *Paul* had planted ) after *Pauls* departure thence, with the Churches of *Asia* thereunto adjoyning, even till *Trajanes* daies; and that though he were banished thence by *Domitian* for a season, yet after his exile he returned thither again, writing an Epistle to that Church during the time of his banishment, *Rev.* 2. 1. which he names before all the other Curches of *Asia*. If St. *John* then kept his residence at *Ephesus*, and ruled that Church by his Apostolical power, even till *Trajanes* daies; how could *Timothy* be sole Bishop and Superintendent thereof? there being no need of a Bishop, where an Apostle was present and resident to govern, by whose divine superior authority and presence all Episcopal Jurisdiction was suspended. To cloze up this particular point, *Petrus de Natalibus*, *l*. 1. *c*. 14. *Nauclerus Chronogr. vol.* 2. *gen.* 6. *Pantaleon de viris Illustribus, Germ. part* 1. *Bartholomeus Anglicus in Chronico de sanctis*, and Bishop *Usher* out of them, *De Britanicarum Ecclesiarum Primordiis, c.* 3. *p.* 31. record; That *Timothy* the Disciple of *Paul*, came into *Britain*, and baptised *Lucius* King thereof, with the whole Nation, and that he was Bishop of *Curie* in *Germany*, and suffered Martyrdom therein on the 3d. day of *December:* Therefore he neither was nor continued Bishop of *Ephesus*, if this be truth. On the other hand. l *Bucolcerus*, m *Fasciculus Temporum*, the n *Centuary* writers, and o some others record, that *Timothy* survived St. *John*, living till about the year of Christ 108. and was then Martyred in the third-Persecution under *Trajan*, or under *Nero*, or *Domitian*. If this were true, and that *Timothy* continued Bishop of *Ephesus* till his death, as the Patriots of

our

d *Adverj. Hær. l.* 3. *c.* 3.
e *Eccles. Hist l.* 3. *c.* 23.
f *Eccles Hist. l.* 2. *c.* 42, 44, 46.
g *In Lipom. De vitis Sanct. l.* 1. *de Johanne.*
h *Cata l. Script. Eccles Johannes.*
i *Onomast. in Joan.*
k *Annal. Tom.* 1.
* *August. Epist.* 86.

l *Chronol. Isag. m De Timotheo.*
n *Cent* 1. *l* 2 *c* 10. *Col.* 616.
o *Niceph l.* 3 *c.* 7 † *Vincentius Spec. Hist l* 38. *c.* 10.

our Prelates affirm, then by their own doctrine it will necessarily follow, *that Timothy was the Angel of the Church of Ephesus* (which they interpret to be the *Bishop of that See*) *to whom S. John writes,* Rev. 2 1, 5. charging him, *that he had left his first love;* and therefore admonished him, *to remember whence he was fallen, to repent, and do the first works, &c.* But it is not credible nor probable, that *Timothy*, a man so pious, so laborious, so vigilant, and so much applauded by *Paul* in most of his Epistles, should be this backsliding Angel of the *Church of Ephesus*, which (to omit all other [a] *Commentators*) the contents of *our authorized Bibles* of the last translation, affirm *to be the Ministers* (not the *Bishop of that Church*, as some Apostatizing Prelates glosse it, against Acts 20. 28, 29, 30.) therefore from thence, and all other the premisses, I may now safely conclude, that *Timothy* was not a Bishop, nor yet the first, sole or any Diocœsan Bishop of *Ephesus*, as our Prelates groundlesly affirm; whose allegations to the contrary I shall next propose and refell, that so the truth may be more perspicuous.

*Object.* 1. The first allegation to prove *Timothy* a Bishop when *Paul* writ the first Epistle to him, *is the Postscript of the second Epistle*, which runs thus; *The second Epistle unto Timothius, ordained the first Bishop of the Church of the Ephesians, was written from Rome, when Paul was brought before Nero the second time.* Hence [b] Bishop *White and others,* conclude *Timothy* to be a Bishop.

*Answer.* To which I answer; *First,* that this Postscript is no Scripture, and all others, (as in Mr. *Perkins* works is proved at large) no part of the Epistle, no Appendix of S. *Pauls,* but a private observation annexed to it, by some Expositor, Scribe or other, after the Epistle written, without any divine inspiration; as the words themselves demonstrate; *The SECOND Epistle unto Timotheus ordained the first Bishop of the Church of the Ephesians, was written from Rome, when Paul was brought before Nero the second time.* Where observe, First, that this Postscript is written, not in the name of *Paul,* but of some third person, as the whole frame of it demonstrates;

[a] *Beda in Apoc. l. and 2. Aretas in Apocal. 2. & 3. Ambros Ansbert in Apoc. l. 2. & Primasius in Apoc. 2. Brightman. Gersomus Bucerus De Gubern. Eccles. p. 205, 393, 408, 419, 421, 433, usque 466. 472, 484, 485.*

[b] *Preface to the Treatise of the Sabbath. Bishop Downham in his consecration Sermon, and Bishop Hall since.*

[c] *Comment on Gal. 6. p. 497, 498, 499.*

E 2 Secondly,

*Secondly*, that this Postscript is no direction given by *Paul* to *Timothy*; as the words (*the second Epistle unto Timotheus, ordained the first Bishop of the Church of the Ephesians, was written, &c.*) evidence, but a direction of some Notary or * Commentator to the Reader, who here speaks both of *Paul* and *Timothy* in the third person.

> * Perchance *Theodoret*, the first in whom I find any Postscripts 430. years after *Christ*.

*Thirdly*, the words *WAS WRITTEN, &c.* in the preterperfect tense, shews this Postscript to be a meer addition of some Scribe or Expositor, some good space after the Epistle written, not of *Paul* himself, at the time when he writ it; all the Postscripts of his other Epistles, appearing manifestly not to be his, by the same reason.

*Fourthly*, it is here call'd, *the second Epistle unto Timotheus*, in relation to the *first*; and the first Epistle to him, written many years before it, is likewise stiled in the Postscript of it, *The first to Timothy*, with reference to the second. As therefore the Postscript of the first Epistle was certainly added by some Notary after the second Epistle written, since it is called the first in relation to it: so no doubt the Postscript of the second Epistle was annexed to it after the first Epistle, and the second were transcribed and bound up together, by the same party that added the Postscript to the first; the Postscript stiling them thus, the 1, and 2. in regard of their mutual relation one to the other, after they were both conjoyned, and the New Testament and *Pauls* Epistles, digested into that order and method, wherein now they are placed, both in manuscripts and printed Coppies.

*Fifthly*, it is very unlikely, that *Paul* would make such a Postscript as this. For as these words (*was written from Rome, when Paul was brought before Nero the second time*) sound not of *Pauls* language, but some others; so the second Epistle unto *Timotheus ordained the first Bishop of the Church of the Ephesians*, favour not of his inditing; who never in any of his Epistles to him or others stiles him a Bishop, much lesse ordained the *first Bishop of the Church of the Ephesians*, neither would he have made such a description of *Timothy* as this, to *Timothy* himself.

*Sixthly*, None of the other Apostles have any Postscripts added to any of their Epistles; it is likely therefore that *Paul* guided by the same Spirit, added none to all, or any of his, but that they * were added by some other, who either transcribed and collected his Epistles together, or commented on them; as were the several Titles both before and over his several Epistles, and the contents before each Chapter, both in manuscripts, and printed Coppies.

Seventhly, it is apparent, that the Postscripts of many of *Pauls* Epistles are forged and false, as * *Mr. Perkins* in his works *Baronius* and *Beza* prove them; and that the Postscript of the first Epistle was written not only after the second penned, but likewise three hundred years after Christ or more. For it runs thus, *The first to Timothy was written from Laodicea, which is the chiefest City of Phrygia Pacatiana.* Now *Phrygia* was not surnamed *Pacatiana* (as * *divers affirm*) by any Historians or Geographers till at least three hundred years after Christ; from one *Pacatius*, a General, as is conceived, who subdued it. Since therefore it was not so stiled till about two hundred years after Christ, this Postscript must needs be added after that time; and so in all likelihood the Postscript of the second Epistle too, being both made by the same author, at the same time; and the first, first, both in time and order, as is most probable neither would *Paul* doubtlesse make such a Postscript to tell *Timothy, that Laodicea was the chiefest City of Phrygia Pacatiana*, it being so near to *Ephesus*, and as well known to *Timothy* as to *Paul*. Who, as * the *Rhemists* and *Baronius confesse, was never at Laodicea*, which they proove by *Gal*. 2. 1. and so this Postscript is but a meer falsitie.

Eightly, This Postscript is directly contrary to the very preface and body of the Epistle, written no doubt by *Paul*; which as it expresly stiles *Timothy an Evangelist*, not a Bishop; exhorting him to make full proof of his Ministry; not of his Bishoprick, c. 4. v. 5. So *Paul* therein, and in the first Epistle, ever terms him, *his dearly beloved Son*, 2 Tim. 1 2. c. 2. 1. 1 Tim. 1. 2, 18. *A man of God*, 1 Tim. 6 11. 2 Tim. 3. 17. not a Bishop: and in the 2 Tim. 4. 12. but a little above the Postscript, *Paul* writes expresly to him he had sent

* See Mr. Perkins comment. on Gal. 5. p. 497. 498, 499. where this is largely prooved.
† Comment on Gal. 6. p 497, 498, 499.
* See Tripart. Hist. l. 11 c. 3. Theodoret Eccl. Hist l. 4. c. 7. the Title of the Chapter. Socrat. Eccl. Hist. l. 7. c. 3. Niceph Eccl. Hist. l. 14. c. 11. (the first who stile it Pacatiana) and those who have lately commented on, and written against this Postscript. Surius Conc. Tom. 1. p. 453. Tom. 2, 3. p. 11, 12, 221, 438, 461, 475, 480, 483, 488, 493, 499, 503, 505, 520, 553, 580, 589, 599, 601. Carolus Sigonius de occidentali Imperio. l. 3. p. 90 Cambden Britania.
p. 5.
* Mr. Perkins Commenter on Gal 6. p. 497, 798, 799.

*Tychicus* to *Ephesus* to know *their affairs, comfort their hearts, and make known to them all things.* He being a beloved brother and faithfull Minister in the Lord, Ephes. 6. 21, 22. and neither *Timothy* his Curate and underling, much lesse his Successor at *Ephesus*, as is probable.

*Ninthly*, This Postscript is directly contradictory to many fore-alleged Scriptures, which prove *Timothy* to be no Bishop, much lesse the first or sole Bishop of the Church of the *Ephesians*; therefore not to be believed, See *Acts* 20. 28.

*Tenthly*, The Postscript it self, but especially the clause of it, ( *ordained the first Bishop of the Ephesians* ) whereon this objection is grounded, is but a late addition, not extant in any of the Fathers works who have commented on this Epistle, (except *Oecumenius*, who lived 1050. years after Christ ; the first in whom this clause of the Postscript is found ) nor in the most antient, best *Greek*, *Latin*, *Arabick*, *English*, or other Copies and *Translations*, *whether manuscript, or printed,* ( of which more anon ) therefore to be rejected, as counterfeit coyn.

*Eleventhly*, d *Eusebius* writes, that *Timothy WAS REPORTED TO BE,* ( not that he verily was) *the first Bishop of Ephesus*; therefore this Postscript either was not in being in his age, or else it had no more credit then a bare report, not sufficient to resolve that *Timothy* was undoubtedly of a truth Bishop of *Ephesus* : The first who makes mention of any of these Postscripts is *Theodoret*, 430 years after *Christ*, who perchance then added them to *Pauls* Epistles ; but in his Postscripts this clause ( *ordained the first Bishop of the Ephesians,* With that of *Titus*, *ordained the first Bishop of the Church of the Cretians* ) cannot be found.

*Secondly*, Admit this Postscript true, and authentical, that *Timothy* was Bishop of *Ephesus* when this second Epistle was written, being but a e *little before Pauls death,* yet this is no good proof, that he was Bishop of *Ephesus*, when the first Epistle was penned, being some 10. or 12. years before, as most conjecture ; for if it be a good argument, That *Timothy* was Bishop of *Ephesus*, when the second Epistle was written to him; because the Postscript of it only stiles him so :

d Ecclef. Hist. l. 3. c. 4. as Meredith Hammer an English Bishop Englished it, in his English translation of Eusebius,

e 2 Tim. 4. 6, 7, 8, 9. with all Expositors on this Epistle and the Postscript of it, if of any force or truth.

## The Un=biſhoping of Timothy and Titus.     23

ſo: it is as good or a better argument for me to ſay, that *Timothy* was no Biſhop of *Epheſus* when the firſt Epiſtle was directed to him, becauſe neither the body nor Poſtſcript of that Epiſtle; nor any other Scripture whatſoever, ſtiles him, either a Biſhop, or Biſhop of Epheſus, *though he * was reſident at Epheſus, when the firſt Epiſtle was written to him; ‖ but not when the ſecond was ſent him;* and ſo ſhould much more have been ſtiled a Biſhop, in the firſt Epiſtle and Poſtſcript, than in the ſecond. Now all the Prelates and Papiſts arguments, by which they would prove *Timothy* a Biſhop, are drawn from his firſt Epiſtle, (which *Ludovicus Capellus, Baronius,* and others acknowledge to be written many years before *Paul* was Biſhop of *Epheſus*) not from his ſecond; the Poſtſcript therefore of his ſecond Epiſtle is no argument to prove, that he was a Biſhop when the firſt Epiſtle was written: for why then ſhould not the Poſtſcript of the firſt Epiſtle ſtile him a Biſhop as well as the ſecond? yea, rather than the ſecond? ſince the firſt hath much matter in it, both concerning the offices and qualities of a Biſhop, the ſecond very little, or nothing, ſave only of *f diligent and conſtant preaching in ſeaſon and out of ſeaſon;* which belongs indifferently to all Biſhops and Miniſters, and is ſo far from being proper and peculiar to Biſhops in theſe dayes, that it is hardly common to or with any of them; Rare to moſt of them, and altogether improper for ſome of them, who *g like the dunſtical Biſhop of Dunkellden, think it no part of their Epiſcopal office, and that they were never ſo much as ordained to preach, but rather to ſit mute and domineer like Lords, and that preaching belongs only to Curats, and inferiour Miniſters, not to Lordly Prelates,* who ſeldom climb now into a Pulpit above once a year, whereas *Chryſoſtom, Auguſtin, Ambroſe, Cyril, Hooper,* and other Biſhops antiently preached once at leaſt every day.

*Obj.* 2. The ſecond objected allegation is this; that *Paul* deſcribes to Timothy *the office, qualities, carriage, and duties of a Biſhop, inſtructing him how to demean himſelf in that office,* 1 Tim. 3. c. 4, and 5. Therfore he was a Biſhop.

*Anſw.* 1. To this I anſwer : firſt, that *Paul by a Biſhop in.*

*† 1 Tim. 1, 3, 4.
‖ 2 Tim. 4. 12.
Epheſ. 6. 21, 22.*

*f 2 Tim 4. 1, 2.
g Fox Acts & Monuments, p. 1153. Nicolas de Clemangiis de corrupto Eccl. Statu c. 14, 15, 16, 17, 18, 19. Biſhop Latymers Sermon of the plough.*

See the Rhemiſts in their Preface to this Epiſtle.

in this Epistle means no Diocæsan Bishop in dignity and degree above a Presbyter, but only such a Bishop as was equal, the same, and no wayes different from an Elder ; as all the h Fathers and most modern Expositors on this and other Texts accord. Such a Bishop I acknowledge *Timothy* to be and so this instruction to him implyes; but that he was a Diocæsan Bishop, superior in dignity to, or different in order from a Presbyter, this text and argument cannot evince.

h *Hierom, Ambrose, Chrysostome, Sedulius, Primasius, Theodoret, Theophylact, Remigius, Rabanus Maurus, Anselmus, Oecumenius, Alensis, Lombard, Bruno,* with all late Expositors on 1 Tim 3. Phil. 1. 1. Tit. 1. 5, 7. Acts 20. 17. 28. and Mr *Cartwright* in his Answer to the Rhemists Preface.
i *Non solum Timotheum sed & omnem per hoc admonet Episcopam,* Oecumenius in 1 Tim. 5. 1.

Secondly, Admit it meant of a Diocæsan Bishop, yet it follows not thence, that *Timothy* was such a one : this Epistle being written rather to instruct others than *Timothy*, who was so well tutered before, both by his Grandmother *Lois*, and *Paul*, 1 Tim. 6. 12. 20. c. 4, 6, 14. 16. 2 *Tim.* 1. 5, 6, 13,14. c. 2. 2. c. 3. 10, 14, 15. but *for a pattern of the qualification and duty of Ministers* ; to direct the Church in all future ages, (who have inserted it into their Canons, Pontificals, and forms of ordinations or consecrations of Bishops and Ministers,) *rather then to inform* Timothy *at that time: whence in both these Epistles there are some predictions of the Apostacy and degeneracy of the last times* ; more necessary for i others than Timothy to know, 1 Tim. 5. 24, 25. c. 6. 15. c. 4. 1, to 7. 2 Tim. 3. 1, to 10.

k 2 Tim. 3 16
l Tim. 6.1, to 21.

Thirdly. There are in the same Chapter instructions given, concerning *Deacons, Widows,* and others; yet *Timothy* was neither Deacon nor Widow ; which being necessary for the Church of God, and for *Timothy* also to know, as he was an Evangelist, a Fellow-helper and Assistant of *Paul* in his Ministerial and Apostolical function, and as his delegate to order and regulate the Church accordingly, argue him to be no more a Bishop, as is surmised; then that every *Minister and Christian* for k *whose instruction and direction this Epistle was written as well as for* Timothies are Bishops; or then any Archbishops, or Bishops instructions to their Archdeacons, Vicars Generals, Chancellors or Officials for Ecclesiastical affairs, or Visitations, argue them to be Archbishops or Bishops.

Fourthly, We read of divers books, concerning the office and regiment of Kings, of Magistrates, and dedicated

to

# The Un-bishoping of Timothy and Titus.

to young Princes, and others who were neither Kings, Magistrates, nor Captains; of divers tractates concerning Bishops, inscribed to such who were no Bishops; yet the dedicating of such Treatises to them, did neither constitute or necessarily imply them to be Kings, Magistrates Captains, Bishops. Why then should this Epistle to *Timothy*, wherein are some things concerning the Office, Qualities, and Duties of a Bishop, prove him convincingly to be such a one.

*Obj.* 3. The third evidence to prove *Timothy* a Bishop, is taken from the 1 *Tim.* 5. 22. Where he is enjoyned, *to lay hands suddenly on no man*; that is, to ordain no man suddenly, a Minister. Therefore certainly he was a Bishop, because none but Bishops have power to ordain Ministers.

*Answ.* 1. I answer first, that the laying on of hands hath divers significations in Scripture. Sometimes, it is taken, *for an apprehension of another as a Malefactor, to punish, or bring him to judgement for his offences*, Exod. 24. 11. Esther 8. 7. Gen. 37. 22. Exod. 6. 13. Nehem. 13. 21. Luke 21. 22. in which sence it may be well taken here, as the preceding verses evidence. Sometimes it is used for *reconciliation of persons at variance*, Job 9. 33. Sometimes for *benediction* or blessing of *another*, Mat. 9. 15. Sometimes for *curing and healing*, Mark 5. 23. Mat. 19. 18. Mark 6. 5. Luke 4. 40. Sometimes for *confirmation*, as many affirm, Acts 8. 17, 18, 19. Sometimes for *ordination*, as Acts 6. 6. cap. 8. 17, 11. cap. 13. 3. 1 Tim. 4. 14. 2 Tim. 1. 6. Acts 19. 6. In which of these sences it is here meant is * *not certainly resolved*, and so no inference can be infallibly raised thence.

* *Divus Basilius ita interpretatus est, quasi nihil hujus capitis ad ordinationem pertineat. Oecumenius in* 1 *Tim.* 5. 22.

Secondly, Admit it meant of ordination, as most conceive it; yet that proves not *Timothy* to be a Bishop, since not only *Apostles, Evangelists, and the Apostles fellow-helpers* had power of ordination, as they were such, Acts 1. 22, 25, 26. c. 6. 6. c. 8. 17, 18. c. 13. 1, 2, 3. c. 14. 23. c. 19. 6. Tit. 1. 5. 2 Tim. 1. 6. but even *Presbyters themselves*: Acts 9. 17. c. 13. 1, 2, 3. c. 14. 23. 1 Tim. 4. 14. and *Timothy* might exercise this power in all or either of these respects, not as a Bishop, which for ought appears he never was; neither read we in Scrip-

Scripture that ordination belongs of right to Bishops, as Bishops; muchlesse, that it is appropriated unto them. Of which more fully hereafter.

*Obj.* 4. The fourth Objection to prove *Timothy* a Bishop, is this; *that he is commanded to rebuke such as sinned openly before all men, that others might fear,* 1 Tim. 5. 20. Therefore he was a Bishop.

*Answ.* I answer, that the argument is an inconsequent.

*First,* Because he might do this as an Evangelist, or as *Pauls* associate or substitute, by vertue of his Apostolical authority, not of his own Episcopal Jurisdiction, as Bishops Officials, Chancellors and Vicars General, rebuke, correct and visit others, not in their own names, or by their own authority, but their Lord Bishops.

*Secondly,* He might do this as a Minister, *every Minister having power sufficient in the publick Ministery of the word, openly to rebuke all sins and sinners,* Isaiah 5.8, 1, &c. Ezech. 2. 2 Tim. 4. 2, 3. Tit. 1. 13. c. 2. 15. Mark 6. 18, 19, 20. 2 Sam. 12. 7.

*Thirdly,* He might do this as a private Christian; every Christian being enjoyned *in any case to rebuke his Neighbour, and not to suffer sin upon him,* Levit. 19. 17. Prov. 9. 8. Eccles. 9. 5. *and so is every Magistrate to do,* Nehem. 13. 11, to 31. Psal. 141. 5. Psal. 101. 5. 8. This therefore is no argument of any Episcopal Jurisdiction; the rather, because this rebuke was to be *publickly in the Church before all,* not in a private Chamber or Consistory Court, ( as all expositors accord ) in which our Bishops pronounce their Censures.

*Obj.* 5. The fift argument to prove *Timothy* a Bishop, is the 1 Tim. 5. 19. *Against an Elder receive not an accusation, but before two or three witness s.* He had power to receive an accusation against Ministers, that so he might correct them; therefore he was a Bishop.

*Answ.* I answer first, that this is a meer *Non sequitur.*

For 1 He might have this power, to receive such accusation as an Evangelist, and *Pauls* Coadjutor.

*Secondly,* As *Pauls* Delegate or Official ; as our Bishops Officials, Vicars and Chancellors now exercise Episcopal Jurisdiction under them ; as their substitutes only, not by

any

any inherent Episcopal dignity or authority in themselves.

*Thirdly*, He might do it by the appointment and mutual consent of the people, *who had power in any differences, to constitute any man a Judge, though no Bishop*, 1 Cor. 6. 1, to 7.

*Fourthly*, He might do it only as an Elder; *Elders having power to rule well*, 1 Tim. 5. 17. and so by consequence, to receive *accusations,* and *to correct Delinquents by reproofs or Ecclesiastical Censures, with the consent of the Congregation*, 1 Cor. 5. 4,5,11,12. c. 6. 1, to 7. Gal. 6. 1. 2 Thess. 3. 14, 15. Mat. 18. 17.

*Fifthly*, I had almost added, that he might have done it as an Ecclesiastical high Commissioner, but that I considered, that he was not so much as *to receive an accusation, against an Elder, but under two or three witnesses at least*, first examined; and *our Ecclesiastical Commissioners and Bishops are so far from this divine Apostolical precept*, by which they would prove *Timothy* and themselves to be Bishops *Jure divino*, that they will *pursevance, silence, suspend, imprison Ministers and Elders, and put them to self-accusing* ex officio *oathes, upon every apparitors jealosie, suspition, and private accusation of any Drunkard, Rascal, without two or three witnesses or accusers, first examined against them, and brought face to face.* A direct proof, that neither they nor their present proceedings are *Jure divino*.

*Answ.* 2. *Secondly*, I answer, that by *Elder* in this Text, (as * many conceive) is not meant a Presbyter, or Minister, *but an antient man*, as it is taken in the *first verse of the Chapter*: so as it proves not, that *Timothy* had any Ecclesiastical Jurisdiction over the Elders that were Ministers of *Ephesus, who ruled that Church*, v. 17 and *were the Bishops of it*, Act. 20. 28. Where *Paul* enjoyns them, *to take heed to themselves*; as having no superintendent paramount them; not giving *Timothy* any charge to take heed to them.

*Thirdly*, Admit these Elders were Ministers, yet *Timothy* had no judiciary power over them, to suspend or correct them: since *v.* 1. he is expresly enjoyned, *not to rebuke an Elder, but intreat him as a Father*: which is far from giving him any such Episcopal Jurisdiction over them as our Bishops now exercise and usurpe; using godly Ministers and

* See *Gersomus Bucerus*, and Mr. *Rutherfords due Right of Presbyteries.*

* *Conference at Hampton Court*, p 89, 90. *Melvini Cessae Commissionis Anatomia. Fullers argument*, 1607. *The Petition of Grievances 7. Iacobi.*
* *Chrysost. Theodoret. Theophilact. Oecumenius, and others on this text. The Brethren of London in K. Henry the 8. his dayes in their Letter to Thomas Philips. Fox Acts and Monuments, p. 951.*

rating and treating them, rather like dogs and scullions, than Elders, or Fathers.

*Fourthly,* The words are not, that he should not excommunicate, suspend, convent or censure an Elder, but *that he should not receive an accusation against him, but before two or three witnesses.* Now to condemn or censure, is one thing, to receive an accusation, another. The first none but a Judge or chief Officer can do; the second, every Register, Clerk, Informer, or under Officer; *Yea, *every private Christian is capable to receive an accusation, and every ordinary Minister too, against another superior to him in age, estate, or place, either privately to admonish him that is accused, of his fault, or to reprove him for it; or to counsel him how to repent and redress it; or to comfort him if he be dejected with it, or to inform against him to the Magistrate, or whole Congregation, or to pray to God for his amendment,* Mat. 18. 15, 16, 17. Levit. 19. 7. Gal. 6. 1. 2 Thess. 3. 14, 15. 1 Tim. 5. 20, 24. Tit. 1. 10, to 14. 2 Johan. 10. 11. Jud. 22. 23. which well expound this text.

* *See Davidis Blondelli Apologia, Sect. 3, 4.*

*Fifthly,* The true meaning of this text is this, that *Timothy* and other Christians of what quality soever, especially Ministers, should not lightly receive or believe any ill report, chiefly of an Elder or Minister, without sufficient testimony of the truth thereof by two or three able witnesses; as will plainly appear by paralelling it with Psal. 15. 3. Numb. 35. 30. Deut. 17. 6. c. 19. 15. 17. Heb. 10. 28. and with Mat. 18. 15, 16, 17. where our Saviour saith thus. *Moreover, if thy Brother shall trespass against thee, go and tell him his fault between him and thee alone: if he shall hear thee, thou hast gained thy Brother: But if he will not hear thee, then take with thee two or three more, that in the mouth of two or three witnesses, every word may be established; and if he shall neglect to hear them, tell it to the Church, and if he neglect to hear the Church, let him be unto thee as an heathen man and publican.* A perfect Commentary on this text of *Paul,* and a direct censure of our Bishops ex officio Oaths, and proceedings by the parties own self-accusing Oath and answer, without or before witnesses produced.

*Sixthly,*

*Sixthly*, This text (admit it gives power to *Timothy* to take an accusation against an Elder before two or three witnesses;) yet it excludes not the other Elders of *Ephesus* from having like power with him; it gives him not any sole power to hear and determine complaints without the other Elders assistance or consent, * *but together with them*, Mat. 18. 19. 1 Tim. 5. 17. Act. 20. 28. Hence the *fourth Council of Carthage*, Can. 23 and after it *Gratian Caus*. 15. *Quest*. 7. *Cap. Nullus*, Decree, *That a Bishop should hear no mans cause without the presence of his Clerks; and that the sentence of the Bishop should be void, unlesse it were confirmed with the presence and assent of the Clergy.* Which is likewise affirmed and practiced by *Tertullian*, Apologia c. 29. St. *Cyprian* Epist. 6. 22, 28, 46. *Clemens Alexandrinus*, Strom. l. 7. *Origen*. Homil. 11. in Exodum & Hom. 7. in Josh. Basil. Epist. 75. *Ambrose* Epist. l. 20. Epist. 80. ad Syagrium. *Ruffinus* Hist. l. 10. c. 9. Cyril. Epist. ad Johannem Antiochenum Gregory Epist. l. 11. Epist. 49. *Hierom*. Epist. ad Demetriadem and others. Yea, *Gratian*. *Caus*. 15. qu. 7. proves out of the *Councils of Hispalin, Agatha the first, Carthage the second and fourth*, and *Gregory* (whose words and Canons he recites at large) *that a Minister, Presbyter, or Deacon cannot be punished, or deprived by the Bishop alone, but by a Synod or Council, and that the Bishop cannot hear or determine the causes of Clergy men alone, without associating the Elders of the Church or other adjoyning Bishops, with him*; for which cause * many antient Councils decreed, *that there should be two Councils kept, in each Province every year, to hear and determine all Ecclesiastical causes and controversies*. This text therefore proves nothing for *Timothies* Ecclesiastical or Episcopal Jurisdiction, *being written rather for the Churches, and Ministers future, than Timothies present instruction*, as || *Gersomus Bucerus* rightly observes. Finally learned * *Doctor Whitaker* hath long since assoyled this objection in these words: *That Timothy is commanded not rashly to admit an accusation against an Elder, this proves not, that Timothy had power or dominion over Elders. For according to the Apostles mind, to receive an accusation, is to bring a crime to the Church, to bring the guilty person into Judgement, openly to reprove*, which

* See *Davidis Blondelli Apologia*, Sect. 3. *Smectimnuus*, Mr. *Rutherfords* due Right of Presbyteries.

* *Concilium Antiochenum*, Can. 20. Gratian Distinct. 18. *Cons. Aphricanum*, Can. 18. *Chalcedonense*. Can. 19 Nicænum Can. 5 Toletanum 3. Can. 18. *Synodus Francica*. Anno 42. Conc. *Melense*, Can. 31. with many others.
|| *Dissertatio de Guber. Ecclesiæ* p. 506, 507, 508.
* *Controv*. 4. Quest. 1. c. 2. Sect. 16.

not only *Superiors may do, but also equals and inferiors*. In the Roman Republike, *Knights did judge not only the people, but also the Senators, and Patricii*. And certainly it seems not that *Timothy had such a Consistory or Court, as was afterwards appointed to Bishops in the Church*. What this authority was, may be understood by that which follows ; *Those that sin rebuke before all, which equals also may do*. Thus Bishops heretofore, if any Elder or Bishop had an ill report, referred it to the Ecclesiastical Senate or Synod, and condemned him, if he seemed worthy by a publick judgement, that is, they did either suspend, excommunicate or remove him. The Bishop condemning nocent Elders and Deacons, not with his own authority alone, but with the judgement of the Church and Clergy Those who were thus condemned, might lawfully appeal to the Metropolitan ; but he could not presently alone determine what seemed good to him, but permitted the Synod to give sentence, and what the Synod decreed was ratified. The same Answer *Martyn Bucer. De vi & usu. S. Ministerii*, Dr. *Andrew Willet Synopsis Papismi. Cont.* 5. *Gen. Quest.* 3. part 3. in the *Appendix*, and *Gersomus Bucerus De Gubernat. Ecclesiæ* * page 300, to 398. (where this objection is most fully cleared by Councils, Fathers, and other authors testimonies) give unto this place: so that it makes no proof at all, that *Timothy* was a Bishop. From all these premises I may now safely conclude, *that Timothy was neither a Bishop, nor Bishop of Ephesus, nor first, nor sole Bishop of that See*, as many overconfidently, and erroniously affirm.

* *Vide p.* 450, *usque* 514. *and David Blondellius. Apologia pro sententia Hieronima de Episcopis & Presbyteris, Sectio* 3.

* See *Gersomus Bucerus p.* 518, 519.

Obj. 6. If any in the sixt place object, that * *diverse of the antient Fathers, as Dionysius Areopagita, Hierom, Ambrose, Dorotheus, Theodoret, Chrysostom, Epiphanius, Eusebius, Gregory the great, Policrates, Primasius, Isidor Hispalensis, B. da, Anselm, Rabanus Maurus, Oecumenius, with many modern writers affirm, Timothy to be Bishop, and first Bishop of the Ephesians*; therefore he was so.

*Answ.* I answer first, that as some of these Fathers are spurious, and not to be credited, so many of their testimonies are ambiguous, if not contradictory. p *Eusebius* writes, *that Timothy IS REPORTED to be the first Bishop of Ephesus, and Titus of the Church of Crete*: which is rather a denyal than

p *Ecclif Hist. l.* 3 *c.* 4 *m Meredith Hanmer, a Bishop Englisheth it.*

an

## The Un-bishoping of Timothy and Titus.

an affirmation that he was Bishop there in truth. *Theodoret* and *Beda* affirm him, *to be Bishop of all* Asia, *not of* Ephesus *only, and so an Archbishop rather than a Bishop.* Their Testimonies therefore being so discrepant and dubious, are of no validity. \* *In* 1 *Tim* 3.

Secondly, ‖ Many of the Fathers affirm Peter to have been Bishop of Rome, and to have continued Bishop there for divers years; yet q *Marsilius Patavinus*, r *Carolus Molinæus*, with sundry f other late Protestant Writers, both forein and domestique, affirm, and substantially prove by Scripture and reasons, that Peter was never at Rome, nor yet Bishop thereof. As therefore their bare authorities are no sufficient argument, to prove *Peter* Bishop of *Rome*, (the foundation of the Popes Supremacy) so neither are they sufficient to evince *Timothy* Bishop of *Ephesus*.

‖ *See Dr* Reynolds *conference, with* Hart, *p.* 213. q *Defensor Pacis, pars* 2 c 16. *Ulricus Velenus, Petrus non venisse Romam, neque illic passus est.* r *Senatus Consultus Franciæ contra abusus Paparum. p.* 162, *to* 172. f *Dr.* Reynolds *conference with* Hart, *c.* 6. *Divis.* 3 *p.* 210, to 218. *Balæus in Act. Rom. Pontif. l.* 1. *Præfatio.* Christopher Carlile *his S.* Peters Life *and* Peregrination, *proving that* Peter was never at Rome. R. Bernard *his fabulous foundation of the Popedom.*

Thirdly, These Fathers affirm not *Timothy* to be sole Bishop of *Ephesus*, or to be a Diocæsan Bishop, or such a Bishop as is superiour to a Presbyter in Jurisdiction or Degree; the thing which ought to be proved; and if they affirmed any such thing, yet seeing the fore-alledged Scriptures contradict it in a most apparent manner, they are not to be credited against the Scriptures testimony.

Fourthly, The Fathers term him Bishop of *Ephesus*; not because he was any sole Diocæsan domineering Bishop there, as the objectors pretend; but because *he was left by Paul to teach and instruct them for a space, till he returned from* Macedonia, and to order that Church joyntly with the other Bishops and Elders thereof; and being one of the eminentest Pastors of the Church, next after *Paul*, who planted it, the Fathers term him, *the Bishop of Ephesus*, in that sence only as they styled *Peter, Bishop of Rome and Antioch, James Bishop of Jerusalem, Mark Bishop Alexandria*, and the like; (\* *not that they were Bishops properly so called*, or such as ours are now, but only in a large and general appellation,

\* *Fox* Acts *and* Monuments. *p.* 1465 Geisimus Buserus *De* Gubernat Eccl. *p.* 432 *usq;* 500, 519, 520, *to* 540.

pellation, because *they first preached the Gospel to these Churches) And that to no other purpose, but to prove a perpetual succession of Presbyters, and doctrine in those particular Churches, from the Apostles time till theirs,* naming the eminentest Minister *for parts and gifts in each Church, the Bishop of that Church;* all which appears by t *Irenæus,* u *Tertullian,* and x *others;* who call them Bishops only for this purpose, *to derive a succession of Ministers, and doctrine from the Apostles.* He that would receive a lager answer to this objection, let him read *Gersomus Bucerus, de Gubernatione Ecclesiæ,* p. 518, to 524. 436, to 498 *usque* 530, 438, 539. and *Davidi Blundelli Apologia;* which will give him ample satisfaction.

t *Adverf. Hæreses, L 3. c. 2, 3. l 4 c. 43, 44, 45.*
u *De Præscriptionibus adverf. Hæreticos.*
x *Eusebius Ecclef. Hist. l 5. c. 12. 22.*
*Fox Acts and Monuments,* p. 1465.

*Obj.* 7. If any finally object, that *Paul desired* Timothy to abide still at Ephesus, *when he went into* Macedonia, 1 *Tim:* 1. 3. and that the Greek verb προσμεινα *signifies a constant residence or abiding in one place.* Therefore *Timothy* was Bishop of *Ephesus:* which if it be a solid Argument, proves many of our Court Non-resident Prelates and Ministers, to be no Bishops (because they reside and abide not, much lesse preach and keep hospitality on their Bishopricks, and Benefices) rather than *Timothy* to be Diocæsan Bishop of *Ephesus.*

*Ansv.* 1. To this I answer, first, that the argument is a grosse inconsequent. For *Timothy* might abide thus at *Ephesus* as an Evangelist, as an Elder, as *Pauls* assistant, or substitute only; as an ordinary Minister, not as a Bishop; his abiding therefore at *Ephesus* is insufficient to prove him a Diocæsan Bishop of that See.

Secondly, Paul *and* Titus *ordained Elders, in every Church to abide and continue with their flocks,* Acts 14. 23. Tit. 1. 5. 7. yet the Opposites deny these Elders to be Diocæsan Bishops.

Thirdly, *Every ordinary Minister is to reside and abide upon his Cure,* Rom. 12. 7, 8. 1 Cor. 7. 20. Jer. 23. 1. 5. If this argument therefore were solid, every Minister should be a Diocæsan Bishop : and that more properly then our Non-resident Bishops, Curates, who are seldome at their Cures.

\* Acts 18. 18, 19.

Fourthly, Paul *left* \* Aquila *and* Priscilla *at* Ephesus *to abide*

## The Un=bishoping of Timothy and Titus.

*abide there*; Will it therefore follow, that they were Diocæsan Bishops of the *Ephesians*? If not, then the argument is invalid.

*Answ.* 2. *Secondly*, I answer, *That* Timothy *was to abide at* Ephesus *only for a season*, *till Pauls return out of* Macedonia, *and no longer*, 1 Tim. 3. 14, 15. c. 4. 13, 14. *after which he went with* Paul *from* Macedonia *into* Asia *to* Troas, *Acts* 20. 4, 5. *and from thence to* Italy, Philippi, *and* Rome, *Heb.* 13. 23. *Phil.* 1. 1. c. 2. 19. Col. 1 1. 1. *Tim.* 4. 9, 13. he being never resident at *Ephesus*, (for ought appears in Scripture or authentique story,) after *Pauls* return out of *Macedonia*. His abode therefore at *Ephesus* being but for so short a time, and he so great a Nonresident from it afterward, cannot possibly argue him to be a Diocæsan Bishop of that Church.

*Answ.* 3. *Thirdly*, the Greek word προσμένειν *to abide*, is oft applyed in Scripture to *a short abode*, *for a day or two*, *or some little space*, as well as to a perpetual fixed residence; *Mat.* 15 32. *Mark* 8. 2. So it is in the objected text; where it is put only in opposition to *Pauls* journey into *Macedonia*; in respect whereof *Timothy* continuing at *Ephesus* till his return, might be truely said, *to abide there*, though after his return he removed thence to other Churches; as *Gersomus Bucerus*, *De Gubernatione Ecclesiæ*, *p.* 532. *to* 581. observes.

*Answ.* 4. *Fourthly*, Paul did not injoyn, *but beseech* Timothy *to abide at* Ephesus : therefore his residence there was but arbitrary at his own pleasure, not coactive, not injoyned by vertue of any Episcopal office, or obligation : this Text therefore cannot prove *Timothy* to be Bishop of *Ephesus*, no more than his stay at *Corinth*, and other places whether *Paul* sent him, prove him to be Bishop of those Churches.

*Answ.* 5. *Finally*, Admit *Timothy* to be both the first and sole Bishop of *Ephesus*, which is false; yet this makes nothing for, but against, our Hierarchical and Diocæsan Bishops : for *Ephesus was but one City*, *one Parish*, *one Church*, *one Flock and congregation*; as is evident by Acts 20. 17, 28, 29.

*Timothy no Diocæsan Bishop of Ephesus.*

c. 18.

c. 18. 24, 25, 26. c. 19. 1, to 18. Ephes. 1. 1. c. 4. 4, 16. c. 21, 22, 23. 1 Tim. 1. 3. c. 5. 17, to 23. Rev. 1. 20. c. 2. 1. So that the argument from this examples is but this, *Timothy* was only Bishop of one City, Parish, Church, Flock and Congregation, not of many: Therefore all *Bishops* ought to be so too, as well as he.

*Obj.* If any object, that the City of *Ephesus* was a Diocess; for it had *many Elders,* therefore many Parishes, and Congregations? *Acts* 20. 17. 28. 1 *Tim.* 5. 17.

*Answ.* 1. I answer, that the argument follows not; For first, in *the Apostles times, and in the primitive Church, every particular Church and Congregation had* \*many *Bishops, Elders, Ministers, and Deacons in it, who did joyntly teach, and instruct it, and likewise govern and order it by their common Counsel and consent;* as is evident by Acts 1. 14, to 26. c. 2. 1, to 47. c. 3. 1. c. 4. 3, 8, 9, 20, 21, 23, 31, to 37. c. 5. 18, to 33, 42. c. 6. 1, to 9. c. 11. 29, 30. c. 14. 23. c. 15. 2, to 23, 25, 32. c. 20. 17, to 30. c. 21. 18. Phil. 1. 1. 1 Tim. 5. 4, to 14. c. 5. 17. Tit. 1. 5, 7. James 5. 14. 1 Cor. 14. 23, to 33. Hebr. 13. 17. 1 Thes. 5. 12. *Ignatius Epist.* 5, 6, 8, 9, 10, 11, 13, 14. *Policarpus Epist. ad Philippenses, Irenæus contra Heres. l.* 3. c. 2. *l.* 4 c. 43, 44. *Tertul. A lversus Gentes,* Apolog. c. 39. St. *Cyprian Epist.* 6, 12, 28. *Clemens Alexandrinus, Strom. l.* 7. *Ambrose Epist. l.* 10. *Epist.* 80. *Hieronimus, Sedulius, Chrysostomus, Primasius, Remigius, Haymo, Rabanus Maurus, Oecumenius, Theophylact, Anselmus, Petrus, Lombardus,* and sundry others, in their Commentaries, and expositions upon Phil. 1. 1. 1 Tit. 5. Acts 15. and 20. 17, 28. The fourth Counsel of *Carthage,* Can. 22, 23, 24, 24. The Council of *A ex,* under *Ludovicus Pius.* Can. 8. 10, 11. Tb 12. Council of *Toledo,* Can. 4. and all Writers generally accord.

*Secondly,* We at this day, have many Prebends, Canons, and Ministers in every Cathedral and Collegiate Church, yea in every Colledge in our Universities, and elsewhere; yet but one Church and Congregation.

*Thirdly,* We have in many other Churches in the Country where the Parishes are large, and there are divers Chapels of ease, many Curates and Ministers; yet but one Church,

\* *See Gersonius Bucerus Dissertio De Gubern. Ecclef. p. 213, 246, 281, 302, 303, 304, 307, 308, 416, 417, 461. Davidis Blund. Apollog. Section. 3. accordingly.*

Church, one Parish, not a Diocess; neither is the chief Minister either a Bishop or Diocæsan, though he have divers Curates and Ministers under him, to assist him in his Ministery: yea in many places where there is but one Church, no such Chapels of ease, and the Parish great, we have several Ministers, Lecturers, and Curates, in some 4. or 5. in most 2. or 3. yet no Diocess, no Bishoprick. Neither is this a Novelty, but an antient constitution, not only instituted by the Apostles, and continued ever since, but likewise enjoyned by the * *Council of Oxford under Stephen Langhton Archbishop of Canterbury in the year of our Lord, 1222.* which decreed, *That in all Parish Churches, where the Parish is great, there should be 2. or 3. Presbyters at the least, according to the greatness of the Parish, and the value of the Benefice; lest that one only Minister being sick, or otherwise debilitated, Ecclesiastical Benefits (which God forbid) should be either withdrawn, or denied to the Parishioners that were sick, or willing to be present at divine offices.* The multitude or plurality therefore of the Elders in the Church of *Ephesus*, is no argument at all to prove, that it was a Diocess; or that *Timothy* was a Diocæsan Bishop, because he had Ministers and Curates under him; for then our Deans, Archdeacons, and Pluralists, who have many Livings, Chapels, (and so many Curates and Ministers) under them, should be Diocæsan Bishops too by this reason.

* *Johannes de Alco, Constit. provin. fol. 122. Lynd provin. Constit. L 3. Tit. De Parochiu, fol. 134.*

Secondly, I answer, that admit there were divers Churches and Congregations in *Ephesus*, which is very improbable, *the greatest part of the Citizens being Idolaters, and the City it self a great Worshiper of the Goddesse Diana*, *and of the Image which fell from Jupiter*, Acts 19. 21. to 41. yet it cannot be proved, that *Timothy* was chief Bishop and Superintendent over all these Churches, but only of one of them: as every Minister and Bishop of *England* is a Minister and Bishop of the Church of *England*, but not a Minister and Bishop in and over all the Churches of *England*, but in and over his own Parish-Church, and Diocess only. For *Paul* himself (who planted that Church, ‖ *resided in it for three years space*, during which time there was no Diocæ-

‖ *Acts* 19. 10. c. 20. 31.

(an Bishop of it but himself) expresly calls the *Elders of the Church of Ephesus*, BISHOPS *and Overseers of that Church, and that by the Holy Ghosts own institution*; and thereupon exhorts them, *to take heed to all the flock; and to feed and rule that Church of God, which he had purchased with his own blood*, Acts 20: 28. 1 Tim 5. 17.

Since therefore every one of these Elders by the Holy Ghosts institution, and *Pauls* resolution was no other, but a *Bishop* over his own flock, (if several,) both to instruct and rule it; it is certain, that *Timothy* (if he were a Bishop of *Ephesus*, and there were many Churches in it) was only Bishop of one of them, not of all; and so no Diocæsan Bishop, as our Prelates and their Flatterers vainly pretend. *Timothy* therefore * being neither a Bishop, nor first, sole, or any Bishop of *Ephesus*, or of any other place, or if a Bishop, no Diocæsan Bishop, but of one Church and congregation only, as these premises evidence; all our Prelates inferences drawn from his example to prove their Episcopal Authority and Jurisdiction *Jure Divino*, (which for the most part hang upon his Episcopal rochet only) fall quite to ground, and their pretended *divine* Episcopal Authority together with it.

*See Smectymnuus Answer to Bishop Halls Remonstrance, p. 48. to 54. printed 1640.

Question 2.

I now proceed to the next Question, *Whether Titus were Bishop, or Archbishop of Crete?* Wherein I shall likewise discuss these two Questions. *Whether the power of ordination belongs only to Bishops, not to Presbyters? And whether this Paradox of the Prelates be true, that Ordainers are greater in Jurisdiction and degree than those that are ordained?*

What ever the common bruit and error of these or former times conceive, under correction, I perswade my self, that *Titus* was no Bishop nor Archbishop of *Crete*: and that for these ensuing invincible reasons.

*First*, Because the Scripture never terms him a Bishop; nor S. *Paul*, who often stiles him, *his Partner and Fellow-helper concerning the Corinthians*, (not Cretians;) *the Messenger of the Churches*, (not Bishop) *and the glory of Christ*, 2 Cor. 8. 2, 3. 6, 16. his *Son*, *Titus* 1, 6. his *Brother*, 2 Cor. 7. 6, 13, 14. never a Bishop, as some would make him.

*Secondly*,

# The Un=bishoping of Timothy and Titus.

*Secondly,* Because his *chiefest imployment was to the Church of Corinth, after that he had been left by Paul at Crete, as Paules partner and fellow-helper in that Church,* 2 Cor. 2. 13. c. 7. 6, 13. c. 8. 6, 16, 23. c. 12. 18.

*Thirdly,* Because he *was Pauls companion, attendant, partner, fellow-helper, Messenger, fixed to no setled place of residence,* as Bishops were, 2 Cor. 2. 13. c. 7. 6, 13. c. 8. 6, 16, 23. c. 12. 18. Gal. 2. 1, 3. 2 Tim. 4. 10. *sent by him from Rome, long after his being in Crete, into Dalmatia,* 2 Tim. 4. 10.

*Fourthly,* Because *Paul* writes expresly to him, *Tit.* 1. 5. not that he ordained him Archbishop or Bishop of *Crete,* but *that he left him in Crete* (for a season) *for this cause, that he should set in order, the things that were wanting, and ordain Elders in every City, as he had appointed him:* Therefore was he left there only as *Pauls* Vicar general, Commissary or substitute, to order those things, which *Paul* could not dispatch, *in such sort, as he had appointed him,* whiles he was there residing, not as the Archbishop or Lord Bishop of *Crete,* to order all things there, by his own Episcopal Jurisdiction and authority alone as he listed himself.

*Fifthly,* He expresly charged him, *to come to him diligently to Nicopolis when he should send Artemas or Tychicus to him, for there he intended to winter,* Tit. 3. 12. By which it is evident, that his stay in *Crete* by *Pauls* appointment, was very short, not above half a year, if so much; after which we never read he returned thither, though we find, *he was sent to Corinth, and Dalmatia, that he went up to Hierusalem with Paul, and came to him during his imprisonment at Rome,* Gal. 2. 1, 3. 2 Cor. 2. 13. c. 7. 13, 14. c. 8. 6, 16, 23. c. 12. 8. 2 Tim. 4. 10. His short abode therefore in *Crete,* without returning thither, proves him to be no Bishop in, or of it.

*Sixthly, Paul* chargeth him, to bring *Zenas* the *Lawyer,* and *Apollos diligently on their way, that nothing might be wanting to them,* Tit. 3. 13. Now it is very unlikely, that an Archbishop or Bishop of *Crete, wherein were* *90. *walled Cities,* would stoope so low, as to wait thus upon a Lawyer, as *Zenas* was, or a Disciple, as *Apollos* was, unlesse he were far more Humble than any Archbishops or Prelates in these our times;

* *Homer. Odyss.* 19.

times; who are commonly so insolently proud, as to disdain all familiar conversations with Lawyers, or Ministers.

*Seventhly, Paul* left *Titus* Bishop of no one City in *Crete*, and he expresly enjoyns him, *to ordain* (not one but many) *Elders* (in the plurall number) *in every City of Crete*, Tit. 1. 5, 7. where there were no lesse than 90. *walled Cities in Homer's time*; which Elders were no other but *Bishops*, and so termed by him v. 7. (*For a BISHOP must be blamlesse, &c.*) as *Hierom, Chrysostom, Ambrose, Theodoret, Sedulius, Primasius, Remigius, Beda, Rabanus Maurus, Bruno, Theophilact, Oecumenius, Anselm, Lyra, Hugo Cardinalis, Aquinas*, with other modern Commentators on this text accord. If then *Paul* gives expresse directions to *Titus*, to ordain many *Elders and Bishops in every City of Crete*, constituting him a Bishop in none of them, that we read of, (an apparent argument, that he was no Bishop there, because he had there no Bishops See at all, and was no sole Bishop of any one City:) it is not probable that he constituted him sole Archbishop, or Bishop of all Crete, (*which had* ‖ *anciently no lesse than 4. Archbishops, and 21. Bishops in it*) *it being the Apostles practice to place many Bishops and Elders in one Church, but never one Bishop or Archbishop over many Churches*, Phil. 1. 2. Act. 20. 28. Hence * *Athanasius, Chrysostom, Oecumenius* and *Theophilact*, on Titus 1. 5. 7. write thus, *Here he will have Bishops to be understood for Presbyters or Ministers, as we have elsewhere often said, neither verily would he have the charge of the whole Island to be permitted, or granted to one man, but that every one should have his own proper cure and charge allotted him: for he knew that the labour and pains would be the lighter, and that the people would be governed with greater diligence, if that the Doctor or Teacher should not be distracted with the Government of many Churches, but should only give himself to the Government of one, and study to compose and adorn it with his manners*. So also *Peter Lombard,* * *Alphonsus de Castro,* * *Doctor Barnes*, and others on and from this text, determine.

*Eightly*, All generally † accord, that *Archbishops*, yea *Metropolitanes*, and *Diocæsan* BISHOPS themselves are not of *Divine* or *Apostolical*, *ut Papal and Humane Constitution*; witnesse Pope *Nicholas*.

‖ *Mercators Atlas in English London*, 1635. p. 812.

* *Quoted by Dr. Barns in his Works,* p. 210. *See Gersomus Bucerus de Guburn. Ecclesia* p. 520, 521. * *Adversus Hæreses. Tit. Episcopus.* * P. 210.

† *See Gersomus Bucerus* p. 233. 261, 398, usque 402, 554. *Tho. Cartwright* 2, *Reply to Whitgift,* p. 404, to 616.

*Nicholas apud Gratianum Distinct. 22. c. 1. Omnes sive Patriarchæ cujuslibet apicem, sive Metropoleon primatus, aut Episcopatuum Cathedras, vel Ecclesiarum sive cujuscunque ordinis dignitatem,* IN-STITUIT ROMANA ECCLESIA. Which Pope * *Anacletus* in his 3. *Epist. c.* 3. doth likewise aver, and Pope *Lucinus,* and *Clement,* in *Gratian, Distinct.* 80. affirm as much; informing us, *that Archbishops and Primates are the Successors of the Heathenish Arch-Flamens, and to be placed only in those Cities where the Arch-Flamens had their Sees:* with which *Peter Lombard* accords, *lib.* 4. *Distinct.* 24. Hence our † *Historians* record of King *Lucius,* the first Christian Prince of this our Realm, *that he instituted* 3. *Archbishopricks, and* 25. *Bishopricks and Bishops, instead of the* 3. *Arch-Flamens, and* 2. *Flamens, changing their Sees into Bishopricks, and Archbishopricks;* by which it is evident, that Archbishops, Patriarkes, and Metropolitans (*instituted only at first by* * *several Councils and Princes*) are no Divine or Apostolical, but only a humane institution; This *all the Archbishops, Bishops and Clergy of England in their institution of a Christian man,* dedicated to King *Henry* the 8. fol. 59, 60. resolve in these termes. *IT IS OUT OF ALL DOUBT, that there is no mention made neither in Scripture, neither in the writings of any authentical Doctor or Auctor of the Church being within the time of the Apostles, that Christ did ever make or institute any distinction or difference to be in the preeminence of power, order or Jurisdiction between the Apostles themselves, or between the Bishops themselves, but that they* WERE ALL EQUAL IN POWER, AUTHORITY AND JURISDICTION: *And that there is now and since the time of the Apostles any such diversity or difference among the Bishops,* IT WAS DEVISED BY THE ANTIENT FATHERS of the Primitive Church, *for the conservation of good order, and unity of the Catholike Church; and that, either by the consent and authority, or else at least* BY THE PERMISSION AND SUFFERANCE OF THE PRINCES AND CIVIL POWERS *for the time ruling. For the said Fathers, considering the great and infinite multitude of Christian men so largely increased through the world, and taking examples of the old Testament, thought it expedient to make an order of Degrees among Bishops,*

*and.*

* See *Anacleti Epist.* 3. c. 3. *Surius Concil Tom.* 1. p. 165.

† *Galfridus Monumetensis, hist.* l. 5. c. 19. *Ponticus Verunnius Brit. hist.* l. 4. p. 106. *Polichron.* l. 4. c. 16. f. 163. *Antiquit. Eccles. Brit* p. 7. with *sundry others.*
* *Surius Concil Tom.* 1. p. 140, 163, 195, 342, 305, 392. *Tom,* 2. p. 1046 *Trim.* 3. p. 547. *Socrat. Eccles hist* l. 5 c. 8. *Evagirus Eccles. hist.* l. 2. c. 18.

and spiritual governers of the Church, and so ordained some to be Patriarks, some to be Metropolitans, some to be Archbishops, some to be Bishops; and to them did limit severally (not onely) their certain Diocesse and Provinces, wherein they should exercise their power and not exceed the same, but also certain bounds and limits, of their Jurisdiction and power, &c. The same is averred by learned Bishop Hooper, in his Exposition upon the 23. Psalm, fol. 40. who sayth, That Archbishops were first ordained in Constantines time: yea * Archbishop Whitgift himself confesseth as much, that Archbishops are neither of Divine, or Apostolical, but humane institution, since the Apostles times. And ‖ Patrick Adamson Archbishop of S. Andrews in Scotland, in his publick recantation, in the Synod of Fiffe in Scotland, Anno 1591. professed sincerely, (ex animo) that Bishops and Ministers by Gods word were all equal and the very same; That the Hierarchy and superiority of Bishops over other Ministers, NULLO NITITUR VERBI DEI FUNDAMENTO, had no foundation at all in the word of God, but was a meer humane Institution long after the Apostles times, from whence the Antichristian Papacis of the Bishop of Rome hath both its rise and progresse; and that for 500. years last past, it hath been the cheifest instrument of persecuting and suppressing the truth and Saints of God in all Cuontries and Kingdoms, as all Historians manifest. Thus this Archbishop in his Palinody, disclaiming not only Archbishops, but even Diocæsan Bishops to be of divine, but only of humane institution long after the Apostles, giving over his Archbishoprick thereupon, and living a poor dejected life. This being then granted on all hands, not only by Protestant Prelates and Divines, but likewise by Popish Canonists and Schoolmen; as *George Cassander, a learned moderate Popish writer, affirmes in these positive words. *An Episcopatus inter ordines ponendus sit, inter Theologos & Canonistas non convenit. Convenit autem* INTER OMNES *olim Apostolicorum* ÆTATE INTER EPISCOPOS ET PRESBYTEROS DISCR MEN NULLUM FUISSE. *Constat autem sacros ordines proprie dici Diaconatum & Presbyteratum, & quos solos primitivam Ecclesiam in usu habuisse legatur.* It is clear, that Titus could not be Bishop of all *Crete*; for then he should be an Archbishop having

---

\* *In his Reply to Tho. Cartwright. See Cartwright his second Reply against Whitgift. Tract. 8 fol. 414, 1061 6;* ‖ *An. Melvini Petri Adamsoni Palinodia printed An. 1610.*

\**Georgii Cassandri Consultatio. Artic. 14.*

having divers Bishops under him, those Elders which he placed in every City of *Crete* being no other *but Bishops*, Tit. 1.7. as all acknowledge; and Archbishops were not instituted till after the Apostles and *Titus* daies; For these reasons I conceive, that *Titus* was not Bishop of *Crete*, having no Episcopal or Archiepiscopal See there appointed to him; which learned \**Gersomus Bucerus* hath at large manifested, to such who will take pains to peruse him.

\* *De Guberna Eccles p. 233, 10 238. 299, to 390. 394, 395, 396, 397, 450, to 493. 580, 581.*

Obj. 1. If any object 1. that the *Postscript of the Epistle to Titus*, stiles him, *Titus ordained the first Bishop of the Church of the Cretians* : Ergo he was Bishop or Archbishop of *Crete*.

*Answ.* 1. I answer first, that *this and all other Postscripts are ∥no part of the Scripture, or Epistles, as Beza and others attest*, and \**Mr. Perkins* proves at large, but an *addition of some private person since,* as is evident by the words themselves in the preterimperfect tense, & third Person. *IT WAS WRITTEN TO TITUS, &c.* therefore no convincing authority. 2ly. That this clause (*ordained the first Bishop of the Church of the Cretians*) is no part of the Postscript, but a late appendix to it, not found in any of the Copies of this Epistle which the Fathers follow, in their Commentaries, in few or no antient Greek, Latine or English Copies and Translations of this Epistle, in few or no Translations of late Commentators. 3ly. Had *Titus* been Bishop of *Crete*, it is like *Paul* would have given him this Title in the Epistle, (where he stiles him, *Titus his own Son after the common Faith, c. 1. v. 4.*) as well as in the Postscript; which in truth is none of his, but some others. 4ly. \* *Ludovicus Capellus*, \* *Baronius*, and others observe, that the Epistle to *Titus*, and 1. Epistle to *Timothy* were both written before *Pauls* first going to *Rome*, and before *Titus* or *Timothy* were Bishops, (as Bishop *Hall* in his *Vindication*, p. 97. and *Smectymnuus*, in his answer thereunto, p. 115, 116, 127, 128. confess. Therefore all the arguments drawn from these Epistles and Postscripts, to prove them Bishops before they were such, and the sole power of ordination to be in Bishops, as Bishops, must be most ridiculous and absurd. 5ly. This Postscript stiles *Titus, Ordained the first Bishop* of the Church of the *Cretians*:

∥ *David Dickson his short explanation on the Epistle to the Hebrews, p. 331, 333.*

\* *Mr. Perkins his Commentary on Gal. 6 p. 496, 497, 498, 499.*

\* *Chronolog Tab.*
\* *Annal. Tom. 1.*

There-

H

Therefore, if true, it must needs be added long after this Epistle written; because he could not be styled the FIRST BISHOP, till he had one or more Successors in his See; in relation to whom he is, and only properly could be styled, *First Bishop of the Church of the Cretians.* 6ly. It is observable, That the Postscript styles him only, *First Bishop of the Church* (in the singular, not Churches in the plural number) *of the Cretians.* Therefore Bishop only over one Church in *Crete*, not over all the Churches and Cities in it; who had many Elders, the same with Bishops, and so styled in the beginning of the Epistle by *Paul* himself, *Tit.* 1. 5, 7. as all * antient and modern Expositors attest. 7ly. That these Postscripts to *Pauls* Epistles were first added to them by *Theodoret*, not to the Text, but in his *Commentary* on these Epistles 430. years after Christ; there being no Postscripts to St. *Peters*, *Johns*, or *Judes* Epistles on which he did not comment; nor in the works of any Father before or after him, till *Oecumenius*, Anno 1050. nor in any Greek or Latin Copies of these Epistles in that Age. 8ly. That these Postscripts both in *Theodoret* and *Oecumenius* are placed not immediately after the Original Text it self, as now they are in some of our late *English Bibles*, new Testaments, and some modern Commentators; but after the end of their Commentaries, as a part of them; and no part or appurtenance of the Text it self. 9ly. That these clauses (ordained the first Bishop of the *Ephesians*, and ordained the first Bishop of the *Cretians*) whereon our Prelates found the Episcopacy of *Timothy* and *Titus*, and their own Hierarchy too, are not extant in *Theodorets* Postscripts to the Epistles of *Timothy* and *Titus*: which run only thus, *The second to Timothy was written from Rome, when Paul was brought before Nero the Roman Emperour the second time. The Epistle to Titus was written from Nicopolis*: his Postscripts therefore will no wayes ayd but confound their cause, since I may well argue, neither *Paul* in his Epistles, nor *Theodoret* in his Postscripts term *Timothy* or *Titus* Bishops of *Ephesus* or *Crete*, therefore they were no Bishops of these places, unlesse better proofs than these Epistles and Postscripts be produced

*marginalia:*
* *Hierom, Ambrose, Primasius, Remigius, Sedulius, Haymo, Augustin, Theophylact, Oecumenius, and others with them.*

*Secunda ad Timotheum scripta est Roma, quando ad Neronem adductus est Romanorum Casarem. Epistola ad Titum Cretensis Ecclesiæ scripta est Nicopoli oppido Macedoniæ.*

to evidence it. The rare antient Manuscript Parchment Copy of the *Greek Bible*, sent to his Majesty by *Cyrillus* late Patriarch of *Constantinople*, remaining in his Majesties Library at St. *James*, supposed by some to be as antient as *Tecla*: but undoubtedly one of the antientest Copies this day extant; hath no other Postscript to the first Epistle to *Timothy*, but this, Περὶ τιμόθεον A ἐγράφη ὑπὸ λαοδικείας: No other to the second to *Timothy*, but this Περὶ τιμόθεον B. ἐγράφη ὑπὸ λαοδικείας: not from *Rome*: And no other Postscript to *Titus*, but Περὶ Τίτον ὑπὸ Νικοπόλεως (all written in Capitals) with which the *Syriac* Copies accord. So that all the residue is but a late spurious addition. The first Author I find these additional clauses (ordained first Bishop of the *Ephesians*, and ordained the first Bishop of the Church of the *Cretians*) extant in, is *Oecumenius*, who flourished not till the year 1050. being a patcher together only of other mens Commentaries, and none of the Orthodoxest or most judicious writers. And withall, this is observable,

1. That *Oecumenius* placeth these Postscripts after his Commentaries, as a part of them, not immediately after the Text as a part or appendant thereof.

2ly. That he first cites his own additions to these Postscripts after his Commentaries in one distinct line, and then placeth *Theodorets* Postscript in another different line some good distance under it, in this manner.

Περὶ Τιμόθεον διδάξα τ ἐφεσίων Ἐκκλησίας πρῶτον ἐπίσκοπον χειροτονηθέντα.

Ἐγράφη ὑπὸ ῥώμης, ὅτε ἐκ διδέρε πρέσῃ παῦλος τῷ καίσαρι νέρωνι.

Περὶ Τίτον τ κρητῶν Ἐκκλησίας πρῶτον ἐπίσκοπον χειροτονηθέντα.

Ἐγράφη ἀπὸ νικοπόλεως τῆς μακεδονίας.

3ly. From *Oecumenius* till about 450. years after him these Additional clauses are not extant in any Commentators or Translations of the Epistles into any other Language, and but in few Greek copies, and those taken out of *Oecumenius*. Therefore doubtless he was the first Author of them. And so they are of no great Antiquity or credit.

Now that you may more clearly discern what a sandy foundation these Postscripts are to build the weighty Hierarchy of our Lordly Prelates on, give me leave to inform you of some observable particulars touching these Postscripts upon mine own search and observation.

1. That *Athanasius, Ambrose, Jerome, Sedulius, Chrysostom, Primasius, Remigius, Rabanus Maurus, Haymo, Hugo Cardinalis, Bruno, Aquinas, Nicholaus de Lyra, Ghorran, Dionysius Carthusianus, John Salesbury, Anselm,* and *Peter Lombard,* the antientest Commentators on the Epistles of *Paul*, have no Postscripts at all extant in them, neither after the Text, nor after their Commentaries; no nor yet *Erasmus, Melancton, Zuinglius, Zanchius, Alfonsus Salmeron, Benedictus Justinianus, Ambrosius Caterinus, Cornelius a Lapide, Claudius Espeneaus, Antonius Scaynus, Estius, Hemingius, Joannis Arboreus, Sotto Major*, nor any other Commentator almost, whether Protestant or Papist.

2ly. That in sundry antient *English* and *Latin Manuscripts, New Testaments* and *Bibles* which I have seen; in the printed *New Testament,* set forth in *Greek* and *Latin* by *Franciscus Xemenez, in Academia Complutensi;* in the Bible of *Isiodor Clarius Venetiis*, 1557. in all the *Latin vulgar Bibles,* attributed to *Saint Jerome;* In the *New Testament*, set forth by *Erasmus;* in the *Latin Bible* printed at *Rome* by command of Pope *Sixtus* the fifth, *Anno* 1592. In the New Testament, comprising the Latin vulgar translation, that of *Guido Fabricius* out of the *Syriack*, that of *Arias Montanus*, and *Erasmus*, set forth altogether by *Laurentius Bierlinke Antwerpiæ*, 1616. In the New Testament set forth by *Miles Coverdale* in Latin and English, *Anno* 1536. in *Master Tyndals* English Bible, and in the English Translation, which *Doctor Fulk* follows in his Answer to the Rhemish Testament, and in many antient Greek Copies, there is no Postscript at all to be found.

3ly. That in the *Latin Bible*, set forth and printed by *Robert Stepken*, *Parisiis* 1532. And in the Latin Bible of *Joannis*

*annis Benedictus*, Parisiis 1558. the Postscripts are thrust out of the page, and put into the Margin, as not worthy to stand under the Text, and being of small or no account.

    4ly. That in the *Latin Bible* set forth by *Robert Stephen* Parisiis 1532. In the *Latin* and *Greek* Bibles of *Philip Melanctons* Edition *Tiguri* 1543. and *Basiliæ* 1545. In *Sebastian Castalio* his Edition of the Bible, *Basileæ* 1551. In the translations of the New Testament out of the *Syriack* both by *Guido Fabritius*, and *Emanuel Tremelius*, in the *Dutch Bible* set forth by *David Walderus*, *Hamburgæ* 1596. In the *French Bible* set out by the *Doctors of Louvain* a Paris 1616. In the Latin Bible of *Joannis Benedictus*, Parisiis 1558. In the Bible translated into English by *Thomas Mathew*, Anno 1537. In the English Bible set forth by diverse excellent *Learned men*, Printed *Cum Privilegio* by *Thomas Petit* and *Robert Redman*. London 1540. In the *English Bible appointed to be read in churches*, printed at London, 1568. In the great Bible lately published by Doctor *Walton*, London. 1657. in the *Syriack* and *Æthiopick* versions. And in sundry other Bibles and New Testaments which I have seen, these clauses (*ordained the first Bishop of the church of the Ephesians*, and *ordained the first Bishop of the church of the Cretians*) are not to be found in the Postscripts to the Epistles to *Timothy* and *Titus*; And indeed you shall seldom find them in any but Master *Beza*, and those that follow his Edition, (as Master *Calvin* and some few others do in their Commentaries) whereas both he and they are professed Enemies to Episcopacy, and disclaim those Postscripts as false and spurious.

    5ly. Master *Beza*, and the Setters forth of the Greek Bible, printed by the Heirs of *Andrew*, Francofurti, 1597. passe this sentence upon these Postscripts: and this clause, *ordained the first Bishop of Ephesus*, or, *of the church of the Ephesians. Non extat in quibusdam vetustis codicibus, & sane suppositum fuisse puto*. And he further addes, that these Postscripts were added by some *vel indoctis, vel non satis attentis. Gulielmus Fstius*, a famous Roman Doctor, in his Commentary on 2 *Tim.* 1. 4. writes thus of the Postscript to it. *Græca subscriptio post finem Epistolæ sic habet; Scripta è Roma ad Timotheum secunda, cum Paulus iterum sisteretur Cæsari Neroni*,
(where-

(where he omits this addition *Ephesiorum Ecclesiæ primus Episcopus*) and then passeth this verdict upon it, *Sed hujusmodi Græcæ subscriptiones, ut incerti sunt authoris ITA NON Magnæ authoritatis.* And *Thomas de Vio Cajetanus, Serracius, Andreas Hyperius, Estius* with others, refute the subscription to *Titus, That this Epistle was written from Nicopolis of Macedonia*; and the * Century writers with others, that the *Second to Timothy was written from Rome at Pauls second appearing before Nero*, censuring it for falshood and mistake: All which considered, I wonder our great learned Prelates, Bishop *Downham*, Bishop *White*, Bishop *Hall*, and especially our great Antiquary * Bishop *Usher*, should so much insist upon these *spurious false Postscripts*, and draw a main Argument from them, to prove their Episcopacy of Divine institution, when *Bellarmine* and those Papists, who write most eagerly for the Prelates Hierarchy, are ashamed to produce such a false and impotent proof for their groundlesse Episcopal jurisdiction.

* *Cent. Mag. 2. fol. 557.*

* *The judgement of Dr. Reynolds, touching the Original of Episcopacy, more largely confirmed out of an antiquity by James Archbishop of Armagh, p. 5.*

Secondly, I answer; that this Postscript is directly false; for it saith, *that this Epistle was written from Nicopolis of Macedonia*. Now it is clear by the 12. verse of the third chapter of this very Epistle, that *Paul* was not at *Nicopolis* when he writ it, but at some other place; for he writes thus to *Titus, when I shall send Artemas unto thee or Tychicus, be diligent to come unto me to Nicopolis, for THERE* (not here) *have I intended to winter*. Now had *Paul* then been at *Nicopolis*, he would have written thus, for *here* (not there) *I have intended to winter*; there being ever spoken of a place from which we are absent, *here* only of a place present. The Postscript therefore being false as * Mr. *Perkins* and others hence conclude it, can be no part of Canonical Scripture, or of this Epistle, none of *Pauls* penning, but a mere Appendix of some ignorant Scribe or commentator of after times, and so no solid proof to manifest *Titus* Bishop or ArchBishop of *Crete*, nor yet of *Nicopolis* when this Epistle was written.

* *Commentary on on Gal. 6. Vol. 2. p. 459.*

*Obj.* 2. If they secondly object; that *Paul* left *Titus* in *Crete* to set in order the things that were wanting, Tit. 1. 5. *Ergo* he was a Bishop.

*Ansr.* I answer, that this is a mere inconsequent; and I may

## The Un-bishoping of Timothy and Titus.

may argue in like nature; Our Archbishops and Bishops (especially those who turn Courtiers, Counsellors of State, and Nonresidents,) leave || their Archdeacons, Chancellers, Commissaries, Vicars general, and Officials, to visit, order, correct their Diocess, and to set in order these Ceremonies, Altars, Images, and Church-ornaments, which were well wanting (now too much abounding) in them; Ergo Archdeacons, Chancellers, Vicars general, and Officials, are Archbishops, and Bishops of those Diocesses: The King sends his Judges, Commissioners and under Officers to some Counties or Cities, to set Causes, Counties, People, Armies, Forts, Cities in good order, and to see defects in these supplyed. Ergo Judges, Commissioners and Officers are Kings: *Churchwardens ought by the Canons of* 1571, *and* 1603. *to set in order and provide such books, ornaments, and other necessaries as are wanting in Parish Churches, and see them well repaired*: Ergo Churchwardens are Bishops: For *Titus* was here left, *to set in order the things that were wanting*, AS PAUL HAD APPOINTED HIM, and no otherwise, *Tit.* 1. 5, 6, 7, 8, 9. he did all by his direction and authority, not his own. There is nothing therefore in this, *of ordering things that were wanting in the Church of Crete*, which favours of Episcopal Jurisdiction. And I may better argue hence, *Titus* did nothing at all in *Crete* but by *Pauls* special appointment and commission; Ergo he was no Bishop; or if a Bishop: Ergo *Bishops should order nothing in their Bishopricks, nor keep any visitations, but by special direction and Commission from the Apostles,* *King, or State, authorizing them; Then the Objectors conclude; Ergo he was a Bishop; and Bishops, Archbishops, (yea Archdeacons too without any special commission from the Apostles, King and State) may make and institute what orders, constitutions, articles, and ceremonies they please, as now they do in their illegal Courts and Visitations, kept in their own names, without any Patent from the King.

*Obj.* 3. If any object in the third place, That *Titus was left to ordain Elders in every City in Crete*; Tit. 1. 5. Ergo he was a Bishop: because none have power to ordain Elders,

but

|| *Bish. p Lat. mers fourth Sermon of the Plough, Fox Acts and Monuments, p.* 119, 120.

* *So the Statutes of* 25 H. 8. c. 29. 37 H. 8. c. 17. 27 H. 8. c. 15. 1 E 6 c. 2. 1 Eliz. c. 1, 2. 8 Eliz. c. 1. 25 H. 8. c. 21. 31 H. 8. c. 9, 14. 31 H. 8. c. 15, 15. 2 H. 5. c. 1. '4 Eliz. c. 5. *expessly resolve.*

but Bishops; since none ordained Elders in *Crete* but *Titus*, who was a Bishop.

*That the power of ordination of Ministers belongs not only to Bishops.*

*Answ.* 3. I answer first, that this is as bad a consequence as the former, and a mere circular argumentation: For first they will needs prove *Titus* a Bishop, because he ordained Elders; and none but Bishops can ordain *Elders*; and then next they prove, that none but Bishops can ordain Elders because *Titus* forsooth was a Bishop, and he only did ordain Elders in *Crete*. A mere circle, and *Petitio Principii*: yet this is the Logick of our great Rabbi Prelates.

*Secondly*, I answer, that this Proposition whereon they ground themselves and their *Prelacy*, *that none have any right Jure Divino to ordain Elders or Ministers, but Bishops*; and that *quatenus Bishops too*, ( which they must adde, or else their argument is unsound, ) is a notorious falshood, and mere sandy foundation; For first, not to remember how *Moses* a civil Magistrate, *ordained and consecrated Aaron and his Son by Gods own appointment*, Levit. 8. 5, to 32. Exodus 29. 9, 35.

*First*, The *Apostles themselves were ordained Apostles and consecrated Ministers by Christ himself*, Matth. 28. 19, 20. Mark 16. 15, 16. John 20. 22, 23, 24. Acts 1. 4, 5. Rom. 1. 5. 2 Cor. 3. 6. *To whom the power of ordination originally and principally appertains*, Ephes. 4. 11, 12. 1 Cor. 12. 28. Acts 20. 28. 1 Pet. 1. 4.

*Secondly*, The *Apostles and Evangelists ordained Elders in every Church*, Acts 14. 23. c. 19. 1, 6, 7. c. 7. 6. yet they were properly no *Bishops* as e all learned men, and our Antagonists themselves acknowledge.

e Fox Acts and Monuments, p. 1465.

*Thirdly*, *The Disciples* ( inferiour to the Apostles and E-vangelists as the Objectors teach ) *ordained Ministers and Elders too*, though they were no such Bishops as the Objectors mean, Acts 14. 1, 2, 3. c. 9. 10, to 22.

‖ Acts 13. 1, 2, 3.

*Fourthly*, ‖ *Presbyters and ordinary Ministers ordained Elders and Ministers, yea Timothy himself was made a Minister by the imposition of the hands of the Presbytery*, 1 Tim. 4. 14. Thus did they in the Primitive Church; this do they still in our own Church, as the *book of Ordination it self confirm-*
*ed*

ed by * two *Acts of Parliament*, the 35. *canon*, and experience witnesse; this do they in the reformed Churches now, which should have no lawfull Ministers, and so no true Churches, if the power of Ordination were *Jure Divino* appropriated only to Bishops, and not common with them unto other Ministers.

\* 5. *&* 6 E. 5. c. 1. 8 E 1. 12 c. 1.

*Fifthly*, Popes, Patriarks, Metropolitans, Archbishops and Choral Bishops (neither of which are properly Bishops in the objectors sence) usually ordain Ministers: if then all these have ordained Elders, Ministers, though no Bishops, by sufficient divine Authority, (as the objectors cannot deny of the four first, and dare not contradict it in the last,) then it is most false; that the power of ordination *Jure divino* belongs only to Bishops, as Bishops, in the objectors sence; for then none of those five, being not properly such Bishops, or *Jure divino* could lawfully have ordained Ministers or Presbyters, as they did and do.

*Thirdly*, There is no one syllable in the Scripture to prove, that the power of ordination belongs only to Bishops *quatenus* Bishops; neither is there any one example to warrant it. We read of Apostles, Evangelists, Disciples, Presbyters, that laid hands on others to ordain them Ministers; but of Bishops, (I mean distinct from Presbyters,) we read not a word to this purpose, how then can this be true, that the power of ordination belongs only to Bishops *quatenus* Bishops, *Jure divivo?*

*Fourthly*, We read not a word to this purpose in Scripture of any Bishops distinct from, or superior, in order, degree and dignity to Presbyters; if therefore such Bishops themselves be not *Jure divino*, the power of ordination cannot possibly belong to them *Jure divino*; the rather because we read of no man whom the Scripture expresly calls a Bishop, ordaining Ministers.

*Fifthly*, Admit there were such Bishops *Jure divino*; yet that the power of ordination belongs to them *Jure divino quatenus* such Bishops, is most false, but only *quatenus* they are Presbyters: For it appertained to the Apostles, to the Evangelists, to Disciples and Presbyters *Jure Divino*, though

I no

no such Bishops as ours; and the objectors will, must and do acknowledge, that it belongs to Popes, Patriarkes, Metropolitans and Archbishops, though they neither were nor are properly such Bishops, and are no divine, but meer humane institutions; therefore it must appertain unto them only, as they are Presbyters, (in which respect they all accord, and are not differenced one from another;) not *quatenus* Bishops; for then the Apostles, Evangelists, Disciples, Presbyters, Popes, Patriarks, Metropolitans, and Archbishops, being not properly such Bishops, could not lawfully ordain. The power therefore of ordination belonging to the Apostles, Evangelists, Disciples, Presbyters and others as well as to Bishops, not to Bishops only, or to them as Bishops, but as Ministers, (it being a g *meer Ministerial act, inferior to * preaching, administring the Sacrament and baptizing, as all acknowledge*) it can be no good evidence to prove *Titus* a Bishop.

g *Gersomus Bucerus p 33.158, to 162. 262, 499, 500, 517, 518, 540, 622, 623. 318, to 367.*
* *Mat. 28. 19. 20. Mar. 16. 15.*

Now because this power of ordination which our Prelates would Monopolize unto themselves, is the main pillar and foundation whereon they now suspend and build their Episcopal Jurisdiction over other Ministers, I shall produce some humane authorities, to prove the right and power of ordination and imposition of hands to be by Gods Law common to Presbyters as well as to Bishops; I shall begin with Councils. The 4. h *Council of Carthage, Can.* 3. about the year of our Lord 418. prescribes this form of ordination of Ministers. *When a Minister is ordained, the Bishop blessing him, and holding his hand upon his head, all the Presbyters or Ministers likewise that are present, shall lay their hands vpon his head by the Bishops hand.* This Canon is incorporated by *Gratian, into the body of the Canon Law*, and hath been practised and put in ure in all ages since, till now; The very *Glosse* on i *Gratian*, yea k the *Rhemists* and ‖ *Roman Pontifical* too, *assuring us, that when a Priest is ordained, all the Priests standing by, do lay their hands vpon him*; neither is there any other form of ordaining Ministers, prescribed in the Canon Law, or Councils, but this alone, which all Churches have observed, and yet retain. Since therefore no Bishop may or ought of himself to ordain Ministers, without the assent and

h *Surius Tom. 2. p. 513.*

✢ *Distinct. 13.*

i *Distinct. 23.*
k *Notes on the 1 Tim. 4. 15.*
‖ *Pontificale Romanum p. 42.*

and concurrence of the Clergy, people and others there present, as l *Gratian*, m *Illyricus*, and n *Gersome Bucerus*, prove at large; and since *all Ministers present ought to joyn with the Bishop in the imposition of hands, in all ordinations of Ministers, and have ever usually done it joyntly in all ages and Churches*; how this prerogative of ordination should be peculiar to Bishops (who may not do it without the Ministres concurrence, no more than Ministers without theirs) or advance them in degree above Presbyters by divine or canonical right, I cannot yet conjecture. True it is, that the o *Council of Ancyra*, ( which I take to be spurious ) about the year of our Lord 308. Can. 3. ordained; *That Choral Bishops should not ordain Presbyters or Deacons; nor yet Presbyters of the City in another Parish; but when and where the Bishop should permit them by his Letters*; And the p Council of *Antioch* under Pope *Julius*, Can. 10. decrees; that *Choral Bishops should not ordain Ministers and Deacons without the Bishops privity.* From whence I observe.

l *Distinct.* 23, 24, 25.
m *Appendix ad Catal. Testium Veritatis.*
n *Dissertat. de Gubernat. Eccl.* p. 318, to 357. 464, 465, 493, 498, 499, 524. *See Canon.* 35.
o *Surius Tom.* 1. p. 296.

p *Surius Ibid.* p. 403, 404.

*First*, That before these spurious Councils restrained the power of Choral Bishops and Presbyters, they did and might lawfully ordain Ministers and Deacons without the Bishops privity or assent.

*Secondly*, That by his assent and licence both the one and the other, without the Bishops presence, might lawfully ordain Ministers and Deacons. These Councils therefore plainly resolve, that there is an inhærent right and power of ordination in Presbyters and * Choral Bishops, as they are Ministers, and that with the Bishops consent, and licence they may lawfully execute it, and confer Orders: Therefore the right and power of ordination is not invested only in Bishops, as they are Bishops, for then none else could ordain but they alone. The forged *Constitutions of the Apostels*, fathered on Pope q *Clement*, prescribe; *That Presbyters and Deacons, may not ordain other Priests and Deacons, but Bishops only.* And the r *Council of Hispalis* or *Spaw*, about the year 657. Canon. 5. 7. out of Pope *Leo*, Epist. 86. decrees; that *Presbyters and Choral Bishops, which are all one, should not presume to ordain Priests or Deacons, or to consecrate Altars or Churches*;

* See *Davidis Blundelli Apologia* sect. 3 p 120, to 130. *De Chorepiscopis.*

q *Constit. Apost.* l. 3 c 10, 11, 20.
r *Surius Tom.* 2. p. 719. Tom. 1. p. 800.

*Churches*; *For in holy writ, by Gods command,* ᶠ *Moses only erected the Altar in the Tabernacle of the Lord; he only annointed it, because he was the High Priest of God, as it is written;* ᵗ *Moses and Aaron among his Priests. Therefore, that which was commanded only to the chief Priests to do, of whom Moses and Aaron were a Type, Presbyters who carry the figure of the sons of Aaron, may not presume to encroach upon. For although they have in most things a common dispensation of Mysteries with Bishops, yet they must know, that some things are notwithstanding prohibited them by the authority of the old Law, some things* BY NEW ECCLESIASTICAL RULES (or CANONS) *as the* CONSECRATION OF PRESBYTERS, DEACONS, *and virgins; as also the Constitution, Benediction, or Unction of the Altar. Verily it is not lawfull for them to consecrate Churches or Altars, not to give the Holy Ghost the comforter by imposition of hands to the faithfull who are to be baptised, or to those who are converted from heresie, nor to make Chrism, nor to sign the forehead of those that are baptised with Chrism.* ᵘ *nor yet publikely to reconcile any penitent person in the Masse, nor to send formed Epistles to any. All these things are unlawfull to Presbyters or Chorall Bishops, because they have not Pontificatus apicem, the highest degree of the High Priest-hood, which by the* AUTHORITY OF THE CANONS, *is commanded to be due only to Bishops, that by this the distinction of the degrees, and the hight of the dignity of the High Priest, might be demonstrated. Neither shall it be lawfull for the Presbyters to enter into the Baptistery before the Bishops presence, nor to baptise or sign an Infant, the Bishop being present, nor to reconcile penitents without the Bishops command, nor to consecrate the Sacrament of the body and blood of Christ he being present, nor in his presence to teach, or blesse, or salute the people, no nor yet to exhort them, all which things are known to be prohibited by the* \* *See* *A ostolick.* These two last authorities are the chief the Papists, Jesuits, and our Prelates insist on, to prove that the power of ordination belongs only to Bishops not to Presbyters.

But to remove these two obstacles, consider, *First*, that there is not a word in either of the two Constitutions, (restraining Ministers from Baptising, consecrating the

*Lords*

---

ᶠ *Exod.* 40.

ᵗ *Psal.* 98.

ᵘ *See Concil. Carthag.* 2. An. 428 c. 3, 4. *Gratian Causa.* 20 qu. 6. *Conc. Carthag.* 3 c. 26. *Gratian Causa* 16. qu. 6.

\* *Leo Epist.* 86.

Lords Supper, and Preaching as much as from Ordinary Ministers) that the power of Ordination, belongs only to Bishops by divine right and institution; or that Presbyters by Gods Law have no power to ordain Ministers and Deacons, the thing only in question.

*Secondly*, That this Council expresly resolves, *that the power and right of ordination is prohibited to Presbyters, and appropriated only to Bishops, not by any Law of God*, or antient Constitutions of the Apostles, or those who immediately succeeded them, *but only by some Ecclesiastical Canons and Constitution then newly made*, and *by the authority only of the See of Rome*; which cannot deprive Ministers of that power of ordination, which the Scripture and God himself hath given them. The rather, because these Canons and Constitutions monopolizing the sole power and right of Ordination to Bishops, were made by Popes & Bishops themselves; who by the * Civil, † Common ‖ Canon Law, *ought not to be Judges or Arbitrators*, ( much lesse sole Judges ) *in their own causes and controversies, nor to determine the rights, bounds of their own Jurisdiction, or to exalt themselves by debasing and prejudicing their fellow-Ministers, through force, power or terror, or to take advantage of their own wrong and usurpation over them, in their divine rights*, which God himself hath equally conferred on them: especially because the very *Roman Pontifical* it self, set forth by Pope *Clement* the 8. and the Romish Pontifs allow and enjoyn Priests and Ministers, to joyn with Bishops in the imposition of hands and ordination of Priests and Ministers, & in their examination before they be ordained. Witnesse these Rubricks. * *Quando Episcopus Ordinationes facere disposuerit, &c. Episcopus* SACERDOTIBUS *& aliis prudentibus viris, peritis divinæ legis, ac in Ecclesiasticis functionibus exercitatis,* SIBI ASCITIS, *ordinandorum genus personam, ætatem, institutionem, mores doctrinam & fidem diligenter investigat & examinet*. At his ordination, *Pontifex stans ante faldestorium suum, & imponit simul utramque manum super caput cujuslibet ordinandi successive, nihil dicens,* IDEMQUE FACIUNT POST EUM OMNES SACERDOTES QUI ADSUNT. *Quod &, tum Pontifex quam Sacerdotes,* TENENT MANUS DEXTERAS EXTENSAS SUPER ILLOS. *Et Pontifex*

*Cedius l 2 Tit 5 c... Digest. l 50. Tit. 17. sect. 45, 54, 74, 170. 175, 150, 205. Davidis Blondelli Apologia. p. 178, 179.
† Cooks 1 Instit. p. 141. Litleton sect 212.
‖ Gratian Distinct. 4. qu. 4.

* Pontificale Romanum, Clementis octavo Antuerp. 1627. p. 4. 40 41. De Ordinatione Presbyterii.

*Pontifex stans cum mitra dicit.* Oremus, FRATRES *charissimi, Deum Patrem Omnipotentem, ut super hos famulos suos, quos ad Presbyterii munus elegit cœlestia dona multiplicet,* &c. And if the Pope and Popish Bishops allow ordinary Priests and Ministers a joynt right & authority in the imposition of hands, & examination and ordination of Ministers in the Church of *Rome* it self; how can or dare our Bishops or Prelatical Clergy deny this right and power to Protestant Ministers in the Church of *England*, and appropriate it to themselves alone?

*Thirdly*, That after the Apostles times before these late Canons, and Constitutions, Presbyters might lawfully ordain Ministers, and Deacons,

*Fourthly*, That the chief reason why the power of ordination was in some sort taken from Ministers, and thus monopolized to Bishops, ( only by their own Constitutions, wherein they have ever favoured themselves,) *was only to advance the power, authority, dignity, ambition, pride of the Pope and Prelates, and to distinguish them in degree and order from ordinary Ministers*, which of right are, and otherwise would be their equals, both in Jurisdiction, power and degree.

*Fifthly*, That they bring not one syllable out of the new Testament, to prove that the power of ordination belongs only to Bishops, not to Ministers; which they would have certainly done, had there been any Text to warrant it; but that all they allege is out of the Old Testament; to wit, *that Moses only consecrated the Tabernacle and the Altar; Ergo none but Bishops must consecrate Ministers, Altars, Churches.* A learned Argument; Ergo none but Kings, and Temporal Magistrates, no, not Bishops themselves, may do it, had been a better consequent. For *Moses* was no Priest, much lesse a Bishop; or High Priest, ( which was x *Aarons office, not his, there being but* y *one High Priest at once*, and he a z *type of our High Priest Christ* ) but a civil Magistrate; yet God commanded him a to consecrate Aaron with his Sons, the Tabernacle and Altar; and after him, b King Solomon ( not the High Priest ) consecrated the Temple, Altar, Court, and all the furniture of the Temple and Altar: So that if these examples prove

x *Exod.* 18. 1, to 43 c. 29. 5, to 45 c. 30. 7. 1 c. 30. *Heb.* 5 4, 5. c. 7. 11.
y *Numb.* 25. 35.
z *Heb.* 4. 14, 15. c. 5. 1, to 11. c. 6. 10 c 7. 20, to 28. c. 8. 1, to 7. c. 9. 1, to 28. c 10. 11, to 13.
a *Exod.* 29. 1, to 37 c. 30. 25, to 31. c. 40. 1, to 34.
b 1 *King* 8. 2 *Chron* 6. 8.

# The Un-bishoping of Timothy and Titus. 55

prove any thing, it is but this alone: That the power of ordination, of consecrating Bishops, Ministers, Churches, Altars, &c. appertains not to Archbishops, Bishops, Popes, Priests, Ministers, but to the chief Temporal Magistrates. But admit that *Moses* was a Priest, or an High Priest, and that the power of consecrating Priests, Temples, Altars appertained to him in that regard; yet this is no argument to prove, that the right and power of Ordination should now belong to Bishops only; and that for these three reasons.

*First*, because the *Aaronical Priesthood was* c *utterly extinct and abolished by Christ, as merely typical and ceremonial*; and so all the appurtenances thereunto belonging.

*Secondly*, Because the High Priest was no Emblem, type Pattern or resemblance of Bishops, which are many, changeable, mortal, *but * only of Christ our true High Priest, who is but one, and remains an High Priest for ever without succession or change*. So that this allusion proves the power of ordaining Ministers to belong originally *to none but* d *Christ, our* e *High Priest, chief Shepheard, and* f *Bishop of our Souls*, as the g *Scripture expresly resolves*; and ministerially, secondarily, to h *every Minister of Christ, as his Embassador, instrument, and Vicegerent.*

*Thirdly*, Because, the office and power of the High Priests and Bishops are different, distinct, yea incompatible one with the other, and the manner of ordination of Priests and Levites under the Laws, different from that of Ministers and Deacons under the Gospel, as the || *Scriptures*, and * all *Authors* joyntly witness: the one of them therefore can be no solid, or convincing argument to make good the *Authority, Jurisdiction*, or *Practise of others*. So that this Council and Constitution, makes nothing against the divine Right and Title of Presbyters to

c Heb 7. & 8. 9. & 10.

* Augustin. Serm. 99. de tempore. Whitaker. Contr. 4. qu. 1. c. 2. Willet. Synopsis Papismi. Cont. 5. q. 3.
d Heb. 9. 14, 19. c. 5. 1. to 1'. c. 6. 20. c. 7. & 8. 9. & 10.
e Heb. 6. 20.
f. Heb. 13. 20.
1 Pet. 5. 4.
g 1 Pet. 2. 25.
h Mat. 18. 1, &c. c. 28. 19. Mark 16. 15. Ihn 15. 16.

4. Ephes. 8. 11, 12, 13 1 Tim. 4. 14. Acts 13. 1, 2, 3. || Exod c. 29. & 30 compared with Acts 6. 1, to 8. c. 14. 23. c. 13. 1, 2, 3. Tit. 1. 5. 1 Tim. 4. 14. c. 12. * Gersomus Bucerus de Gubernat. Eccles. p. 264, 255, 269, 291, 299, 300, 309, 446, 501, 502.

ordain

to ordain, or for the Bishops sole Monopoly of imposition of hands, by any divine Charter from Christ or the Holy Ghost.

*Finally,* Neither of these Councils or Constitutions simply debar Ministers from the imposition of hands on others together with the Bishop, which they *k ever practised, and were authoried to do, both by God himself, and the fourth Council of Carthage, Can. 3.* But from laying on hands and ordaining Ministers of themselves alone without the Bishop, (when there was one) who *cannot ordain, or lay hands on any Ministers by virtue of these constitutions without them.* Since therfore the Bishop of himself alone cannot impose hands on any Minister without their assistance or consent, nor they without the Bishops, it is apparent, that the right of ordination is not wholy and originally vested in the Bishop, by any divine or humane right; but equally and joyntly in them both. *The * Council of Aquisgran or Aken, under Ludovicus Pius An.* 816. *c.* 8. out of *Isidor. Hispalensis De Ecclesiasticis Officiis l.* 2. *c.* 7. determines thus: *The dispensation of the Mysteries of God are committed to Presbyters as they are to Bishops, for they are over the Church of Christ, and are consorts with Bishops in the confection of the body and blood of Christ, and likewise also in the instruction of the people, and in the office of preaching, and only the Ordination and Consecration of Clerks is reserved to the High Priest or *Bishop, because of his authority, lest the Discipline of the Church, challenged or exercised by many, should dissolve concord and engender scandals; For Paul the Apostle calls Elders and Priests by the name of Bishops,* Tit. 1. 5, 7. Acts 20. 28. Phil. 1. 1. 1 Tim. 3. *D. Rabanus Maurus De Instit. Clericorum, l.* 1. *c.* 6 writes thus: *That Presbyters although they be Priests, yet they have not attained the top or highest degree of Priesthood, because they cannot sign the fore-head with Chrism, nor give the Holy Ghost; neither can they ordain Clerks in sacred orders, which is reserved to Bishops for unity and concords sake. The Epistle de* 7. *Gradibus Ecclesiæ in the ninth Tome of Jeromes works, avers in expresse terms; that the ordination of Clerks and consecration of Virgins was reserved only to the High-Priest or Bishop for his greater honour.* And *Tertullian*

*k Acts* 13. 3.
1 *Tim* 4. 14.
*The Rhemists with all late Commentators, Ibidem, & some antient too Davidis Blondelli Apologia Sect.* 3. *Vretius, Desperata Causa Papatus, lib.* 2. *sect.* 2.

* *Surius Tom.* 3. *p.* 299.

* *By Canons made only by Bishops themselves not Christ or his Apostles.*

*de*

*de Baptism c.* 17. writes, *that the High Priest, who is the Bishop, hath the right of giving Baptism, after him Presbyters and Deacons, yet not without the Bishops authority, for the honor of the Church*; By all which it is evident, that Bishops have not the sole executive power of ordination by any divine right or. institution ( of which there is not one syllable, either these or other Councils or Fathers) but only by ‖Canons & humane Constitutions, made by Popes Bishops themselves, to advance their own honour, power, pomp and dignity; yet notwithstanding the right of ordination remaines still in Ministers; and belongs to Bishops, only as they are Ministers by divine right, not as they are Bishops; as is evident by the *m* 9. *Chapter of the same Council of Aken,* taken out of *Isidor. De Eccles. Officiis l.* 2. *c.* 6. where writing of Bishops ordination by imposition of hands, and the original thereof, they use this expression, (which *n H. Rabanus Maurus,* likewise hath:) *But that Bishops are ordained by imposition of hands,* A PRÆDECESSORIBUS DEI SACERDOTIBUS, *by the Priests of God their Predecessors, is an antient constitution. For the holy o Patriark Isaac laying his hands upon the head of Jacob, blessed him, and p Jacob in like manner gave a benediction to his sons, &c.* Where the Council and Fathers both affirm; that even Bishops themselves are ordained by *Priests or Presbyters* (not Bishops) *their Predecessors,* therefore the right and power of ordaining Ministers ( and Bishops too ) belongs to Presbyters as well as Bishops, and to Bishops only as Presbyters, not Bishops; and so can no waies advance them in Jurisdiction, order, or degree above Ministers. The Popish *q Council of Trent Sessio* 23. *De Sacramento Ordinis c.*4. determines, *that Bishops are superior to Presbyters, and that they can confer the Sacrament of Confirmation, ordain Ministers of the Church, and do many other things, which those inferior orders have no power to do. And Can.* 7. *De Sacramento Ordinis: If any shall say, that Bishops are not superior to Priests, or that they have not the power of ordination, or confirmation, or that this power, which they have, is common to them with Presbyters; or that the orders conferred by them without the consent or calling of the secular power are void, let*

\* *Alex Alensis Sum pars* 4. *q.* 9. *m.* 5. *art.* 1.

*m Surius Ibid. p.* 300.

n *De Instit. Clericorum l* 1.*c.*4.

o Gen. 27, and 28.
p Gen. 28.

q *Surius Tomi* 4. *p* 955.

K                                    *him*

him be *Anathema*: Lo here this Council appropriates the power of ordination only to Bishops, by denying it to be common to them with Ministers, and in this regard makes Bishops superior in degree to Ministers; yet not by any divine right or institution, (of which there is not one word) but only by humane and Canonical; (as the r *History of the Council of Trent*, and f *Chemnitius* well observe:) For in the same t *Session de Reform. Can.* 7, 8. it enjoyns; that according to the antient Canons, (& the *Roman Pontifical* too) when Ministers or Deacons ar to be ordained; that the Bishop calling to him the Priests and other Prudent men, skilfull of the divine Law, and exercised in Ecclesiastical constitutions, should diligently enquire and examin before them the stock, person, age, institution, manners, doctrin, and faith of those that were to be ordained; and that those orders should be publickly conferred and celebrated in the Cathedral Church; the Canons of the Church being called to, and present at it; or if in any other place, or Church of the Diocesse, Præsenti Clero Loci, *the Clergy of the place being present*. u Pope *Anacletus*, and the x *Canon Law*, having long before that time ordained; *That Priests and Deacons should be ordained by their own Bishop;* Ita ut Cives & Alii SACERDOTES assensum præbent; *So as the Citizens and other Priests assented thereunto*; which they usually did, and ought to do, as *Gratian* with y others prove at large. So that though this Council, and the other Canons and Constitutions debar Presbyters and Ministers from the act and exercise of ordination, (which yet they ever used, and practiced as assistants to the Bishops, who can ordain none but by their assent, since they ought to joyn with them in the imposition of hands) yet they deprive them not of their inherent right, nor of the exercise of it as assistants to the Bishop, which they have ever used. I passe now from these Councils and Constitutions to the Fathers, who jump in judgement with them. It is true that z *St. Hierom*, a *Epiphanius*, b *Isidor Hispalensis*, c *Ambrose*, d *Augustine*, e *Leo*, and f others affirm, that Bishops

r *Lib. 7.*
f *Examen Concil. Tridentini pars 2. De Sacramento Ordinis.*
t *Ibid. p. 968.*
u *Epist. 2. c. 2. apud Surium Tim. 1. p. 161.* recited by *Gratian Distinct. 67.*
x *Gratian Distinct. 61, 62, 63, 64, &c.*
y *Illyr. Catalogus Testiū veritatis Anno 1562 Appendix. p. 23, to 36. vera demonstratio, quod Electio Præsulum & Episcoporum non ad Ecclesiasticos solum sed & ad Laicos, quos vocant, pertineat, quedque hi hoc jure Electionis inde usque à Christi temporibus annis. 1500. usi sunt.*
z *Epist. ad Evagrium. & in Tit. 1.*
a *Cent. haref. l. 2. haref. 75.*
b *De Ecclef. Officiis l. 2. c. 7.*
c *In Ecclef 4. and 1 Tim 4. 14.* d *Questiones ex utroque Testamento mixtim. quest. 101.* e *Epist. 86.* f *Aquinas Supplementum Quest. 38. Artic. 1.*

*only*

## The Un-bishoping of Timothy and Titus.   59

only in their times ( yet assisted by the Presbyters who joyned with them in the ordination and imposition of hands ) did use to ordain Ministers and Deacons; *and that Presbyters might do all things that Bishops did, except the conferring of Orders, and some other trifles, as consecrating of Altars, Churches, Virgins, Crisme, &c. not warranted by Gods word;* yet none of them determine, that the right and power of ordination belongs only to Bishops, by divine institution and appointment; that Presbyters have no right at all by the word of God to confer Orders; or that they might not do it in any case; but they expresly aver the contrary : For as they did joyn *with the Bishop in the imposition of hands,* as appears by the 3*d.* Canon of the 4*th.* *Council of Carthage,* forecited; so in g *S. Ambrose* his time, in Ægypt, *if the Bishop were absent, the Presbyters use to consign and confer Orders;* as this Father testifieth : and *b* St. *Augustin* records, *That in Alexandria, & throughout all Ægypt, if the Bishop were wanting, the Presbyter conferred orders.* Hence *Aerius* (as i *Epiphanius* reports his words ) reasoned in this manner: *What is a Bishop to a Presbyter? one differs nothing from the other; it is one order ( saith he ) one honor, and one dignity.* Imponit manus Episcopus; ‖ ITA ETIAM PRESBYTER : *The Bishop imposeth his hands, or ordains Ministers; so likewise doth the Presbyter; The Bishop baptizeth, so also doth the Presbyter; The Bishop sits in a Throne, so also doth the Presbyter. And he also alleaged, that the Apostle saith to a Bishop,* \* *Neglect not the gift that is in thee, which thou hast received by the laying on of the hands of the Presbytery: Epiphanius* there denyeth not directly, that the Presbyters then did use to ordain; but demands, *how it is possible for a Presbyter to ordain, not having imposition of hands in the election of Ministers, or to say that he was equal with a Bishop?* A false and miserable shift : since all \* *Histories, Fathers, Authors, Councils testifie, that in that age, Presbyters had alwaies their voyces in the Election, yea their hands in the ordination of*

g *Ambros. in Ephes* 4.
h *Quæstiones ex utroque Testamento mixtim, quæst.* 101.
i *Cont. Hares. l.* 3. *Tom.* 1. *Hær.* 75.
† *See Cent. Magd.* 3. *De Ritibus circa vocationem & ordinationem, Col.* 135.
k 1 *Tim.* 4: 14.

\* *Appendix Catalogo Testium veritatis, p.* 23. to 56. *Gersomus* Bucerus,

*De Gubernat. Ecclef. p.* 25, 130, 131, 328. *usque* 334. 346, *usque* 354, 360, 361, 362, 363, 364, 414. 609.

*Ministers and Deacons.* Firmilianus in his Epistle to St. Cyprian, about 230 years after our Saviours Nativity, asserts, that the power of Ordination as well as of Baptising belongs to Presbyters: *Quando omnis potestas & gratia in Ecclesia constituta sit, ubi præsident MAJORES NATU, qui & baptizandi, ET MANUM IMPONENDI, ET ORDINANDI POSSIDENT POTESTATEM.* And St. *Cypran* himself in his 33. & 58. Epistles, *Presbyteris, & Diaconibus*, relates, that Presbyters, his Colleagues, joyned with him in the ordination of *Aurelius*; and that none were ordained but by their Common Counsel, and weighing of their merits. *In* \* *ordinationibus Clericis, fratres charissimi, solemnus vos ante consulere, & mores & merita singulorum COMMUNI CONSILIO PONDERARE, &c.* After which extolling the merits of *Aurelius*, though young in years, he subjoyns, *Hunc igitur fratres dilectissimi à me &* A COLLEGIS QUI PRÆSENTES ADERANT ORDINATUM SCIATIS; *quod vos scio & libenter amplecti.* And in his 68. Epistle he addes, that in the Election and Ordination of Priests and Bishops, the People have the greatest power, *vel eligendi dignos Sacerdotes, vel indignos recusandi. Quod & ipsum videmus de divina auctoritate descendere, ut Sacerdos plebe præsente sub omnium oculis delegatur, & dignus atque idoneus* PUBLICO JUDICIO AC TESTIMONIO COMPROBETUR: which he proves at large by *Numb.* 10. *Acts* 2. & 6. and other Texts. And then concludes, *Propter quod diligenter de traditione divina, & Apostolica observatione observandum est & tenendum, quod apud nos quoque, &* \* *ferè per universas Provincias tenetur, ut ad ordinationes rite celebrandas, ad eam plebem cui Præpositus ordinatur, Episcopi ejusdem Provinciæ proximi quique conveniant, & Episcopus diligatur plebe præsente, quæ singulorum vitam plenissime novit, & unius cujusque actum de ejus conversatione perspexit, &c.* St. *Hierom* in his Commentary on *Zeph.* c. 2. *Tom.* 5. p. 218. D. writes expresly: *SACERDOTES, &c.* that Priests and Presbyters who give Baptism, & imprecate the Lords advent to the Eucharist, make also the oyl of Crism, MANUS IMPONUNT, impose hands, instruct the Catechumeny, LEVITAS ET ALIOS CONSTITUUNT SACERDOTES;

*\* Cypriani Opera Edit. Parisiis Epist. 75. p. 115.*

*\* Ordinandis.*

*\* Tertul. Apol. c. 39. Ambr. Epist. 32.*

## The Un-bishoping of Timothy and Titus. 61

ordain Levites, and other Priests: Therefore Presbyters in S. Hieronimus time ordained Ministers, Deacons, and layd on hands as well as Bishops. Yea * *Anastatius*, in the life of Pope *Pelagius the first*, records, that this Pope *An. Christi* 555. for want of three Bishops to ordain him; was ordained Pope, by *John* Bishop of *Perusia*, and *Bonus* Bishop of *Florence*, and *Andreas* Presbyter de *Hostia*, which *Luitprandius de Vitis Pontificum*, p. 84. and *Albo Floriacensis in his life*, p. 140. likewise testifie: Lo here a Prebyter or ordinary Minister ordaining not only another Elder, but a Bishop, yea a Pope; and supplying the place of a Bishop, ‖ the general Council of *Nice. Can.* 4. the first Council of *Arelat. Can.* 21. the second Council of *Carthage, Can.* 12 the third Council of *Carthage, Can.* 19. the Council of *Aphricke, Can.* 16. the Council of *Rhegium, An.* 472 the Council of *Arausica, Can.* 21. the Council of *Chalcedon, Acts* 13. *p.* 187. with sundry Popes Decrees, ordaining, *that no man shall be consecrated a Bishop, but by three Bishops at least, and that a consecration made only by two Bishops shall be void*; and so this Pope no lawfully ordained Pope, unles that this Presbyter supplyed the place of a Bishop in his consecration, and his Ordination were good and valid by the Law of God, though invalid, and a mere nullity by these Canons, * Anno 1390. about *John Wickliffs* time there arose in *England* certain bold *Clerks, who affirmed, that it was lawfull for them to make new Presbyters and Clerks, and confer orders, like Bishops: teaching likewise, that they were endued with the same Power in Ecclesiastical affairs as Bishops were, whereupon they layd hands on many, and ordained divers Ministers: who affirmed likewise, that they had equal and the self-same Ecclesiastical power with Bishops*: which was the constant Doctrin of *Wickliff* and the * *Waldenses*. This Doctrin of theirs was true, but their practise discommended, yet the Ministers thus ordained by them, held their ordination lawfull by Gods Law; yea and their ordination of others in those times of darknesse and persecution, was good and valid, when no *Wicklivists, Lollards* or other orthodox Professors of the Gospel could be admitted into orders by the Bishops of that age, unlesse they would subscribe to their

† *De Vitis Pontificum, p. 53.*

‖ See *Surius Concil. Tom. 1. p.* 188. 161, 163. 341, 369, 376, 406, 502, 506, 574. Tom. 2. *p.* 187, 656, Tom. 1. *p.* 699, 718, 467 Tom. 2. *p.* 624. 267, 268. 272, 638. 731.

* *Antiqu. Eccl. Brit.* 302.

* See *Usserius de Statu & Successione Ecclesiæ, c.* 9, 10.

Popish

Popish assertions, as some of our Prelates now will admit none to receive orders, unlesse they will first subscribe to such private positions and Ceremonies, as are directly contrary to the established doctrine, and discipline of the Church of *England*; by means whereof many godly men are kept from the Ministery. And though m *Chrysostome, Primasius, Theodoret, Ambrose, Rabanus Maurus, Oecumenius Theophilact, Haymo*, with some others, interpret that of the 1 Tim. 4. 14. *By the laying on of the hands of the Presbytery*; to be meant either of *Paul* himself, or of the Senate of the *Apostles*, or of such who had Apostolical authority, or of Bishops, and not of meer Presbyters; because (say they) Presbyters (to wit according to the practice of their, though not of former times) could not ordain a Bishop, but only Apostles, or Bishops; yet none of them so much as once affirm, that they cannot by the Law of God ordain Deacons, and ordinary Ministers; or that they ought by Gods Law and divine institution to be ordained onely by Bishops, or Presbyters ordination void: yea n *Theophyl.* on that text writes thus: *Behold a wonderfull thing, See how much the imposition*, SACERDOTALIUM MANU-UM, *of Sacerdotal or Priests hands can do*; A clear demonstration, that Priests as well as Bishops, and Bishops only as they are Priests not Bishops, have power of layng on hands. And o *Theodoret*, thus glosseth the text, *here he calls those the Presbytery who had attained Apostolical grace*; For, saith he, *divine Scripture hath called those who were honored in Israel, Elders.* The Fathers therefore confessing, that Presbyters and Elders might and did in some cases and places Ordain, and Consecrate Ministers without the Bishop, and likewise joyn with the Bishop, (in all places) in the imposition of hands; grant that the right of ordination and imposing hands, belongeth to them by the word of God, as well as to Bishops; the rather, because this is the constant doctrine of the p *Fathers*, that *Bishops and Presbyters, by Gods Law and institution, are both one and the same, and so continued till long after the Apostles times*; Therefore their power of ordination, the same with theirs. Neither do the Papists dissent from this: q *Aquinas* writes; That *the imposition of hands belongs only to those*

*who*

m *In 1 Tim. 4. 14.*

n *In 1 Tim. 4. 14.*

o *In 1 Tim. 4. 14.*
p *Ambrose in Eph. 4. & 1 Tim. 3. Hierom, Sedulius, Theodoret, Primasius, Rabanus Maurus, Remigius, Oecumenius, Theophilact. Anselmus, Beda, Bruno, &c. in Phil. 1. 1 Tim. 3. Tit. 1. 5, 7. Act. 20. 17, 18.*
q *In 1 Tim. 4. 14. Lect. 3.*

*who are the Ministers of Christ. which was double, one which was made by Deacons, the other by Ministers;* and because he adds not the third by Bishops; he plainly intimates, that the ordination made by Ministers and Bishops, is one and the same, and that Bishops ordain only as Ministers, not as Bishops. r *Cajetan* on that text saith, *That Paul relates, that the Imposition of hands SACERDOTALIS OFFICII, is a part of the Sacerdotal or Priests office,* ( not the Bishops ) and *Faber* in 1 Tim. 4. 14. writes, *that Presbyters did use to lay their hands on the heads of those who were to be ordained, purged, or made compleat Ministers, powring forth holy prayers.* I know indeed that ſ *Aquinas* and other *Schoolmen* hold, that it belongs only to Bishops to confer holy orders; yet he, t *Durandus & Alensis* grant, *that this is not by virtue of any divine right, or institution, but only by humane Constitutions and Canons, by reason of the more excellent Power and Jurisdiction that the Bishop hath over and above Ministers, and for order sake;* yea they both affirm, *that Presbyters do, and ought to joyn with the Bishop in the imposition of hands in the ordination of Ministers.* The *Rhemists* in their *Annotations* on the 1 Tim. 4. 14. confesse, *that when a Priest is ordained, the rest of the Priests and Elders present, do together with the Bishop, even at this day among them,* ( *and have antiently used heretofore* ) *to lay hands on those that are to be ordained;* citing the *fourth Council of Carthage: Can.* 3. for proof thereof. And the u *Canonists,* with some x *Schoolmen* grant, *that Priests and Ministers by the Popes Dispensation and License, may without a Bishops concurrence ordain Deacons and Ministers; but a meer Layman, or one that is no Minister cannot do it.* A clear proof, that the imposition of hands appertaines to Presbyters as well as Bishops, and that the power of ordination rests more in the Ministers person, than in the Popes Grant or License; else why might not a Layman as well as a Minister, grant Orders by virtue of the Popes License, or why should Ministers joyn with Bishops in the imposition of hands? But to passe from these to the reformed Churches beyond the Seas. We know that most of them have no Bishops; that all their Ministers and Deacons are ordained by the common Election of the People

and

t *In 1 Tim. 4. 14.*

ſ *Supplementum Qu. 38. Arti. 1.* t *in 4. Sent Dist. 24. Qu. 5, 6. Alensis Summ. pars 4. qu. 9. m. 5. art 1.*

u *Summa Angelica Ordo Sect. 13. and Innocentius there cited.*
x *Filiuc. Jesuita De Casibus Consc. pars 1. Tract. 9. c. 5. Alex. A'ensis Sum. Theol. pars 4. qu. 9. m. 5. Artic. 1.*

Magistrates, and imposition of the Senate or Colledge of Ministers hands; yet none of our Prelates (till * some of late) have been so impudently shamelesse, as to deny their ordination and Ministers to be lawfull, or their practice to be dissonant from the Scriptures, or them to be true Churches. What their writers have determined concerning the power of ordination, incident to Ministers as well as Bishops, and to Bishops only as Ministers, and servants to the Church, not Lords, these ensuing passages will declare: y *Joannes Lukawitz* in his *Confession of the Taborites against Rokenzana* c. 13. of the *Sacrament of order*, writes thus, *They confess, that the conferring of Orders only by Bishops, and that they have more effectual authority of this nature then other Ministers, is not from any faith or authority of the Scriptures*, Sed ex consuetudine habetur Ecclesiæ, *but from the custom of the Church.* This being the *constant doctrine of the* z *Waldenses and Taborites, that the power of giving orders, and imposing hands, belonged to Presbyters as well as Bishops; and that Bishops and Ministers by Gods Law were both one; and no Bishop greater than any Presbyter in honour, or Jurisdiction.* a Melanchton writes, *That if Bishops and Ordinaries are enemies of the Church, or will not give orders, yet the Churches retain their right; For wheresoever there is a Church, there is a right of administring the Gospel; wherefore there is a necessity that the Church should retain the right of calling, electing and ordaining Ministers. And this right is a gift given to the Church, which no humane authority can take from the Church; as Paul witnesseth in the fourth of the Ephesians, where he saith, When he ascended up on High, he gave gifts unto men; and he reckons Doctors and Pastors among the proper gifts of the Church, and adds, that such are given for the Work of the Ministery, for the edifying of the body of Christ, &c. where therefore there is a true Church, there must needs be a right of electing and ordaining Ministers. One thing had made a difference of Bishops and Pastors, to wit, ordination, because it is instituted that one Bishop might ordain in many Churches; but seeing that by Gods Law there are not divers degrees of a Bishop and Pastor, it is evident, that an ordination made by a Pastor in his Church, is ratified by Gods Law.* Marsilius Patavinus *in his Defensoria Pacis,*

*pars*

---

\* See *Canterburies Doom*, p. 335, 390, 392.

y *Lydii Waldensia* p. 23.

z *Fox Acts and Monuments* p. 110. Catal. Testium Veritatis tit *Waldenses* p. 445.

a *Argument. & Respons. pars 7. De Potestate Episcopi, Arg. 2.*

# The Un=bishoping of Timothy and Titus. 65

*pars 2. c. 15. 17. affirms, that the power of ordaining Ministers belongs not to Priests and Bishops, but to the Magistrates and people, where he is to be a Minister. That every Priest by divine authority, may confer all Sacraments, and give orders, as well as any Bishops; and that every Priest hath power to ordain and promote any Believer that is willing to the Priesthood, he preparing him Ministerially, but God simply and immediately impressing the Sacerdotal power or character; the orginal property of ordaining Ministers being only in Christ, the head of the Church.*
|| *Hyperius* thus seconds him, ' The imposition of hands in || *In 1 Tim. 4.*
' the election of a Bishop, or Deacon, to approve the per- 14.
' son to the multitude or people, was made by THE EL-
' DERS, in whom this authority rested, whence it is here
' added, with the *laying on of hands by the authority of the Priest-*
' *hood*, or as it is more significantly and plainly expressed in
' in the Greek, with the *laying on of the hands of the Presbyte-*
' *ry*, which signified the whole Congregation of Elders. And
' they agreed, that he *who was elected by the Consent of many*,
' should be commended and approved as a fit person, by
' this external sign. Which is thus backed by * *Hemingius*, * *In 1 Tim. 4.*
' The imposition of the hands of the Presbytery, is the right 14.
' of ordination, which the SENATE ( or Eldership ) of the
' Church, or other Ministers of the Gospel did administer.
' Learned *Gerardus, Locorum Theolog. De Ministerio Ecclesia-*
' *stico* proves at large, That the power of Ordination be-
' longs to Presbyters, & that Ministers ordination by Pres-
' byters alone, is a good ordination by the word of God,
' refuting the Papists Cavils to the contrary. || *Pezelius* || *Argum. &*
thus jumps in judgement with him. ' Heretofore the au- *Resp. pars 7.*
' thority of Ordination was granted to the Bishops at least *De Ordin Mi-*
' by a humane institution, yet so that the suffrages of the *nist. in Argum.*
' Church might not be excluded from the Election of Mi- 1.
' nisters, and that the other Presbyters should be present at
' the examination, and lay their hands together on him,
' that was to be ordained: For so *Gratian Can. Presbyter. Di-*
' *stinct.* 23. when a Presbyter is ordained, the Bishop bles-
' sing him, and holding his hand upon his head, all the
' Presbyters likewise that are present, shall hold their

L hands

'hands upon his head, close to the Bishops hands: which tended to this purpose, that the Presbyters likewise might retain the right of consecrating, or ordaining to themselves, and that so they might manifest, that whatever the Bishop should do, that he did it not in his own name alone, but in the name of all. ǁ *Musculus* harps upon the same string thus, 'It must plainly be confessed, that the Ministers of Christ heretofore were elected, the people being present and consenting, and they were ordained and confirmed OF THE ELDERS, by the laying on of their hands." This *form of electing Ministers is Apostolical and lawfull;* which he there proves at large.

ǁ *Loci Com. De Ministr. Verbi Dei.*

The Noble *Mornay, Lord of Plessis,* sings the same tune in these words, 'These things being thus proved, we adde, that the right of laying on of hands, and ordaining Ministers, is in the power of the Presbyters. And this verily concerning the Apostles daies is more apparent, than that it can be so much as doubted: For saith Paul to *Timothy, Neglect not the Gift that is in thee by the laying on of the hands of the Presbytery,* that is, of the Presbyters or Elders. Moreover *Timothy* himself ordained Elders, and since a Bishop and a Presbyter are names of one and the same function; if the Bishops challenge this right to themselves from the Scriptures, the Presbyters also may do the same: but if they deny it to Presbyters, in this very thing they abrogate this right to themselves. And verily this was a good form of Argument in the Church in Antient times. ǁ He can baptize, he can consecrate and administer the Sacrament of the Lords body, (which are the greater and more honourable Actions, because Sacraments of undoubted truth, of highest note and use,) Therefore he may lay on hands. (which is lesse;) Now in ordaining Elders, the Bishop laying his hands on the heads of those who were to be ordained, the rest of the Elders likewise did lay on their hands, as appears out of many places of the Decrees. The ǁ Century writers inform us, That in the Apostles

* *De Ecclesia Cap. 11.*

ǁ *M gist Sent. tat. l. 4 c. 25.*

ǁ *Cent 1. l. 2 c. 6. Ritus Vocationis & Ordinationis, Col. 502.*

## The Un-bishoping of Timothy and Titus. 67

'Apostles time, the Apostles did not assume to themselves
'the power of electing and ordaining Elders and Deacons,
'but they had the suffrage and consent of the whole
'Church; and that they, and the other Ministers of the
'Church with them, did ordain and lay hands on them;
'which they prove by *Acts* 6. and 13. and 14. and 19. and
'1 *Tim.* 4. 14. And in the 2d and 3d Century following, c 6.
'they affirm, That Bishops and Ministers were thus elected
'and ordained, the Elders as well as the Bishops laying their
'hands on them. The \*Confession of *Saxonie*, c. 12. re- \* *Harmon. Con-*
'solves, That it belongs to the Ministers of the word to *fess. pars* 2.
'ordain Ministers lawfully elected and called. The ‖ Synod
'of *Petrocow*, (in *Poland*) *Artic.* 6. decreed, That no ‖ See *Gersomus*
'Patron should receive or admit any Ministers to teach in *Bucerus de Gu-*
'his Church, unlesse he were lawfully ordained and sent by *bern. Eccl. p.*
'the Superintendents, and the Elders, and had a good and 618.
'certain Testimonial from them; and the Synod of *Wlodisla-*
'*via*, *Artic.* 8. and 12. determines thus: The ordination
'and mission of Ministers in certain places to work in the
'Lords Vineyard, is committed to the Superintendents,
'and to the Ministers and Elders their Colleagues; (not to
'Bishops:) *Georgius Major* in his *Enar. in Philip.* 1. 1. writes
'thus, That there is no difference between a *Bishop* and
'a *Presbyter*, *Paul* witnesseth in the 1 *Tim.* 4. 14. where
'he saith, *Neglect not the grace that is in thee, &c. by the lay-*
'*ing on of the hands of the Presbytery*; that is, of the Order or
'Colleadge of the Presbyters: by which it is shewed, That
'*Timothy* was called and ordained to the Episcopal functi-
'on by the Presbyters. Therefore at that time PRESBY-
'TERS HAD THE RIGHT OF ORDINATION, as well
'as Bishops, neither was there any difference between
'them. To these I might adde, *Master John Calvin*, *Pisca-*
'*tor*, *Marlorat*, and most other Protestant Commentators on
'the 1 *Tim.* 4. 14. *Zanchius De statu peccati & Legal. in*
'*quartum Praceptum*, *Chemnitius Loc. Com. pars* 3. *De Ecclef.*
'c. 4. and *Examen Concilii Tridentini pars* 2. *De Sacram. Or-*
'*dinis*, p. 224, 225, &c. (where he proves at large, 'That
'the election & vocation of Ministers belongs to the whole
L 2                                 Church,

*Gal. Voetius Desperata Causa Papatus, l. 2. Sect. 2.*

'Church, to the people as well as the Clergy; that the imposition of hands belongs to Presbyters as well as Bishops. Wherefore the Apostle saith, 1 *Tim.* 4. 14. that *Timothy* had a grace and a gift by the imposition of hands, neither saith he only of my hands, but he adds also of the Presbytery, that there should be thought no difference, whether any one were ordained either by the Apostles, or by the Elders.) *Antonius Sadeel. Responf. ad Repetita Turriani Sophism. pars* 2. *Locus* 12. *B·za de diversis Ministrorum Gradibus. Junius Contr.* 5. *l.* c. 3. *n.* 3. *Chamierus Paustratia Cathol. Tom.* 2. *de Occum. Pontif.* c. 6. with sundry * other writers of the reformed Churches, who aver and prove against the Papists and Jesuits; that the power of election and ordination of Ministers by the word of God, belongs to the whole Church and Congregation, and the imposition of hands to Ministers, Elders, and Presbyters, as well as to Bishops, and to Bishops only as they are Presbyters. But he that hath handeled and proved this most largely and fully of all others, is *Gersomus Bucerus de Gubernat. Ecclesie* (being an answer to *Bishop Downhams Sermon of Bishops*) p. 261, 262, 283, 287, 292, 294, 299, 310, 318, to 367. 464, 465, 493, 498, 499, 524, 618. & *David Blondellus* Apol. pro Sent. *Hieron.* sect. 3. p. 309. to 379. where this point is so learnedly and substantially proved by Scripture, Reason, and Authors of all sorts, that none, which read these passages of theirs, can ever hereafter call this into question more.

† *Presbyteri & Episcopi sunt Jure divino pares, id est, administrant idem officium, eodem modo, & eadem authoritate, unde Presbyteri impositionis manuum in pastoribus ordinandis jus habent.* 1 *Tim.* 4. 14. *Can. Presbyter. Distinct.* 93. *See Amandus Polanus Syntagm. Theol. l.* 7. c. 11.

Having run thus long abroad, I now in the last place return to our own Church and writers. *The Book of ordination of Ministers, ratified by two several Acts of Parliament, namely* 3 *Edw.* 6. c. 12. *and* 8 *Eliz.* c. 1. *and subscribed to by all our Prelates and Ministers* * *by virtue of the* 3*d. Canon as containing nothing in it contrary to the word of God, expresly orders, that when Ministers are ordained;* ALL THE MINISTERS PRESENT AT THE ORDINATION SHALL LAY THEIR HANDS TOGETHER WITH THE BISHOP ON THOSE THAT ARE TO BE ORDAINED: *And the* 35. *Can.* made in Convocation by the Bishops & Clergy *An.* 1603. prescribes, *that the Bishop before he admit any Person to holy Orders, shall diligently*

* *Canons* 1603. 35, 37.

### The Un=bishoping of Timothy and Titus. 69

gently examine him in the presence of those Ministers that shall ASSIST HIM AT THE IMPOSITION OF HANDS. *And if the said Bishop have any lawfull impediment, he shall cause the said Ministers carefully to examine every such Person so to be ordered. Provided that they who shall assist the Bishop in examining* AND LAYING ON OF HANDS, *shall be of his Cathedral Church, if they may be conveniently had, or other sufficient preachers of the same Dioceße, to the number of three at the least.* And according to this book of Ordination and Canon, when ever any Ministers are ordained, all the Ministers there present joyn with and assist the Bishop in laying on of hands, on every one that is ordained. So that both by the established Doctrine and practice of the Church of *England*, the power of laying on hands, and right of ordination, is common to every of our Ministers, as well as to our Bishops; who as they cannot ordain or lay hands on any Ministers without the Bps. so the Bp. can ordain or lay hands on no Ministers without them; so that the power & right of ordination rests equally in them both. With what face or shadow then of truth our Prelates now can or dare to Monopolize this privilege to themselves alone, against this book of Ordination, their own Canons, Subscriptions, yea their own and their predecessors common practice to the contrary (which perchance their over great imployments in temporal businesses, and secular state affairs, have caused them wholly to forget, as least not to consider:) let the indifferent judge. But to passe from them to some of our learned writers: *Alcuvinus De Divinis Officiis c. 37. writes, that Bishops, Presbyters, & Deacons were anciently, and in his time too,* An. 790, 800. * *elected by the Clergy & People, and that they were present at their Ordination and consenting to it: That the Bishops consecration in his daies used in the Church of Rome, wherein two Bishops held the Gospel or New Testament over the head of the Bishop consecrated, and a third uttered the blessing, after which the other Bishops present laid their hands on his head, was but a Novelty, not found in the Old or New Testament, nor in the Roman Tradition.* And then he proves out of *Hierom his Epistle to Evagrius*, and his *Commentary on the first to Titus*, that the ancient consecration of Bishops, was nothing else but their election and

* *See Bishop Jewel's Reply to Harding Art. 4. Divij. 15. Euſebius Eccl Hiſt l. 3. c. 11. l. 6. c. 29. l. 3. l. 7. c. 2. Socr. Eccl Hiſt. l. 1. c. 6. l. 5 c. 8, 9, 9, 15 c. 7. c. 3. 12. 26, 28, 29, 34, 35, 3 45. l. 4 c. 6. Evag im Eccl. ſ. hiſt. l. 2. c. 8. 11. l. 2. c. 11, 12 l 4. c 6. 36. Gratian Diſtinct. 03. 29. Appendix ad Catalogum Teſt. Veritatis.*

and inthronization by the Elders, who chose out one of their company for a Bishop, and placed him in a higher seat than the rest, and called him a Bishop, without further Ceremony; just as an Army makes a General, or as if the Deacons should choose one from among them and call him an Archdeacon, having no other consecration but such as the other Deacons had, being advanced above others only by the Election of his fellow-brethren, without other solemnity.

By which it is plain, that in the Primitive Church, Presbyters did not only ordain Presbyters and Deacons, before there were any Bishops elected and instituted; but likewise, that after Bishops were instituted, they elected and ordained Bishops ( as well as Elders and Deacons ) and that the sole ordination and consecration of Bishops in the Primitive and purest times, was nothing but the Presbyters bare election and inthronization of them without more solemnity; So that the other Rites and Ceremonies now used, are but Novelties. *Anselm Archbishop of Canterbury* on the 1 Tim. 4. 14 expounds these words, *with the laying on of hands of the Presbytery; in this manner,* He *calls that the laying on of hands which was made in his ordination; which imposition of hands was in the Presbytery, because that by this imposition of hands, he received an Eldership, that is, a Bishoprick. For a Bishop is oftentimes called a Presbyter by the Apostle, and a Presbyter a Bishop.* ( whom in his *Commentary* on the third Chapter on Phil. 1. 1. Tit. 1. 5, 7. he proves to be one and the same in the Apostles time, and in the Primitive Church. So that by his resolution the imposition of hands, and power of ordaining Elders and Bishops, belongs to Presbyters as well as to Bishops. Our *English* Apostle m *John Wickliff*, and his Coætanian n *Richard Fitzralphe*, otherwise called, *Richardus Armachanus* Archbishop and Primate of *Ardmagh* in *Ireland*; if we believe either *their own writings*, or o *Thomas Walden*, who recites their own opinions, argument. , and takes a great deal of pains (though in vain) to refute them : affirmed and taught:

*First*, That in the defects of Bishops, any one that was but a mere Priest, was sufficient to administer any Sacrament

m *Wickliff*, De c. Sectis No c'-lu, c 6. De Papa, c. 11.
n *Richardus Armacharus* Ad Quæst. Armenorum, l. 11. c. 1.
o *Waldensis* Cont. Wicl Tom. 3. c. 60, 61, 63. & Tom. 1. l. 2 Artic. 3. c. 57.

ment or Sacramentals whatsoever either found in Scripture, or added since.

*Secondly*, That one who was but a mere Priest might ordain another, and that he, who was ordained only by a simple Priest, ought not to doubt of his Presbytership, or to be ordained again, so as he rightly performed his Clerical Office, because the Ordination comes from God, who supplies all defects.

*Thirdly*, That mere Priests may ordain Priests, Deacons and Bishops too; even as the inferiour Priests among the Jews did ordain and consecrate the High Priest, as Bishops consecrate Archbishops, and the Cardinals the Pope.

*Fourthly*, That the power of Order is equal, and the same in Bishops and Priests, and that by their very Ordination they have power given them by Christ to administer all Sacraments alike; therefore to confer Orders and confirm Children, which is the lesse, as well as to baptise, administer the Sacrament of the Lords Supper, and preach the Gospel, which are the greater.

*Fifthly*, That Christ sitting in heaven hath given the power of consecrating and ordaining Priests and Deacons, of Confirmation, and all other things, which Bishops now challenge to themselves, to just Presbyters; and that these things were but of late times, even above 300. years after Christ, reserved and appropriated to Bishops, only by their own Canons and Constitutions, to increase their *Cæsurian* Pomp and pride. And *Waldensis* himself (who undertakes to refute these Propositions) saith expresly, 'That *no man hitherto hath denyed, that God in an urgent case of necessity gave the power of ordination to any one that is but a mere Priest, to wit, in the want or defect of Bishops. All the Archbishops, Bishops, Archdeacons, and Clergy of England in their Book, intituled, The Institution of a Christian man, subscribed with all their hands, and dedicated to King Henry the 8th. Anno 1537. Chapter of Orders, and King Henry the 8th. himself in his Book styled, A necessary erudition for any Christian man, set out by authority of the Statute of 32 H. 8. c. 25. approved.* \* Tom. 3. c 35. Sect.

'proved by the Lords Spiritual and Temporal, and Ne-
'therhowſe of Parliament, prefaced with the Kings own
'Royal Epiſtle, and publiſhed by his ſpecial command in
'the year 1543. in the *Chapter of Orders*, expreſly reſolve,
'That Prieſts and Biſhops by Gods Law are one and the
'ſame, and that the power of Ordination and Excommuni-
'cation belongs equally to them both. Learned *Martin
Bucer* in his Book *of recalling and bringing into uſe again the
lawfull ordination of Miniſters, and of the Office of Paſtors*, in
his *Scripta Anglicana*, written here in *England*, p. 254, 255,
259, 291, 292, 293. and on *Matth.* 16. layes down theſe
Concluſions.

*Firſt*, That the power of ordination reſts principally and
originally in Chriſt himſelf, the Prince of Paſtors.

*Secondly*, That this power is ſecondarily and derivately
in the whole Church, whoſe conſent is requiſite in the election and ordination of Miniſters.

*Thirdly*, That the actual power of Ordination and impoſition of hands belongs as well to Presbyters as to Biſhops, that they ought to joyn with the Biſhop in the
laying on of hands; and that *Timothy* was ordained by the
byters.

*Fourthly*, That Biſhops and Miniſters have the power of
impoſition of hands in them only inſtrumentally, not originally as Servants, to the whole Congregation.

*Fifthly*, That the examination and ordination of Miniſters ought to be made publickly in the Church where they
are elected to be Miniſters, before all the Congregation; *All
which he proves by ſundry Scriptures and Hiſtories*. *Peter Martyr* his Cœtanian, ( *Regius Profeſſor in the Univerſity of Oxford, in the daies of King Edward the ſixth*, ) in his *Commentary upon the* 2 *Kings* 2. 23. and in his *Common places*, printed
at London. *Cum privilegio, Anno* 1 76. *Claſs*. 4. *Loc*. 1. *Sect*.
23. *p.* 849. writes thus, 'The Papiſts cannot object grie-
'vous ſins againſt the Miniſters of the Goſpel, but they op-
'poſe only ſome ſlight, that I ſay not ridiculous things: they
'ſay that our Paſtors have no impoſition of hands, and
'thence they endeavour to conclude, that they are not to
'be

# The Un-bishoping of Timothy and Titus.

'be reputed just Governours of the Church; and that the
'Congregations which are taught and governed by them,
'are no true Churches, but Conventicles of Revolters.
'And this they say, as if the imposition of hands were so
'necessary, that without it there can be no Ministry in the
'Church; when notwithstanding *Moses* consecrated *Aaron*
'his Brother and his Children, offering divers kinds of
'Sacrifices, on which no man formerly had laid on hands.
'Likewise *John the Baptist* brought in a new right of Bap-
'tism, and administred it to the Jews, when as yet no hands
'had been laid upon him, and he himself had been baptised
'of no man. *Paul* also called by Christ in his journey, did
'not presently go to the Apostles that they might lay hands
'upon him, but he taught in *Arabia* three years space, and
'ministred to the Churches, before that he went up to
'the Apostles his Antecessors, as himself witnesseth in *his*
'*Epistle to the Galathians*. We reject not the imposition
'of hands, but retain it in many Churches; which if we re-   Nota.
'ceive not from their Bishops, we are not to be blamed for
'it, for they would not confer it on us, unlesse we would
'depart from sound Doctrin, and likewise bind our selves
'by Oath to the *Roman Antichrist*.' In which words he
resolves,

*First*, That the imposition of hands is no such essenti-  \* See *Davidis*
al part of Ministers ordination,\* but that it may be omit-  *Blundelli Apo-*
ted; and that those who are elected and lawfully called   *logia, sect.* 3. De
to the Ministery by the suffrage of the whole Church and  *Ordinatione, &*
People, are Ministers lawfully called and ordained without *Plebis in Ele-*
this Ceremonie.   *&tionibus jure,*
p. 309, to 448.
*Secondly*, That the imposition of hands belongs to Mini-  *where this is*
sters, as well as Bishops; and that those who are ordained *largely proved.*
Ministers in the reformed Churches, where they have no
Bishops, only by the laying on of hands of other Ministers,
are lawfully ordained.

*Thirdly*, That this position, that the power of Ordination belongs only to Bishops, that those who are no true
Ministers who are ordained without a Bishop, is but a vain
ridiculous Popish Cavil. Our Prelates therefore should be
M                 ashamed

ashamed to ground both their own, and *Titus* his Episcopal Hierarchie upon it. The Papists and Jesuites have made use of this errovious Paradox, on purpose to render the Ordinations of Ministers, by *Luther, Zwinglius, Calvin, Melanchia*, and other first Reformers of the Protestant Churches, and their Successors since their separation from the Church of Rome, mere *Nullities*, their *Ministers* no *Ministers*, and by consequence the Protestant Churches and Sacraments no Churches or Sacraments at all; Whence * *Bellarmine*, b *Cornelius Jansenius*, and other Papists argue thus: *Lutherus, Zwinglius, Calvinus, Melanthonus, &c. Non fuerunt à veris Pastoribus Episcopi ordinati, sed Presbyteri tantum. Ergo nec illi qui primis illis successerunt, ab iis ordinati fuerunt veri Pastores. Sed Ecclesia sine Pastoribus esse non potest*; SEQUITUR IGITUR, ADVERSARIOS VERAM ECCLESIAM NON HABERE. Which they style ARGUMENTUM INDISSOLUBILE. This Popish and Jesuitical position and opinion, though at large refuted by *Peter Martyr*; *Chamier, Gersomus Bucerius, David Blondellus, Apologia pro sententia Hieronimi, De Episcopis & Presbyteris*, Sectio 3. *Gisbertus Voetius* in his *Desperata Causa Papatus, ubi imprimis magna illa præjudicia de Reformatorum Vocatione, successione & secessione funditus subruuntur*, Lib. 2. Sect. 2. with other forein Protestant, and our own Domestick Divines; yet Archbishop c *Laud*, in his Relation of his Conference with *Fisher*, p. 175, 176. is not ashamed to shake hands with the Papists and Jesuites herein; and positively to conclude, *That no mere Priest had the power of Ordination*, BUT A BISHOP ONLY: and thence he infers, NO BISHOP NO CHURCH: wherein he is seconded by Bishop *Mountague Originum Ecclesiasticarum*, Tom. 1. pars posterior, p. 464. by Bishop *Hall*, in his *Episcopacy by Divine Right*, p. 18, 19, 91. and Part 2. Sect. 15. *Power of Ordination* IS ONLY IN BISHOPS. Upon which account Bishop *Hall* re-ordained * Mr. *John Dury*, formerly ordained by Presbyters in a Reformed Church beyond the Seas; whenas all our Bishops admit the Ordination of *Masse-Priests* in the Church of Rome it self by *Popish Bishops*, to be a *lawfull Ordination*, and never re-ordained d any *Popish Priest*

a De Clericis.

b Notarum Spongia Cent. Gul. Voetium.

c See Canterburies Doom, p. 389, 390.

* See the Time-serving Proteus.

d Mr. Samuel Rutherford's due Right of P. esbyterys, p. 237, 238, 239, &c.

or

## The Un-bishoping of Timothy and Titus.

or *Jesuit*, if he became a Protestant, but admitted him to exercise his Ministry freely amongst us, without renouncing his *Popish Orders, and taking new from them*. In imitation of whose Jesuitical opinion, and Romish practise our present Bishops, and Vicars Generals are now so rigedly *Popish* and *Extravagant herein*, that they refuse to own any of our Ministers, ordained by *Presbyters* during the late troubles, to be *Ministers*; and will not admit them to Benefices or Fellowships, unlesse they *will renounce their Presbyterial Ordination*, as NULL & VOID, and receive a NEW ORDINATION FROM BISHOPS, notwithstanding their promised and expected moderation and reformation of these their former *Exorbitances*, the principal occasions of our late wars and miseries. I shall therefore seriously beseech and desire our Prelates and their Vicars Generals to be ashamed of, and renounce this their Popish and Jesuitical practice and position; whereby they not only greatly offend, but even Un-church most Protestant Churches in forein parts, and Un-minister their Ministers, amongst whom his Majestie and themselves have been harbored & relieved in their greatest Extremities. Especially seeing *Erastus Junior* ( newly published by a * *Popish Priest*, under the disguise of a Sectary ) doth not only argue and declaim against all *Presbyterian Ministers* and *their Ordinations*; but even against their own *Episcopal Consecrations and Ordinations*, as meer NULLITIES because not derived from the Roman Pontif, nor warranted by those Canons and Councils which they urge against Presbyterial Ordinations. And to reclaim them from their error herein, I shall desire them for their own honour, and our Churches peace, with unpassionate spirits, and dis-ingaged affections, seriously to consider what our learned writers and professors of Divinity have formerly written in this particular. Learned * Dr. *Whitaker*, writing against *Bellarmine*, saith; *that this text of the* 1 Tim. 4. 14 *makes very much against the adversaries*; For from this place we understand, that Timothy received imposition of hands from the Elders, who at that time governed the Church by a common Council; and against * *Duraeus*, he argues thus: Luther, Zwinglius,

* London, 1660

* Controv. 2. qu. 5. c. 5.

† Contra Duraeum, l. 7 sect. 55.

Zwinglius, Oecolampadius, Bucer and others were Presbyters; and Presbyters by Gods Law are the same with Bishops; therefore they might lawfully ordain other Presbyters; Dr. Fulk in his Confutation of the Rhemish Testament: Annot. on Tit. 1. Sect. 2. and Dr. Willet in his Synopsis Papismi, the 5. general Controversie quest. 3. part 2. write thus, ‘Although in the Scrip-
‘ture a Bishop and an Elder is of one order and authority
‘in preaching the word, &c. yet in government, by antient
‘use of speech, he is only called a Bishop, which is in the
‘Scripture called chief in government, to whom the ordi-
‘nation or consecration by imposition of hands was alwaies

*Nota.* ‘principally committed. Not that imposition of hands be-
‘longeth only to him, for the rest of the Elders that were
‘present at ordinations did lay on their hands, or else the
‘Bishop did lay on his hands in the name of the rest. We
‘differ from the Papists in this; They affirm, that not
‘principally and chiefly, but solely and wholly the right of
‘consecrating and giving Orders appertaineth unto Bishops.
‘But concerning the power of giving Orders we say; that
‘though it were chiefly in the Apostles, yet the Pastors and
‘Elders together with them laid on their hands, *Act.* 13.3,
‘4. and as St. *Paul* speaketh of his laying on of hands, 2 *Tim.*
‘1. 6. so he maketh mention of imposition of hands by the
‘Eldership, 1 *Tim.* 4. 14. And the *Rhemists* on that place
‘mislike not the practice of their Church, that their Priests
‘do lay on their hands together with the Bishop upon his
‘head that is to be ordained. What else doth this signifie,
‘but that they have some interest in ordaining together
‘with the Bishop? The 4. Council of *Carthage* Can. 3. De-
‘crees thus: Let all the Priests that are present, hold their
‘hands next to the Bishops hand, upon the head of him
‘that is to be ordained. Again Can. 14. of the same Coun-
‘cil: The Bishop must not give orders, but in the presence
‘and assembly of the Clergy. By this then it is manifest,
‘that imposition of hands doth not wholly and soly belong
‘to the Bishops, seeing the rest of the Elders were wont to
‘lay on their hands likewise, or the Bishop in the name of
‘the rest. So that the Elders were not excluded. Dr. *Field*
in

in his 5. *Book of the Church*, c. 27. is of the same opinion; where he proves out of *Durandus and other Papists*, 'that the power of consecration and order is not greater in Bishops than in any other Ministers; that the power of ordination was reserved to Bishops, not by any divine, but humane Constitutions only, rather for to honour the Bishops priestly place, than for that it might not be done by any other, and for the avoiding of confusion and schism in the Church: Concluding, that in cases of necessity; as when Bishops are extinguished by death; or fallen into heresie, or obstinately refuse to ordain men to preach the Word and Gospel of Christ sincerely, and the like, then Ministers only may ordain other Ministers, without any Bishops assistance. And Mr. *Cartwright* in his *Confutation of the Rhemish Testament*, on the 1 Tim. 1. 14. Sect. 18. and on Tit. 1. Sect. 2. proves, both by the *Rhemists* own practise and confession, by the 4. Council of *Carthage*, cited by them, and the History of *Eradius* his ordination, who succeeded *Augustine*, to which six Elders, as well as two Bishops were called, and by the text of *Timothy* it self, that the imposition of hands belongs to Elders as well as Bishops, which he manifests to be one and the same by divine institution.' Finally, acute and learned Dr. *Ames* in his *Bellarminus Enervatus Tom. 2. l. 3. c. 2.* of the *vocation and ordination of Ministers*, Sect. 4, &c. *De Ordinatione*, concludes thus against *Bellarmine*, who affirms, *that the ordination, vocation, and election of Bishops and other Ministers of the Church belongeth only to Bishops*.

*Nota*.

*First*, That it cannot belong *Jure Divino* to Popish Bishops, superior to Presbyters in degree, because they themselves are only, *vel juris, vel injuriæ humanæ*, of humane right, or rather injurie, not of divine institution.

*Secondly*, That the very act of ordination belongs to divine Bishops, that is, to Presbyters, in a Church well ordered.

*Thirdly*, That as to the right, force and virtue which it hath in constituting the Ministers of the Church, it alwaies appertains to the whole Church; as the celebration of Matrimony receives all its force and virtue from the consent of the parties married.

*Fourthly*,

*Fourthly*, That in the corrupted and collapsed State of the Church, the Ministery and Order failing; the very Act of Ordination, so far forth as it is necessary to the constitution of a Minister, may in such a case be lawfully executed by the people.

*Fifthly*, That the Act of Ordination is attributed to Presbyters, 1 *Tim.* 4. 14. And that the Apostles themselves did not ordain ordinary Ministers, but by the concurrence and consent of the people, *Acts* 14. 23.

*Sixthly*, That in the primitive Church, which was governed by the Common Counsel of the Presbyters, before there were any Bishops, the very first Bishops were not ordained by Bishops, which then were not, but by Ministers, and Presbyters only.

*Seaventhly*, That all the Councils, Decrees and Testimonies of Fathers objected to the contrary, prove nothing else, but that the Act and Right of Ordination partly by Custome, and partly by humane Decrees, was given to the chief Presbyter or Bishop after the Apostles time, but not belonging to them by any divine right.

*Figthtly*, That the imposition of hands is not absolutely necessary to the essence of a Pastor, no more than a Coronation to the essence of a King, or the celebration of a Mariage, to the essence of a mariage.

*Ninthly*, That the power of Ordination, according to the Schoolmen and Canonists, is not an Act of Jurisdiction, but of simple Office, which Presbyters may perform without any Command or Jurisdiction.

*Tenthly*, That the Papists themselves teach, that baptism conferred by any Christian, though a lay man or woman, is good, by reason of the necessity of it: that a simple Presbyter by the common consent of the Popish Doctors, may administer the Sacrament of Confirmation, or confer any of the greater Orders, and that all the Pontificians teach with unanimous consent, that a Bishop once consecrated, although he be a Simoniack, Heretick, excommunicate Person, or the like, may yet firmly ordain others. Therefore a *fortiori* Godly Presbyters, or the People and Church

Church of Christ, may lawfully confer orders without the help or concurrence of a Bishop. Which authority of his ought not to be slighted as Scismatical or erroneous, it being consonant to the Doctrine both of our own and other Writers, Churches; *and this book of his printed by Authority, in the University of Oxford*, no longer since than *Anno* 1629. It is evident then by this whole cloud of Witnesses (to omit others) that the power and right of ordination and imposition of hands (which sayth * *Gratian*, *is nothing else but a Prayer over a man*; and as || *Aquinas writes, signifieth only the conferring of grace, which is given by Christ; and not that Ministers*, (he saith not Bishops, who are here but Ministers) *give this grace*; *and so as proper for Ministers as Bishops both by divine and humane right and practise*; belongs to Presbyters and ordinary Ministers as well as Bishops; therefore Bishops cannot be paramount Presbyters and ordinary Ministers in order and Jurisdiction, in this regard; neither will this power of Ordination prove *Timothy* or *Titus* Bishops, as they now vainly surmise. Wherefore I shall retort the Objection in this manner against the Opposites.

* *Manuū impositio quid est aliud quàm oratio super hominem? Cauf.* 1. qu. 1. c. *Manus*, *Ambr. in* 1 *Tim.* 4.
|| *In* 1 *Tim.* 4. *Lect.* 3. See *Gersonium Bucerum De Gubern. Eccl. p.* 337.

> That power or authority which is common by divine right and institution to Evangelical Ministers and Presbyters as well as to Bishops, can neither prove *Timothy* or *Titus* to be Bishops, or Bishops to be superiour to Presbyters or Ministers in Jurisdiction, order, dignity or degree, *Jure divino* or *humano*.
> But the power and Authority of ordaining Presbyters, Ministers, and Deacons, is such; as the premises undeniably evidence.
> Therefore it can neither prove *Timothy* or *Titus* to be Bishops, nor Bishops to be superiour to Presbyters, or Ministers in Jurisdiction, order, dignity or degree, *Jure divino* or *humano*.

*Sixtly*, St. *Paul* in the 1 *Tim.* 3. and *Titus* 1. 6. *&c. makes a particular enumeration and recital both of the qualifications, and offices of a Bishop*; But among all these, he speaks not a word concerning the power or act of ordination; neither doth

doth he make it a part of a Bishops qualification or duty to be apt and able discreetly to confer orders, as he doth particularly require, *he \*should be apt to teach:* How therefore this should be a chief property, or principal sole quality of a Bishop, I cannot yet conjecture, since the Scripture makes it none, but rather a *property and act of the Presbytery*, 1 Tim. 4. 14. Act. 13. 3, 4. I shall desire Bishops therefore, to produce some divine Charter or other for this their pretended Monopolie of ordination, which they would ingrosse unto themselves alone (perchance to make the more advantage by it, it *\*being a sweet and pleasant gain as some handle it now,*) before they lay any further Title thereunto, even as they are Diocæsan Bishops.

\* 1 Tim. 3. 2.

\* Lindewodes Constit. Provinc. l. 3. de Censibus cap. Sena.f 160. 161.
\* See my Breviate of the Prelates intollerable Incroachments upon the Kings Prerogative Royal, and Subjects Liberties.

Seaventhly, I must inform our Bishops for their learning, that \* *An. 31. H. 8. in the Patent Rolls part 4. King Henry the 8. granted a Patent to all the Archbishops, and Bishops of England, to enable them to consecrate Churches, Chapels, and Churhyards, by virtue of his special Patents and Commissions under his great Seal first obtained;* without which they could not do it: and that all the Bishops in King Edward the 6. time, had special clauses in their Letters Patents, authorizing them to ordain and constitute Ministers and Deacons, as *Bishop Ponets, Bishop Scoryes, Bishop Coverdales, Patents* 5 *Edw.* 6. pars 1, &c. with others in his Reign, testifie at large. Neither do or can our Archbishops or Bishops at this day consecrate any Bishop or Archbishop, unlesse they have the Kings own \* Letters Patents, authorizing and commanding them to do it, as the Patents directed to them upon every Bishops confecration and experience witnesse. It is clear therefore that their power to consecrate Churches, Chapels, Churchyards, Ministers and Bishops, belongs not to them as they are Bishops, and that it is meerly humane not divine, since they claim and execute it*\*only by virtu of the Kings Letters Patents*; and as a part of their Ecclesiastical Jurisdiction (not Ministerial function) deprived *only from the King*, as the Statutes of 26 H. 8. c. 1: 37 H. 8. c. 17. 1 E. 6. c. 2. 5 E. 6. c. 1. 1 Eliz. c. 1, 2. 5 Eliz. c. 1. 8 Eliz. c. 1. resolve: Therefore it cannot advance them above Presbyters, by any divine right.

\* See Wests Presidents Warrants Sect. 574.

\* See Erastus Junior.

*Eightly,*

*Eightly*, a All accord, that in cases of necessity, when or where Bishops are wanting, or when there are none but Simoniacal or Heretical Bishops, who refuse to ordain such as are Orthodox, or will not subscribe to their heresies, there Presbyters and ordinary Ministers may lawfully confer Orders, confirm, and do other Acts, which Bishops usually ingrosse to themselves; so *Ambrose*, *Augustine*, *Richardus Armachanus*, *Wicliffe*, *Thomas Waldensis*, *Field*, *Ames*, with others in their forequoted places; and generally all divines resolve without dispute. Yea that learned *Morney* Lord of *Plessis*, in his Book *De Ecclesia*, c. 11. b *Amesius*, with sundry others affirm, that the people alone in case of necessity where there are no Bishops nor Ministers, may lawfully elect and ordain Ministers, as well as baptise and preach (both which c Papists, and d Protestants affirm, that Laymen may lawfully do in cases of necessity) the right of ordination and election of Ministers being originally in the whole Church and People, Ministerially only in Bishops and Ministers as servants to the Congregation, and the imposition of hands no essential, but a ceremonial part of ordination, which may be sufficiently made without it, as *Angelus de Clavasio*, *Peter Martyr*, and others, both Papists and Protestants, affirm. But when *Paul* left *Titus* in *Crete*, e to set in order the things that were wanting, and to ordain Elders in every City, there were present no other Bishops or Elders to ordain Ministers, (as is likely) but *Titus* only and the people; for we read of none else but *Titus* then in *Crete* (which was but newly converted to the faith;) and he is enjoyned, to ordain Elders in every City; which proves there were none there before, for what need then of any, yea of many others to be newly ordained, and that in every City? *Titus* his example of ordination therefore in this exigent and necessity in a Church then newly planted, is no argument to prove him a Diocæsan Bishop; since other *ordinary Ministers* might ordain in such a case, as *all acknowledge, yea and the people too, without either *Minister* or *Bishop* to assist them.

*Ninthly*, I answer, that it is most evident, that *Titus* did not ordain Elders in every City, by virtue of any Episcopal inherent Jurisdiction of his own, but as *Pauls* Substitute, who

a *M. Perkins on Gal. 1.8. Zanchius Com. in Eph. 5. Mr. Rutherford his due right of Presbyteries. c. 8. S A. 8. p. 17 5, 10 140. Robinson and others there quoted. Bishop Downham his Sermon on Apoc. 1. 7.*
b *Bellarminus Ener. Tom. 2. l. 3. c. 2.*
c *Summa Angelica, Baptismus 5. Sect. 12. Conc. Carthage 4. Can. 39, 99. Gratian Distinct. 23. cap. Mulier.*
d *Fox Acts and Monuments, 1610. p 465, 485, 501, 599, 1015, 1016, 1795, 1796.*
e *Tit. 1. 5. Cyprian Epist. 68.*

\* *Saravia de diversis Ministrorum gradibus, c. 1. p. 3. Davidis Bendelli Apolog. Sect. 3. p. 354.*

who *appointed him to do it, and prescribed him what manner of Persons he should ordain:* Tit. 1. 5, 6, 7, 8, 9. This therefore cannot prove *Titus* to be a Bishop; or that the sole right of ordination is appropriated unto Bishops, as Bishops, but rather the contrary.

*Lastly,* Admit, that the power of ordaining Presbyters belonged only to Bishops *Jure Divino*; yet is no good consequent; *Ergo,* they are superior to Presbyters in order and degree *Jure Divino*; since the conferring of orders, (*an fact of service, of Ministry only, not of Authority, and no more then an external complement or Ceremony*) is far g inferior *to the authority of preaching, baptising, consecrating, and administring the Sacrament of the Lords Supper, binding obstinate, and loosing penitent sinners, which Jure Divino every Minister may do as well as a Bishop.* The Bishops and Ministers in the primitive Church had h *many of them the gift of tongues, of prophecy, of healing and working miracles,* which some Bishops then, and all now want; yet these extraordinary endowments made them not superior in Jurisdiction, order, or degree to those Bishops who then wanted those gifts, or to ours now, who take far more state upon them, than those Bishops did. i *Many Bishops there are and have been that could not, at least would not preach, though* k *Bellarmine himself,* yea the l *Council of Trent,* and m *all men acknowledge, that it is the chiefest, and most honourable part of their Episcopal function, as making them Christs Ambassadors:* Are they then inferior in order, dignity, power, degree to Bishops, yea to Ministers, Vicars, and poor Curates who are both able and willing to preach? That which makes any man superior in order, Jurisdiction, or dignity to his equal, must be an authority superior to that which his equal hath, not the accession of any inferior dignity or power. The making of an Earl, a Knight, or Country-Justice, addes nothing to his former honour in point of superiority or precedency: If a Bishop be presented to an ordinary benefice, Prebendary or Deane-

f *Amesius Bellarminus Enervatus Tom. 2. l. 3. c. 2. and others foresayted.*
g See *Gersomus Bucerus de Gubern Eccles.* p. 33, 158, to 162. 261, 262, 499, 500, 517.
h 1 Cor. 12. 9, 10. Act 10. 46.
i *Marsilius Patavinus Defens. Pacis pars 2. c. 20, 24. Fox Acts and Monuments,* p. 1153. *Bishop Latymers Serm of the plough. Nicholaus de Clemangiis de corrupto Eccl. statu. c. 14, 15, 16. Avent Annal. Bojorum l 6. Proœmi.*
k *De Cleric. c. 4.*
l *Sessio 24. Decr. de Reformatione cap. 4.*
m *Thomas B. cons Catechism. The Institution of a Christian man: Chapter of Orders. Gersomus Bucerus de Gubern. Eccles.* p. 33, 138, usque 162, 251, 252, 479 500, 517: 518, 540, 522, 623.

# The Un-bishoping of Timothy and Titus. 83

ry, (as * *some are and have been by way of Commendam.*) it accumulates nought to his Episcopal authority. Therefore the power of ordination being inferiour to the power of the Keyes, preaching and administring the Sacraments, (which every Minister enjoyes *Jure divino*, as absolutely as any Archbishop or Bishop) can no wayes advance Bishops in Jurisdiction or degrees above Presbyters and ordinary Ministers, no more than the Bp. of *Durham his being a* || *Count Palatine, with his large temporal Jurisdiction, far exceeding that of all our Archbishops and Bishops,* advanceth him in order and degree above them all. So that this grand Objection to prove *Titus* a Bishop; yea a Bishop superiour in Jurisdiction, order, and degree to Ministers; is both false and idle.

*Obj.* 4. If any object, *That it is a received Maxime in the Schools,* † *that he which ordains is greater than he who is ordained*; and that the Apostle saith, *That the lesser is blessed of the greater:* Therefore *Titus*, and so likewise Bishops who ordain Ministers, are superior to Ministers, in point of Jurisdiction, order, dignity and degree.

*Answ.* 1. I answer, *First*, that this objection takes that for granted which I formerly refuted, and evidenced to be a falsehood; to wit, That the power of ordination belongs only to Bishops, not to Presbyters; and so is built on a false sandy foundation.

*Secondly*, I answer, that this Proposition, He that ordaineth or consecrateth Ministers is greater in Jurisdiction, power, or degree, than the parties consecrated and ordaineth; is a notorious dotage and untruth, broached at first by *a* Epiphanius, to confute *Aerius his orthodox opinion of the parity of Bishops and Presbyters*; and since that taken up at second hand by *b Bellarmine, and other Jesuites,* the *c Council of Trent, d Bishop Downham,* with other Patriots of the Popes and Prelates Monarchy; and last of all (like Coleworts twice sodde) usurped by *all our Prelates in their High Commission at Lambeth in their Censure of Doctor Bastwick,* who

† *Hobards Reports, p. 107, 150, &c.*
*See Goodwins Catalogue of Bishops, p.70, 72, 1114, 123, 143-164,185, 214, 220,147, 245, 275,345, 381, 412,436, 418, 484, 501, 502,568,569, 570,571,572, 610, 621,622, 630.*
|| *Goodwins Catalogue of Bishops, p. 614, 657, 660, Brook County Palatine, 14, 15, 16, 18, 19, 24.*
† *Bellarmin. de Clericis, l. 3. quæst. 2.*

*a Contra hæreses, l 3. Tom.1. Hær 75. Col. 759, 760.*
*b De Cleri.is, l. 3. Quæst. 2.*
*c Sessi. 23 De Sacramente Ordinis, cap 3. &*

Canon 7. d *His Sermo*, April 17. Anno 1608. *in the defence of the honourable Function of Bishops, and his defence of that Sermon since. Bishop Bilson of the perpetual Government of the Church, c. 13.*

laid the whole weight and burthen of their Episcopal superiority and precedency over other Ministers, upon this rotten, counterfeit Pillar, unable any waies to support it, as these ensuing demonstrations will evidence at large beyond all contradiction.

For first of all we know, e that *Cardinals and Bishops at this day*, ( *as the People and Clergy, yea the Emperours heretofore* ) *do elect and consecrate the Pope*; yet they are not greater in order, dignity, power or Jurisdiction than the Pope, but inferiour, and he far superiour to them in all these. We f read, that *Metropolitanes, Patriarks, Primates and Archbishops are created, consecrated and installed by ordinary Bishops*, as the g *Archbishops of Canterbury and Yorke*, have oftentimes been by the Bishops of *London, Rochester, Winchester, Salisbury, Banger*, and the like: yet are they not greater in dignity, power, authority, place, or order than they, but subordinat and subject to them whom they thus ordain, in every of these? We know by daily experience, that one Bishop consecrates and ordains another, and he a second, and that second a third; yet all of them are of equal power, and Jurisdiction, not different or distinct in order or degree; & sometimes the last of the three in respect of his Bishopricks, takes *precedency of the rest, that ordained him, as the* h *Bishops of London, Durham, and Winchester do here with us, and other Bishops do in foreign parts*. So *Some* i *Ministers joyn with the Bishop in the ordination and laying on of hands on other Ministers*, yet none of them is deemed superior in Jurisdiction, order, or degree to the other. Now were this our Prelates objected Paradox true; the Cardinals should be greater in order, power, & degree, than the Popes; the Bishops, than the Patriarks, Metropolitans, Primates and Archbishops ordained by them; one Bishop, one Minister greater than another; yea there should be so many different degrees, among Bps. and Ministers, as there are successive subordinate ordinations; which is both false and absurd. St. * *Hierom in his Epistle to Evagrius and on Titus*, 1. with *Alcuvinus, De Divinis Officiis* c. 37. affirm, that *in the Primitive Church Bishops were at the first both elected and consecrated by the Presbyters*, and the Scrip-

---

e *Gratian Distinct.* 79, 63., *Pontificale Romanum, Platina in vitis Pontif.*
f *Gratian Di. 79, 63.*
g *See Antiquitates Ecclesiæ Brit. Godwins Catalogue of the Archbishops of Canterbury and York, Malmesbury De Gestis Pontificum Anglia*, with *Mason his Consecration of Bishops*; and *the book of consecration of Bishops*.
h 3 & H. 8. c. 10.
i *The book of Ordination of Ministers: & Can.* 35.

* *See Davidis Blondelli Apol. sect. de ordinatione.*

ture is express, that both *Paul* and *Timothy were ordained by the Presbytery*, Acts 13. 3, 4, 1 *Tim*. 4. 14. If the Bishops reason then be Orthodox; it follows inevitably, That in the Apostles times, and the Primitive Church, Presbyters were superiour in Jurisdiction, order and degree to Bishops, yea to *Paul* and *Timothy*, the one an Apostle, the other an Evangelist, being all ordained by Presbyters, not Bishops Lords paramount over them, as they now pretend; and then farewell their divine Hierarchy which they so much contend for. The *Archbishop of Canterbury* ( who stood much upon this argument at *Doctor Bastwicks* Censure ) both *crowned our Soveraign Lord King Charles*, and *baptised* his Son *Prince Charles*; will he therefore conclude, that he is greater in power, authority, place, and Jurisdiction than they? The k *Archbishops of Canterbury*, *have usually crowned and baptised the Kings of England*, and the Archbishops of *Rhemes the Kings of France*; will they therefore infer, Ergo they are greater in power, dignity, and authority than they; as the l *Popes argue, that they are greater than the Emperors*, *because the Bishops of Rome have usually crowned the Emperors?* Are the Princes Electors in *Germany* greater than the Emperors; or Nobles of *Poland*, *Bohemia*, and *Sweden* greater than their Kings; because they * elect and create them Emperors and Kings? Are the Lord Majors of *London* and *York*, or the Major of other Cities inferiour to the Commons; or the Lord Chancellors of our Universities of *Oxford* and *Cambridge*, lesse honourable, potent than, and inferiour to the Doctors, Proctors, and Masters of Art? or the heads or Masters of the Colleges and Halls in them, subordinate to, or lesse worshipfull or eminent than the fellows, because they are elected, constituted and created by them, to be such? Are the Knights, Citizens and Burgesses of the Parliament, not so good as those Freeholders, Citizens & Burgesses who elect them? Or the Masters of Companies inferior to those that choose them? If not, as all must grant, how is this maxime true, *That he who constitutes, ordains, or consecrates another, is greater than the parties constituted, ordained, or consecrated, and that in Jurisdiction, place, order, and*

k *See Liber Regalis, Antiquitates Eccles. Brit. & Goodwins Catalogue of Bishops. Bochellus Decret. Eccl Gal. 1. l. 5. Tit. 2.*
l *Marsilius Patavinus Defensoris Pacis : pars 2. c 25.*
* *See Mr. flores Cosmography. Grimstons Imperial History.*

*degree*

degree? Our *Popish Priests* are not ashamed to proclaim, m *That in their consecration of the Sacrament, they create their very Creator, and make no lesse than Christ himself*: are they therefore greater and higher in order and degree than Christ, the n *great and only High Priest*, the o *chief Shepheard, and Bishop of our Souls*, whose p *Vicar and Substitute the Pope himself doth but claim to be?* Certainly if this their Popish Proposition be true, they must needs be one order or degree Higher, in point of Priesthood, than Christ himself; who must then loose his Titles of High Priest, and Chief Shepheard, because every Masse-Priest will be paramount him, in that he not only consecrates, *but creates him too.* We read in q *Scripture, that Kings, Priests and Prophets were usually annointed and consecrated to be such with oyle*; was therefore the oyle that consecrated them, greater or better than they? Are the font and water, better than the Children baptised in or with them? The Diadems better than the Kings, because they Crown them? or the very hands of Bishops and Ministers, worthier than Ministers ordained by them? If not, then are not Bishops greater than the Ministers which they ordain or consecrate, since they are but instruments, Servants, not prime original Agents, Lords, or Supreme absolute Actors in these severall consecrations and actions. If we cast our eyes either upon nature or policy, we find this Proposition of our Prelates a mere falsehood. In nature we see, that a Man begets a Man; an Horse an Horse; an Asse an Asse, a Dog a Dog, &c. equal one to the other in nature, quality, species and degree; the Son being as much a Man, a Gentleman as the Father? the Colt as much an horse as the steed that begot him. In Civil or Politique Constitutions, we see the like; in our Universities, Doctors, and professors of Divinity, Physick, Law, Musick, create other Doctors of the same Professions, equal to themselves, and as much Doctors in these arts as they; one Doctor in each of these, being as much and no more a Doctor then another, save only in point of time or antiquity, but not in respect of the profession or degree of Doctorship it self; yea *& every Minister made by any Bishop, is as much, as truly and fully*

---

m *Discip. Sermo. 111. Bishop Jewels Reply to Harding. A tic. 22. Div. 10 p. 452, 453.*
n *Hebr. 4. 14, 15. c. 8. 1. c. 9. 11 c. 10. 21.*
o *Hebr. 13. 10. 1 Pet. 2. 25. c. 5. 4. John 10. 1, &c.*
p *Concil. Constantien. Sessio 24. Bellarm. De pontifice Romano.*
q *Exod. 29. & 35. Lev 4. 3. 16. 1 Sam. 10. 1. c. 16. 6. 11. Psal. 81. 10. 1 Kings 1. 39. c. 19. 15, 16.*

✝ *Bishop Jewels Reply to Harding, Article 4. Divis. 5, 6, 18. Richardus Armachanus De Quest. Armenorum, l. 11. c. 1. 2, 3, 4. 5, 6, 7.*

fully a Minister as the Bishop himself, as all Protestants and Papists do acknowledge; therefore the same in specie with, and equal to a Bishop: Our Bishops pretend themselves *Spiritual Fathers*, and they call the Ministers ordained by them, *Sonnes*; So || *Epiphanius* long since argued against *Aërius*: As therefore in natural generations, a man begets a man, a beast a beast; and in civil respects, a Gentleman begets a Gentleman; a Peasant a Peasant, &c. but not a man a beast, a beast a man, a Gentleman a Peasant, nor a Peasant a Gentleman; So Bishops when they engender natural Children, beget them as men, not Bishops, and their Children are as much men as themselves; when they spiritually ordain or engender Ministers, they do it only as they are Ministers, not Bishops, and those they thus beget and ordain, are as much Ministers as themselves; when they beget and consecrate Bishops, they do it as they are Bishops, and those thus begot and consecrated are as much Bishops as themselves. Since therefore they ordain Ministers only as they are Ministers, not as Bishops; as is clear (else it were an unnatural an incongruous, yea a monstrous generation, to beget one of a different kind, order, quality and degree from themselves, and as much as if a man should beget a beast, an horse, or an asse) and since every Minister is as much, as compleat a Minister every way as the Bishop, and Ministers who ordain him; how this proposition can be true; *that the ordainer is higher in Jurisdiction, or different Jure Divino in order or degree from the ordained*, I cannot yet perceive, neither can our Prelates ever make it good. We know there are now divers Ministers living, who not only baptized, but likewise ordained some of our Bishops to be Ministers, and laid hands upon them with the Bishop at the time of their ordination; yea every of our Bishops and Archbishops were first ordained Ministers by Ministers before they were made Bishops or Archbishops. And *the first Bishops that were ordained in the Church paramount Ministers, were ordained Bishops by Ministers, as Hierom writes in his Epistle to Evagrius*, and * all since acknowledge out of him. Are these Ministers therefore in point of order, honor, jurisdiction,

|| *Contr. hæres. l. 3. hæres. 75.*

* *See Davidis Blondelli Apologia Sect. 3.*

diction, dignity and degree, greater than our Archbishops or Bishops? If so, then the controversie is at end; and the truth most apparent; that our Ministers are greater and higher in degree then our Bishops and Archbishops, not our Bishops and Archbishops higher, greater then they, as they vainly contend. If not, then the Prelates maxime, on which they ground their Hierarchy, is most false, in that sence in which they urge it; and so will yeild no supportation to their Hierarchy.

*Thirdly*, I answer, that this Proposition of theirs is warranted by no Scripture, nor backed with any convincing reason drawn from Scripture; therefore it proves nothing either for *Titus* his Episcopal authority; or for Bishops superiority above other Ministers, by any divine right or institution: As for that text of *Heb.* 7. 7. (*And without all contradiction the lesser is blessed of the greater*;) it is nothing to the purpose.

*First*, Because it is not spoken concerning ordination, or of one Ministers ordaining or blessing another, but *only of Melchizedechs blessing of Abraham*, and Ministers blessing of the people, as the words and * *all Commentators joyntly testifie*.

* *Anselmus Haymo, Rabanus, Primasius, Calvin, Deering, David Dickson and others on this text.*

*Secondly*, Because it is not meant of Ministers, who blesse others only *Ministerially*, or *Instrumentally*, by way of duty and service, as Bishops ordain Ministers: not by inherent original authority; for then Ministers, and other Saints of God, should be better and greater then God, whom they *blesse* and *praise*, *Gen.* 9. 26. c. 14. 20. c. 24. 27. *Psal.* 41. 13. *Psal.* 66. 8 *Psal.* 68. 25. *Psal.* 103. 1, 2, 20, 22. *Psal.* 135. 19, 20. *Luke* 1. 68. c. 2. 28. *James* 3. 9. Then *Jacob* who *blessed King Pharoah*, *Gen.* 47. 7, 10. should be greater then *Pharoah* in his own Realm. *The people who blessed King Solomon*, 1 *Kings* 8. 66. greater then their King; and the Disciples and People *who bless'd our Saviour Christ*, *Luke* 19. 37, 38. greater then Christ: But this Text is meant of Christ himself; who by *Melchizedech* his type, blessed *Abraham* by his own inherent authority and power; as the only † *true high Priest*, and ‖ *chief Shepheard of our soules*. If therefore our

† *Heb.* 4. 14, 15. c. 8. 1 c. 9. 11. c. 10 21.
‖ *Heb.* 13. 10. 1 *Pet.* 5. 4.

Prelates

Prelates take their maxime in this sence, he that ordains Ministers, to wit, originally by his own inherent primitive authority and power, is greater then those who are ordained in Jurisdiction, power and degree; then the proposition thus interpreted, is true and warranted by this text; but yet they gain no advantage by it, because no Bishops, do or can ordain Ministers thus, *but * only God and Christ alone*, whose Ministers and Servants both the ordainers and ordained are. But if they mean, that they who ordain Ministers only Instrumentally and Ministerially as servants to Christ, his Church and the whole Congregation, ( in whom the original and primitive right of ordination is only vested ) are greater in Jurisdiction, order and degree, then those who are ordained, as they do and must do; then the proposition is most false and not justified by this Scripture, as the premised instances manifest. The King, the original of all temporal Honour, Justice, Power, is greater then any Officers, Justices, Powers, derived from and under him; but not his Attorny who draws their Patents or Commissions, nor those who swear or install them in their Dignities and Offices, under the King, as Bishops do Ministers under Christ and the Church.

*Eph 4.10,11. 1 Cor. 12.28. Mat. 9.37,38.

Fourthly, Admit this proposition true; that those who are to ordain others, are greater in power and authority then the parties to be ordained, before their ordination fully executed, because they have an Office, Calling, Ministry which the others want; in which sense the proposition may be true: yet it is not true, that the ordainers are greater in power, office, authority then the parties actually ordained after the ordination past and finished; because the very end of ordination, is to confer the self-same office of Ministry on the parties ordained, which the ordainers themselves have, in as large and ample manner as they enjoy it; and the parties once ordained, are thereby made as compleat, as absolute Ministers every way, in respect of their orders and office, as any of those who ordained them: though they were not so when they came to be ordained. This appears by the examples of † *Mathias* and *Paul*; before they were called and ordained to be Apostles,

† *Act. 1.25,26. Gal. 2.8,9,11, 14. 1 Cor. 12,28, 29. 2 Cor. 11.5.*

O they

they were inferiour to the other Apostles; but being once called and ordained Apostles, *they became equal with the other Apostles in Apostolical power, dignity, degree,* and were not inferiour to them in either. So that from all these premises I may conclude, that this maxime of our Prelates, whereon they build their Episcopal Hierarchie, in that sence they take it, is most false; and neither proves *Titus* to be a Diocæsan Bishop, nor yet Bishops to be superior to other Ministers in dignity, power, order, or degree, by divine right and institution, as they pretend they are.

*Finally,* Admit the Proposition true, yet it proves but this, that Bishops are superiour to those Ministers only which themselves ordain, (so that if they ordain none they are superiour to none;) not to those ordained by other Bishops and Ministers, which may be their equals notwithstanding this allegation, seeing they were not ordained by them; this Proposition extending only to the Act, not to the power of Ordination. If any extend it further, in this sort, that they who have power to ordain Ministers are greater in order, Jurisdiction, degree and dignity, than those who want this power; then it will follow, that Bishops suspended from ordaining others (*either for advancing unworthy Ministers, without due examination, or making Ministers without a Title, as many now do,* for which our own * *Canons prescribe, they shall be suspended from giving Orders for two years space*) are inferiour in order and degree to Bishops, who may execute this power and ordain; and so one Bishop shall be superiour in order and degree to another Bishop; which none ever yet affirmed; yea all our Bishops *being prohibited and disabled by their own* ‖ *Canons to ordain Ministers or Deacon at any time, but only at the 4. solemn times appointed, and that in the presence of the Dean, Archdeacon or two Prebends at the least, or of four other grave Persons, being Masters of Art at least, and allowed for publick Preacher.* It will hereupon follow, that Bishops only at these four times of the year, are greater in dignity and degree than Ministers, because they may then ordain, but not at other seasons, when they have no power or authority to confer orders upon any, being restrained by the Canons as well

* *Canons 33. An. 1603.*

‖ *Canon 31. Which they now violate every day by clandestine Ordinations in their chambers and at other seasons.*

## The Un-bishoping of Timothy and Titus. 91

well as Ministers. All which being layd together, discovers the weaknes, the absurdity of this our Prelates Theory, on which they build both their own, and *Titus* his Hierarchy, which now fall quite to ruine with this their sandy foundation, which I have here for ever dissipated and subverted, if I mistake not.

I shall close up this, concerning the power and right of Ordination, with these ensuing Authorities and memorable examples. a *Joannes Major*, b *Joannes Fordonus*, c *Hector Boetius*, d *David Blondellus*, and others record, That the *Scots* from their first embracing of the Christian Faith, *Anno Christi* 179. till the year 430. when the Pope made and sent *Palladius* to them, to be their *Bishop*, were constantly instructed and governed ONLY BY PRESBYTERS AND MONKS, SINE EPISCOPIS, WITHOUT BISHOPS, *Qui vacarent quod sedulo prædicationi, essentque frequentes in oratione ab incolis* Culdei *id est* Cultores Dei *sunt appellati.* So as the primitive Church of *Scotland* for 233. years space, was instructed and governed only by Presbyters and Monks, who ordained each other Ministers without any Bishops. After this e *Columbanus* a Presbyter and Abbot by profession, comming out of *Scotland* into *Britain* in the year of Christ 656. and preaching to the *Picts* in the *North*, whom he converted to the Faith, they bestowed on him the Island of *Hye*, where he built a Monastery: of which Island * *Beda* gives us this account, that for the space of 200. years (when he writ his History) *Habere autem solet ipsa Insula Rectorem semper Abbatem* PRESBYTERUM, CUJUS JURE, ET OMNIS PROVINCIA, ET IPSI ETIAM EPISCOPI, *ordine inusitato* DEBEANT ESSE SUBJECTI, *juxta exemplum primi Doctoris illius (* Columbani *)* QUI NON EPISCOPUS SED PRESBYTER EXTITIT ET MONACHUS. Lo here even in *Britain* it self we find in the first Conversion of the Northern parts thereof amongst the *Picts*, Bishops themselves for two hundred years space or more, subject even of right and custom to a Presbyter and Monk as their Superintendent, and no way subject to their inferiour Jurisdiction. And this Presbyter and his Monkes

a *De Gestis Scotorum, l. 1.*
b *Scotichron, l. 3. c. 8.*
c *Scotorum Hist. l. 6. f. 92. & l. 7. f. 118.*
d *Apollogia pro sententia Hieronymi, sect. 3. p. 314, 315.*

e *Beda Eccles. Hist. l. 3. c. 4. & 3. 5.*

* *Hist. l. 3. c. 5.*

92       *The Un-bishoping of* Timothy and Titus.

*e Jo. Cassinus, collatio 4. Patrum in Eremio, &c. c. 1.*

*f Eccl. Hist. l. 3. c. 3. 5.*

did not only *ordain and send abroad* Presbyters *and Monks,* (as Abbot * Paphnutius also ordained *Daniel* a Presbyter, about the year 422. though no Bishop but a Presbyter) but even Bishops themselves successively, who instructed the Picts and Northern parts of our Island, and converted them to the Christian faith. Hence our venerable *f Beda* thus writes of King *Oswald, M. x. ubi Regnum suscepit, desiderans totam cui praeesset gentem fidei Christianae gratiae imbui, &c. misit* AD MAJORES NATU SCOTORUM, *inter quos exulans, ipse Baptismatis Sacramentum, cum his qui secum erant militibus consecutus erat, petens, ut sibi mitteretur Antistes, cujus Doctrina & Ministerio gens quam regebat Anglorum Dominicae fidei, & dona disceret, & susciperet Sacramenta. Neque aliquanto tardius quod petiit impetravit. Accipit enim Aidanum, summae mansuetudinis & pietatis ac moderaminis virum, habentem zelum Dei, quamvis non plenè secundum scientiam. Ab hac ergo insula* Hy *ab horum collegio Monachorum ad provinciam Anglorum instituendam in Christo, missus est* Aidanus AC-CEPTO GRADU EPICOPATUS, *quo tempore eidem Monasterio Segenius Abbas* ET PRESBYTER FUIT, (who conferred the degree of a Bishop upon him; though but a Presbyter himself, as learned *g David Blondell* observes.) This Bishop *Aidan* comming to *Oswald* King of Northumberland, to convert his people, is a fit patern for all our Lordly Prelates imitation, which if pursued would much indear both their Persons and Function to God and all good men, *h Cujus doctrina id maximè commendabat omnibus, quod non aliter quàm ipse vivebat, cum suis, ipse docebat. Nihil enim hujus mundi quaerere, nil amare curabat. Cuncta quae sibi a Regibus vel a divitibus seculi donabantur, mox pauperibus qui occurrerent erogare gaudebat. Discurrere per cuncta & urbana, & rustica loca, non equorum dorso, sed pedum incessu vectus, nisi si major fortè necessitas compulisset, solebat. Quatenus ubicunque aliquos vel divites vel pauperes accedens aspexisset, confestim ad hos divertens, vel ad fidei suscipiendae sacramentum, si infideles essent, invitaret; vel si fideles in ipsa eos fide comfortaret, atq; ad eleemosynas bonorumque operum executionem & verbis excitaret & factis: In tantum autem vita illius a nostri temporis*

*g Apolog. pro sententia Hieronymi, sect. 3. p. 367, 1037 l.*

*h Beda Eccl. Hist. l. 3. c. 5.*

*segnicia*

## The Un-bishoping of Timothy and Titus. 93

*fugnicia diftabat, ut omnes qui cum eo incedebant five ad tonfi, five laici meditari deberant, id eft, aut legendis Scripturis aut Pfalmis difcendis operam dare. Hoc erat quotidianum opus illius, & omnium qui cum eo erant fratrum. Ubicunq; locorum deveniffent.* And O that this were the daily work of all our Lodly Bishops, Deans and Chapters now! As this Bp. *Aidan*, so divers of our other first Northern Bishops sent out of *Scotland* from *Hy* Abby, were made both *Priests* and *Bishops* by the Abbots of *Hy*, who was no Bishop but a Presbyter, as *i Finan, Colman, Tuda, Ceollac, Trumkere, Ceadda*, and others, all made Presbyters and Bishops by this Abbot, and his Presbyters and Monks. Yea this was a common practise in that Age, both in *England* and *elsewhere*, for Bishops themselves who were Monks to be ordained by and subject to their Abbots who were Presbyters, as well as in *Hy* Abby, as is evident by this 4. Canon of the *k Council of Herudford* under *Theodor* Archbishop of *Canterbury*, An. 673. *UT EPISCOPI MONACHI non migrent de loco ad locum, hoc eft, de Monasterio ad Monasterium, nisi per dimissionem proprii Abbatis, sed in ea permaneant OBEDIENTIA quam tempore suæ conversionis promiserunt.* Bishops therefore in those daies who were Monks (as * most Bishops were then) were not only ordained Bishops by their Abbots, being only Presbyters, but also subject and obedient to them, even by the Canons of this *Council*, and kept residence in these *Monasteries*, from whence they could not depart to any other place, Church or *Monastery*, but by the licence and mission of their Abbot Presbyters. Enough to curb the pride, and destroy the monopoly of sole Ordination now claimed by their Lordly Successors. The rather, because not only Presbyters in the first plantation of the Gospel and Christianitie amongst the *Picts, Scots, Britains* and *Saxons*, but also amongst the *French* and *Goths*, ordained both their *Priests* and *Bishops* too, by divine and humane right, untill they were restrained by subsequent new Canons made by Bishops themselves, as *l David Blondel.* proves at large. In imitation of them, and upon the forecited Grounds, Presidents and Texts of Scripture, *Anno Dom.* 1389. the *Lollards, Wiclifs*-disciples (as a *Walsingham* a Monk records) winning very many to their Sect, grew so
*audacious*

*i Beda Eccl. Hift. l. 3. c. 17. 21, 22, 25, 26, l. 4. c 4. Davidis Blondelli Apolog. ip. 369, 370, 371 3 2, 373 Muth. Weftm Anno 556, 661 663. k Beda Eccl. Hift. l. 4. c 5. Spelmanni Concil. p 153.* 
* See *Godwins Catalogue of Bishops*.

l *Apolog'a, &c. p. 357, to 374.*

a *Hift. Angliæ, An. 1389. p. 374.*

audacious; that their Presbyters, like Bishops, created and ordained new Presbyters; affirming, *That every Priest had received as much power to bind and loose, and to Minister other Ecclesiastical things, as the Pope himself giveth or could give.* This power of Ordination they exercised in the Diocesse of *Salisbury*: And those who were ordained by them, thinking all things to be lawfull to them, presumed to celebrate Masses, and feared not to handle Divine things, and administer the Sacraments. This wickednesse (as the Popish Prelates and Monks then reputed it) was discovered by a certain man ordained a Minister by them, to the Bishop of *Salisbury* at his mannor of *Sunnyng*; By which it is apparent, that the *Lollards* and *Wiclenists*, (the Protestants of that age) believed, that the power of Ordination belonged as much to Presbyters by Gods Law, as to Bishops or Popes; that one of them might as lawfully ordain Ministers as the other; and b *that as they might lawfully preach the Gospel without the Bishops licence* (first prescribed by the forged Statute, of 2 H.5.c.15. made only by the Bishops without the Commons consent, to suppresse the preaching of the Gospel) so likewise ordain Ministers without it; and that Ministers ordained only by Presbyters without a Bishops privity or assistance, were lawfull Ministers, and might lawfully with a good conscience discharge all Ministeriall offices; This being not only their received Doctrin, but their practice too, Moreover I find that c *Jan.* 20. 1542. *Nicholas Amsdorffius, a noble and learned unmarried man, was ordained Bishop of Newburg, by Martin Luther, Dr. Nicholas Medler Pastor of Newburg, George Spalatine of Aldenburge, and Wolffgangus Steinius of Lucopetra, joyning with him in the imposition of hands;* Which ordination *Luther* afterwards publickly maintained to be lawfull, in a printed Treatise. Lo here we have Presbyters not only ordaining a Presbyter, but a Bishop, of late, as well as former times. If therefore the Prelates Paradox be true; *That he who ordains, is greater in Jurisdiction and degree, then he that is ordained.* It will hence inevitably follow, that these Presbyters (and those who ordained the first Bishops) were greater in Jurisdiction, degree, order then Bishops; And then farewell their pretended Hierarchy: d *Anno Dom.* 1537.

b *This was the Doctrin and practice of all our Martyrs. Fox Acts and Monuments* 1610. p. 83, 485, 500. 02, 521, 541, 52, 553, 556, 68, 588, 590, 92, 598, 599, 02, 604, 639, 105, 874, 883, 884, 911, 931, 50, 916, 1001, 1006, 1007, 1015, 1016, 1099, 1156, 1868, 1889.
c *Chytræus Chro. Saxonia, l.*15.p. 456.
d *Chytræus ibid p.* 434.

1537. *Christian the* 3 *King of Denmark*, removed and suppressed by a publique Edict, all the Bishops of his Kingdom for their intollerable Treasons and Rebellions, abolishing their Lordly Bishopricks, as contrary to our Saviours institution, the means that made them idle, proud, ambicious, unpreaching Prelates, and sedicious, treacherous Rebels to their Princes; and instead of the 7. Bishops of Denmark, he instituted 7. Superintendents, to exercise the Office of Bishops, give Orders to others, and execute all Ecclesiastical affairs; which 7. *Superintendents Aug.* 26. 1537 received their Ordination from *John Bugenhagim* a Protestant Minister, in the Cathedral of *Hafnia*, in the presence of the King, and Senate of Denmark. Lo here all Bishops cashiered, as false rebellions Traytors to their Soveraign, (as they have *e* usually been in all states and ages, there having been more notorious Traytors, Rebels, and Conspirators of Bishops, then of all other ranks of men in the world, as I am able to make good) as contrary to *Divine institution*, ( and so not *Jure Divino*, as they now boast; ) and Superintendents *ordained by a meer Presbyter in their stead*, to confer *Orders unto others* in all *the Danish Churches*. *In the beginning of Reformation in Germany, and other places*, *Luther and other Ministers*, *usually ordained Deacons and Ministers*, *and set out Books of the manner of their ordination, without any Bishops assistance*; Which power of ordination and imposition of hands, have ever since been practised by Ministers in all reformed Churches, who have abandoned Bishops, (such as ours are, and make themselves) as contrary to Gods word. *Patrick Adamson* Archbishop of Saint *Andrews* in *Scotland*, in *g* his *Recantation* publiquely made in the *Synod* of *Fiffe*, *April* 8. 1591. confesseth *That the office of a Diocesan Bishop*, Omni authoritate verbi Dei destituitur, & solo politico hominum commento fundatur; *is distitute of all authority from Gods word, and only founded in the politick figment of men; out of which the Primacy of the Pope or Antichrist hath sprung, and that it is worthily to be condemned, because the assembly of the Presbytery,* (penes quem est Jurisdictio & Inspectio, tum in Visitationibus, tum in Ordinationibus) *which hath the Jurisdiction and Inspection, both in Visitations and in Ordinations, will perform all these things with*

*e See my Antipathy of the English Lordly Prelacy to Unity and Monarchy. Cent. Magd.* 4, 5, 5, 7, 8, 9, 10, 11, 12, 13. c. 7, 8, 10. *Antiq. Ecclesiæ Brit. and Godwins Catalogue of Bishops.*
f *Chytræi Chro. Saxonia l.* 14, 15, 16, 17.

g *Patricii Adamsoni Palinodia*, p. 49, 55.

greater

greater authority, piety and zeal, then any Bishop whatsoever; whose care is for the most part intent, not upon God, or his function, but the World, which he especially serves. A fatal blow to our Prelates Hierarchy: for if Lord Bishops be not *Jure Divino*, and have no foundation in the word of God, then the power of Ordination belongs not to them *Jure Divino*, as they are Lord Bishops, neither can, do, or ought they to confer Orders as they are Bishops, but only as they are Ministers. And if so (as is most certain) then this power of Ordination belongs not at all to Bishops as they are Bishops, but only as they are Ministers; and every Minister as he is a Minister, hath as much divine right and authority to give Orders as any Bishop whatsoever; the true reason why antiently among the Papists, as [b] *Durandus* confesseth, and now too, as the *Rhemists* witnesse; and [i] *even in our own English Church among us at this day, Ministers ought to joyn with the Bishop in the imposition of hands; Neither can our Bishops ordain any one a Minister, unlesse Three or Four Ministers at least joyn with him in the Ordination and laying on of hands.* This being an apparent truth, I shall hence, from the Bishops own principles, prove Presbyters superior and greater then Bishops in jurisdiction, dignity, and degree. Those (say they) to whom the power of Ordination belongs by divine right, are greater in jurisdiction, dignity, and degree, then those who have not this power; and the ordainer, is higher, superior in all these, then the ordained. But the power of Ordination belongs *Jure Divino* only to Presbyters, as Presbyters, not to Lord Bishops; and if to Lord Bishops, yet not as Bishops but Presbyters; and Bishops when they ordain in a lawfull manner, do it only as Presbyters, not as Bishops; Therefore Presbyters are superiour to Bishops in jurisdiction, order, and degree; and Bishops themselves, far greater in all these as they are Presbyters (an office of divine institution) then as they are Lordly Prelates, or Diocæsan Bishops, a meer humane invention. Thus are our great Lord Bishops (who [k] vaunt of the weaknesse of Puritan principles, whereas their Episcopal are far more feeble and absurd) wounded to death with their own

[b] *Rationalis divinorum l. 2. de Sacerdote. Rubrica.*
[i] See the Book of Ordination, and Canon. 35.

[k] See Bishop *White* his Epistle Dedicatory to the Archbishop of Canterbury, before his Treatise of the Sabbath.

own weapons, and all their domineering, swelling authority, overthrown by that very principle, foundation, on which they have presumed to erect it; the antient Proverb being here truly verified, *Vis consilii expers mole ruit sua.* I shall cloze up this with the words of accute *l Antonius Sadeel*, who after a large proof of Bishops and Presbyters to be both one and the same by Divine institution, windes up all in this manner : *We conclude therefore, seeing that superior Episcopal dignity, is to be avouched only by humane institution,* tantum esse humani juris, *that it is only of humane right : On the contrary, since it is evident by the expresse testimonies of Scripture, that in the Apostles times, Bishops were the same with Presbyters,* Jure Divino potestatem Ordinandi non minus Presbyteris quàm Episcopis convenire, *that by Gods law, and Divine right, the power of Ordination belongs no lesse to Presbyters, as to Bishops.*

*l Responf. ad Turriani Sophismata pars 2. loc. 18.*

And with Learned *m David Blondel,* who after a large proof out of Scripture, Antiquity, History, Fathers, Councils, and other writers; *that the right of Ordination belongs to Presbyters as Presbyters,* and not only to *Bishops;* concludes with these 6 Arguments.

*m Apologia pro sententia Hieronymi sect. 3. p. 378.*

1. Those to whom the practice of the Church hath assigned the same functions, *de facto*, the same she professeth to have by themselves the self-same dignity, and parity in all things, from the beginning.

But the practice of the Church hath assigned the same functions of confirming, *ORDAINING PRIESTS AND DEACONS,* preaching, administring the Sacraments, &c. to Presbyters and Bishops.

Therefore she professeth a Bishop and Presbyter to have by themselves the self-same dignity and parity in all things from the beginning.

2. Whatsoever things are known to be prohibited by new Rules and Canons, were free before the Rules and Canons made.

But to confirm, consecrate, reconcile, ordain Presbyters, &c. are known to be prohibited by new Rules and Canons to Presbyters.

There-

Therefore they were free before the Rules and Canons made.

3. What things soever were free before, by accession of a new consent of Churches, may afterwards become free to Presbyters as well as Bishops.

But to confirm, consecrate, ordain, &c. were free before.

Therefore they may (now) by accession of a new consent of Churches, become free again for after times.

4. Novel rules are not the Primordial, truly Divine, and Apostolical Law of the Church, but humane only.

The rules by which these functions of conferring, consecrating, ordaining, Ministers, &c. are known to be reserved to Bishops, and prohibited to Presbyters are Novel.

Therefore they are not the Primordial, truly Divine, and Apostolical Law of the Church, but humane only.

5: All humane Laws may be abrogated by the same will and power whereby they are made and received, to wit humane,

But the rules by which these powers (of ordaining Presbyters,&c.) are known to be reserved to Bishops, and prohibited to Presbyters, are humane Laws.

Therefore they may be abrogated by the same will and power, to wit humane.

6. Whatsoever Church out of her own free Liberty, or will, hath abrogated any humane Law, to which she had in any sort before consented, since she used her proper and indefectable power, ought not to incur the reprehentions of other Churches.

But the Church of the Protestants, in restoring the antient identity & parity of Bishops and Presbyters, & Ordination of Presbyters by the Presbyteries, hath out of her own free Liberty, abrogated the humane Law to which she had before consented.

Therefore the Church of the Protestants in restoring the antient identity & parity of Bishops and Presbyters, and ordination of Presbyters by the Presbyteries (without any Diocæsan Bishop) since she hath used her proper and indefectible power therein, ought not to incur the Reprehension of other Churches. Much

Much lesse then (by all these Arguments) ought any of our Ministers ordained, or Presbyters ordaining Ministers without the Bishops, during our late Wars and Revolutions, to be censured, reviled, or their ordinations proclamed null and void, (and by consequence their baptising, and consecrating of the Lords Supper null likewise) by any of our Bishops or Prelatical Clergy, or their Adherents, untill they are able to demonstrate them to be such, against all the preceding Testimonies, Presidents, Texts and Arguments here produced to the contrary.

*Obj.* 5. If any finally object, *that the Fathers style Titus the first Bishop of Crete, and Timothy of Ephesus*: therefore they were Diocæsan Bishops, and superiour in Jurisdiction and degree to other Ministers, and so by consequence are other Diocæsan Bishops as well as they.

*Answ.* 1. I answer, *First,* that neither S. *Paul* nor S. *Luke,* who lived in their times, and knew them far better than any Father or Writer since, ever so much as once terms or stiled them Bishops; much lesse, the first or sole Diocæsan Bishops of *Crete,* or *Ephesus;* which no doubt they would have done, had they been in truth Diocæsan Bishops there; and the name, the Office of a Bishop so honourable and sublime, above that of Ministers, even *Jure Divino*, as our Prelates and their Flatterers now pretend. Their Testimonies therefore, who stile them only * *Ministers* (or *Evangelists*, never *Bishops*) is to be preferred before all Fathers and Writers, (who stile them Bishops) being neither acquainted with their Persons or Functions, nor living in their Age.   * 1 *Tim.* 6. 2 *Tim.* 4. 5. 1 *Thes.* 3. 2.

*Secondly,* No Father ever stiles them, or either of them a Diocæsan, or sole Bishop of *Crete* or *Ephesus,* (the thing which ought to be proved,) *but Bishops only,* as they stiled other Ministers, *the name, the Office of Bishops and Presbyters being but one and the same, and promiscuously used in the Apostles times; all Presbyters being then called Bishops, and all Bishops Presbyters; as is evident by* Acts 14. 23 c. 20. 17, 28. Phil. 1. 1 Pet. 5. 1, 2, 3. Tit. 1. 5. 5, 7. Tim. 3. 3. 1, 2, 3. 2 John 1. 3. John 1. Philemon 9. and all antient, all modern Commentators

mentators on thefe Texts confeſſe. Whence the *Tranſlators of our laſt authorized Engliſh Bible,* affix theſe Contents to *Titus,* 1. 6, to 10. (which treats of the qualities of Biſhops) *How they that are to be choſen,* MINISTERS *ought to be qualified*: And the Book of Ordination of Miniſters confirmed by two * *ſeveral Acts of Parliament*) preſcribes the 1 *Tim.* c. 3. *Acts* 20. and *Titus* 1. *to be read both at the ordination of Miniſters, and Conſecration of Biſhops*: and ſo intimates, yea interprets, that Biſhops and Miniſters in the Scriptures language, are both one, in name, office, and were ſo reputed in the Primitive Church.

* 5 & 6 Edw. 6. c. 1. 8 Eliz. c. 1.

*Thirdly*, The Fathers uſe the words, *Elders and Biſhops, promiſcuouſly*, calling Elders Biſhops, and Biſhops Elders; Hence *Papias the Auditor of St. John, and companion of Polycarpus,* writes thus *in the Preface of his Books.* * *It ſhall not ſeem grievous unto me, if that I compile in writing, and commit to memory, the thing which I learned of the Elders. If any came in place which was a follower of the Apoſtles, forthwith I demanded the words of the Elders: what Andrew, what Peter, what Philip, what Thomas, or James, or John, or Mathew, or any other of the Lords Diſciples; what Ariſton, and the Elder John, Diſciples of the Lord, had ſaid.* Here he ſtiles, not only Biſhops, but even the Apoſtles *Elders. Polycarpus,* his companion and Cœtanian, writes thus in *his Epiſtle to the Philippians,* ‖ *Be ye ſubject to Presbyters and Deacons as to God: let the Presbyters be ſimple and mercifull in all things.* Now thoſe whom he here ſtiles *Presbyters,* S. Paul expreſly terms *Biſhops,* Philip. 1. 1. *Juſtine Martyr* in his ſecond *Apology,* uſed neither the name Biſhop nor Elder, but terms the Miniſter only, *He who is ſet over the Brethren, He who holds the firſt place,* in reference to the Deacon, who holds the ſecond place, not to any Elders of an inferior order to a Biſhop. And leaſt any one ſhould dream, that *Juſtine Martyr* here ſpeaks of a *Biſhop,* Tertullian, who lived near about that time, or within few years, in his * *Apology* writes thus: *Præſident nobis probati quique Seniores, &c.* Approved Elders (not Biſhops) preſide over us, having obtained this honour, not with any price, *but a good teſtimony.* Whence it is evident, that

* Euſebius, Eccleſ. Hiſt. l. 3. c. 39. p. 55.

‖ Bibliotheca Patrum, Tom. 1. p. 96.

* Apolog c. 39. Tom. 1 p 691, 693, 694.

in

## The Un-bishoping of Timothy and Titus.

in his age, every Christian Congregation had *divers Elders,* (not one Diocæsan Bishop) over it, *to feed and rule it,* according *to the practise of the Apostles times,* Acts 14. 23. c. 20. 17, 28. c. 21. 88, Philip. 1. 1. 1 Tim. 5. 17, Tit. 1. 5. James 5. 14. 1 Pet. 5. 1, 2. Hence learned a *Apollinarius,* calls the Bishops and Elders of the Church of Ancyra in Galatia, Presbyters. And b *Clemens Alexandrinus,* relating the Story of the young man delivered by S. John to a Bishop, to train up in the fear of God, twice together calls him, interchangeably, both a *Bishop and an Elder,* as M:ridith Hamner (a Bishop) Englisheth it. So c *Ireneus,* one of the antientest of all the Fathers, stiles *Polycarpus Bishop of Smyrna,* That *holy and Apostolick Elder :* yea he terms the Bishops of *Rome* themselves *Elders,* d ' They (saith he) that were Elders before *Soter,* 'of the Church which now thou governest, I mean *Ana-* 'cletus, *Pius, Hyginus, Thelesphorus,* and *Xystus,* neither did 'so observe it themselves, neither left they any such Com- 'mandement to posterity. And the same Father *Adversus* '*Heresus,*l.2.c.39.l.3.c.2.& l.4.c.43 44. oftentimes stiles Bi- 'shops Elders; and Elders Bishops; making Presbyters e- 'qual to Bishops in all respects, and Successors to the A- 'postles as well, as much as they. So e *Dionysius Alexandrinus,* in his Epistle to *Xystus,* Bishop of *Rome,* about the year of Christ, 240. writes thus; ' There was a certain bro- ' ther, reputed to be of our Church, and Faith, very aged, ' & priusquam ego etiam creatus Episcopus, and created ' A BISHOP before I was, and as I think, before blessed ' *Heraclas* was made a Bishop. Where he expresly terms this party, who was but a Minister or Presbyter only in that Church, *A BISHOP,* and saith, *he was created a Bishop:* when he was but ordained a Minister. And that famous *Gregory Nazianzen* (three hundred and seventy years after Christ,) in his 9, 13, 15, 21, *and* 28. *Orations,* p. 262, 375, 368, 479. *as Elias Cretensis,* in his *Commentary on those places* testifieth, *useth the words Bishops and Presbyters reciprocally, stiling Bishops Presbyters, and Presbyters Bishops; making them all one by divine institution, and different only by humane invention, which difference he heartily wisheth might be abolished;* himself

a *Eusebius Ecclef. Hist. l. 5. c. 16.*

b *Eusab. Ecclef. Hist. l. 3. c. 23.*

c *Euseb. Ecclef. Hist. l. 5. c.20.*

d *Ibid. c. 25.*

e *Euseb. Ecclef. Hist. l.7. c.8.*

*See his life before his works*

self p voluntarily resigning his Bishoprick of Constantinople, to betake himself to a more private and retired life. The Fathers therefore thus promiscuously using the name Bishop and Presbyter, stiling *Bishops Presbyters*, and *Presbyters Bishops*, and making both of them one and the same by divine institution, their stiling of *Timothy* and *Titus*, Bishops of *Ephesus* and *Crete*, is no argument or proof at all, that they were Diocæsan, or sole Bishops of those places; or that they then had, or any Bishops now have, by divine institution, any Episcopal Jurisdiction and preeminence over other Presbyters or Ministers, or were superior to them, in order, dignity or degree.

Fourthly, The Greek word ἐπίσκοπος, which we English a Bishop, signifies properly nothing else, but *an Overseer, Survayor, Superintendent, or Administrator*, and is oft times applyed both by *Greek Authors*, and the *Septuagint Greek Translators*, to secular offices. * Hence ‖ *Homer* stiles *Hector, the Bishop of the City*: In the *Verses* of *Solon* in *Demosthenes*, *Pallas* is called *the Bishop of Athens*: *Plutarch* in the life of *Numa*, stiles *Venus, the Bishop over the dead*, and he there makes mention of a *Bishop of the Vestal Virgins*. *Suidas* records, that in the *Athenian Republike*, those *who are sent to the Cities under their Jurisdiction, to oversee the affairs of their Companions; were called Bishops*. *Cicero* in his seventh book to *Atticus*, writes thus; *Pompey will have me to be the Bishop of all Compagnia and the Maritine Coasts, to whom the choise and sum of the businesse may be referred*. And in the *Pandects*, the Clerks of the Markets are called *Bishops*. The *Septuagint*, Numb. 13. read *the Bishops of the Army*. 4 *Kings* 11. they read, *the Bishops who are over the Army, and the Bishops over the house of the Lord*. Where Watchmen, Guardians, and Overseers, are called Bishops, 2 Chron. 34. *The Overlookers of the Workmen*, are stiled Bishops; Judges 9. *Zebul is called Abimelechs Bishop* in the Greek; which we now English, *his Officer*: So Numb. 4. 16. The office of *Eliazar, in the Tabernacle of the Lord, and the function of Judas*, Psalm 109. 8. *is termed* ἐπισκοπή *a Bishoprick*, by the Septuagint; and so expresly stiled by the Holy Ghost himself, and Englished by us, Acts 1, 20. *His Bishoprick*

*Aretius. Theolog. Problemata. Locus 62. De Officiis Eccl. Sect. 9. p. 184, 186. Chemnitius Examen Concilii Tridentini pars 2. De Sacramento Ordinis, c. 4. p. 223, 214.*
*Iliad. 1. 10.*

### The Un-bishoping of Timothy and Titus.

*Bishoprick let another take.* Yea, *Constantine* the Great ( as * *Eusebius* records in his life ) inviting some Bishops to a Feast, called himself a Bishop in their presence, uttering these words; *You faith he, are Bishops within the Church, but I am constituted of God a Bishop without the Church.* Our New Translators, Acts 20. 28. render the Greek word ἐπισκόπους Bishops (the title which the holy Ghost gives *to the Elders of the Ch. of Ephesus* ) Overseers; Luke 19. 44. *The time of Gods visitation and overthrow of Jerusalem,* is termed, τ̀ καιρὸν τῆς ἐπισκοπῆς σου, &c. Luke 1.6,7, 8. c. 7. 16. Heb. 2. 6. The Greek word which we translate, *hath visited us,* is ἐπισκέψατο. Whence the day of Gods gracious visitation of his people to convert them to him in mercy, is called *by the Holy Ghost,* 1 Pet. 2.12. ἡμέρα ἐπισκοπῆς *The day of visitation;* yea our very visiting of sick persons, prisoners, Orphans and Widdows, is termed by Christ and the holy Ghost himself, (though a meer act of charity, humility, and Christian duty, * not of Jurisdiction and Lordly Prelacy,) ἐπισκέψασθε Mat. 25. 36. 43. and ἐπισκέπτεσθαι, Jam. 1. 27. *to visit or to play the Bishops part and duty;* which the meanest Christian, yea women ( though uncapable of sacred orders ) may doe and ought to perform, as well as any others. So intermedling with other mens affairs, or coveting of any other mens offices of what condition soever, is termed by the Apostle, 1 Pet. 4. 15. ἀλλοτριοεπίσκοπος *the playing as it were the Bishop in another mans Diocesse.* Yea every Ministers feeding and taking the oversight of his proper flock, is stiled, *the doing of a Bishops office:* and those Presbyters who do thus, are not only said to be ἐπισκοποῦντες 1 Pet. 5. 21 that is, *men executing the office and duty of a Bishop;* but likewise stiled, ἐπίσκοποι ; that is, true and proper Bishops : a name given only to Presbyters (and none but they in holy Scripture, Acts 20. 28. Phil. 1. 1. Titus 1. 7. and to Chr ft himself, who is stiled, ἐπίσκοπον τ̀ ψυχῶν ὑμῶν, the Bishop of our Souls, 1 Pet. 2. 25 but not to any Apostle, Evangelist, Diocæsan or other Prelate; none such being particularly termed *a Bishop* throughout the whole New Testament : The Fathers make Bishops and Overseers all one, *deriving the very name of a Bishop, from a Greek verb, which signifieth to overlook*

* *De Vita Constantini, l. 4. c. 24*

* *So is the word ἐπισκέψασθαι used by Basil. Epist. 52. not to ride in visitation like a Lordly Prelate but to consider of the miserable state of the Church & to be carefull for it ; as Bishop Jewel witnesseth in his Defence of the Apology of the Church of Engl. part 2. c. 3. Div. 5. p. 107.*

look, watch, ward, or take care of. Hence * *Augustin* writes thus; *He did keep, he was carefull, he did watch, as much as he could, over those over whom he was set.* And Bishops do thus. *For therefore an higher place is set for Bishops, that they may superintend, and as it were keep the people. For that which in Greek is called a Bishop, that in Latine is interpreted a Superintendent, because he overseeth, because he seeth from above. For like as an higher place is made for the vineyardkeeper, to keep the vineyard, so an higher place also is made for the Bishops. And a perillous account is to be rendred of this high place, unlesse we stand therein with such an heart, that we may be under your feet in humility, and pray for you, that he who knows your minds, he may keep you; because we can see you entring and going out, but yet we are so far from seeing what you think in your hearts, that we cannot so much as see what you do in your Houses. How therefore do we keep you, like men, as much as we can, as much as we have received. We keep you out of the office of dispensation, but we will be kept together with you; we are as Pastors to you, but under that Pastor (*Christ,*) we are Sheep together with you: we are as teachers to you out of this place, but under that one Master we are Scholars with you in this School. If we will be kept by him who was humbled for us, and is exalted to keep us, let us be humble.* * *Those set themselves before Christ, who will be high here where he was humble. Let them therefore be humble here, if they will be exalted there, where he is exalted.* In an other place he writes thus. * *For this cause the Apostle saith, He that desires a Bishoprick, desires a good work.* He would expound what a Bishoprick is: * *it is a name of labor not of honor. For it is a Greek word, and derived from hence, that he who is made an Overseer, overseeth those over whom he is set, namely by taking care of them.* For ὄπι is over, but σκοπεῖς is intention, overseeing or care: therefore if we will render ἐπίσκοπεῖν in Latine, we may say it is to play the Superintendent; that he may understand, that he is not a Bishop, who delights to be over others, but not to profit them. On which words *Ludovicus Vives* thus Comments; *The name of a Bishop is derived either from* ἐπισκοπεῖν, *which signifieth to consider, or from* ἐπισκέπτομαι, *which signifieth the same, and to visit. Whence Suidas saith, there were some sent from the Athenians*

---

\* *Enarratio in Psal.* 125. *Tom.* 8. p. 725, 727.

\* *Let our great Prelates mark this well.*
\* *De Civitate Dei,* l. 19. c. 19. *Tom.* 1. *pars* 2. p. 516.
\* Episcopatus nomen est operis non honoris: non dominium, sed officium: non honos sed onus, *Hierom, Sedulius, Primasius, Theodoret, Beda, Haymo, Rabanus Maurus, Oecumenius, Anselm in* 1 *Tim.* 3. *Isidor Hispalensis, De Ecclef. Officiis,* l. 2 c. 5. *Gratian Cauf.* 8. qu. 1.

nians to the Cities under them, who should look into their affairs: and these were called Bishops, that is, as it were Overseers, or Visitors, and Observers. In holy Scriptures, a Bishop is commonly called, a Watchman, as in Ezekiel 3. 17. c. 33. 2, 6, 7. and in Hosea 5. 1. The Lord complaineth that the Bishops were made a snare on Mizpah, (or in the watch tower) and a net spread upon Tabor; as if he had spoken of the ‖ Bishops of this age, who lay snares in their Bishopricks and large nets to catch mony, but not with thin holes or threads, lest the gift should swim through: yea now it is so provided by the diligence and wits of certain men, that without evasion of this Law, a Bishoprick may not only be lawfully desired, but likewise bought and sold. St. Chrysostom in his 10. Hom. upon the 1 Tim. St. Hierom in his Epistle to Evagrius, Beda on the 1 Pet. 2. 25. Anselme on Phil. 1. 1. Aquinas secunda secundæ: Qu. 184. Art. 6. Petrus de Palude, de Potest. Coll. Apostol. Art. 1. (all cited by Bishop Jewel in the Defence of the Apologie of the Church of England, part 6. c. 2. Divis. 1. p. 523.) and St. Bernard also, de Consideratione ad Eugenium, l. 2, & 3. joyntly resolve; that a Bishop is nothing else, but a Superintendent, Watchman, or Overseer, and that he is called a Bishop from hence, that he overseeth, survaieth, or watcheth over others, with which all other antient and modern writers, whether Forein or Domestique, Papists or Protestants accord. Hear only Dr. John Ponet Bishop of Winchester, in his Apologie against Dr. Martin, in defence of Priests marriage, c. 4, 5. p. 44, 52, 53, 54. who as he there expresly reckons up *Popes, Cardinals, BISHOPS, Priests, Monks, Canons, Friars, &c. to be the Orders of Antichrist; *taxing them likewise severely and comparing them with the Eustathian hereticks, for refusing to wear usual garments, and putting upon them garments of strange fashions, to vary from the common sort of people in apparel: So he thus determines of the names Bishop and Superintendent: And further whereas it pleaseth Martin not only in this place, but also hereafter to gest at the name of Superintendent, he shweth himself bent to condemn all things that be good, though in so doing he cannot avoid his open shame. Who knoweth not that the name Bishop hath so been abused, that when it was spoken, the people understood nothing else, but a great Lord, that went in a

‖ Note this.

* As did Wicliff and others before him, Dial. l. 3. c. 17, 18. * Fol. 116.

Q                white

white Rochet, with a wide shaven Crown, and that carrieth an oyl box with him, where he used once in 7. year, riding about to confirm Children, &c. Now to bring the people from that abuse, what better means can be devised, then to teach the people their error by another word out of the Scriptures of the same signification: which thing by the term Superintendent would in time have been well brought to passe. For the ordinary pains of such as were called Superintendents, should have taught the people to understand the duty of their Bishop, which you Papists would fain have hidden from them. And the word Superintendent being a very Latine word made English by use, should in time have taught the people by the very Etymology and proper signification, what thing was meant, when they heard that name which by this term Bishop, could not so well be done, by reason that Bishops in the time of Popery were Overseers in name, but not indeed. So that their doings could not teach the people their names, neither what they should look for at their Bishops hands. For the name Bishop, spoken amongst the unlearned, signified to them nothing lesse then a Preacher of Gods word, because there was not, nor is any thing more rare in any order of Ecclesiastical persons, then to see a Bishop preach, whereof the doings of the Popish Bishops of England can this day witnesse; but the name Superintendent should make him ashamed of his negligence, and afraid of his idlenss, knowing that St Paul doth call upon him to attend to himself and to his whole flock; of the which sentence our Bishops mark the first peice right well, ( that is, to take heed to themselves, but they be so deaf, they cannot harken to the second ) that is, to look to their floc. I deny not, but that the name Bishop may be well taken, but because the evilnesse of the abuse hath marrid the goodnesse of the word, it cannot be denyed, but that it was not amisse to joyn for a time another word with it in his place, whereby to restore that abused word to his right signification. And the name Superintendent is such a name, that the Papists themselves ( saving such as lack both learning and wit ) cannot find fault withall. For Presius the Spaniard and an Archpapist, ( out of whom Martin hath stolen a great part of his book) speaking of a Bishop, saith: Primum Episcopi munus nomen ipsum præ se fert, quod est Superintendere, Episcopus enim Superintendens interpretatur

*Acts 20. 27, 28.*

tatur, visitans aut supervidens, &c. *That is to say: The chief office of a Bishop by interpretation, signifieth a Superintendent, a Visitor, or an Overseer.* Why did not Martin as well steal this peice out of *Peresius*, as he did steal all the common places that he hath for the proof of the Canons of the Apostles, and of Traditions in his second and third Chapters? *Martin in the* 88. leaf is not ashamed in his book to divide the signification of the terms, (Bishop and Superintendent) as though the one were not signified by the other. But it may be that Martin as the rest of the Popish Sect would not have the name of (Superintendent) or Minister used, least that name which did put the people in remembrance of sacrificing and Lludsapping, should be forgotten. Since therefore this Title *Bishop,* is thus promiscuously used, both in prophane and Christian writers, and in the Scripture it self, for any *Officer, Overseer, Survayer, Superintendent, Watchman, Guardian, Pastor,* or *Keeper, as well temporal and civil, as Ecclesiastical,* and all these their offices are stiled in Greek, a *Bishoprick:* since every Pastor, Watchman, Presbyter, Minister, Rector, and Curate, who takes care of, watcheth over, feedeth, overlooketh, instructeth, or keepeth the flock and people committed to his charge, is even in the Scriptures Language *called a Bishop,* and said, *to act, to do the office of a Bishop:* since those who out of charity, love, or friendship go to visit others, who are either sick, poor, Fatherlesse, or otherwise distressed, yea God himself when he comes to punish or shew mercy unto others, are in the Greek and Scripture phrase, said, *to visit and play the Bishops*; as appeareth by the forecited Scriptures, and by Acts 15. 36. *Where Paul said to Barnabas,* ἐπισκεψάμεθα τοὺς ἀδελφοὺς ἡμῶν, which we translate, *Let us go again & visit our brethren, in every City, where we have preached the word of the Lord, and see how they do.* From which text the *Rhemists would make Bishops ordinary visitations, to be Jure Divino*; but this was no Lordly Episcopal visitation such as our Bishops now keep, for we read of no visitation Articles, Oaths, Fees or presentments in it; neither were *Paul* and *Barnabas* such Bishops, as now, but it was a meer visitation of love, as one friend visits another, not of Jurisdiction, as the last words: *And see how they*

\* *See Fulk and Cartwright.* Ibid m.

## The Un-bishoping of Timothy and Titus.

they do, together with the *Council of Laodicea*, Can. 57. expound it, and verf. 14. *Simeon hath declared how God hath at the first* ἐπισκέψατο *did visit the Gentiles, to take out of them a people for his name.* And Acts 7. 23 *When Moses was full* 40 *years old, it came into his heart* ἐπισκέψασθαι, *to visit his brethren, the Children of Israel; and sin e these words* ἐπισκέψασθαι and ἐπισκοποῦντες, (that is) *to visit, oversee, or play the Bishop*, ‖ imply no Lordship, Soveraignty, Dominion, Jurisdiction, or Lordly Episcopal authority in them, (at least no such as our Bishops now claim and exercise:) *but rather an Act of humility, charity, service, and inferiority to the persons visited,* as is evident by Mat. 25. 36. 43. Acts 7. 23. c. 15. 36. Jam. 1. 27. Heb. 2. 6. 1 Pet 5. 2, 3, 5. It hence unanswerably follows, that Bishops Episcopal Lordly visitations, are not *Jure Divino*, and that other Ministers are as much Visiters, and may visit as well as they ; that every Presbyter, Minister, Curate who doth faithfully discharge his duty, * *is as much, as truly, as properly a Bishop, both in the Scriptures language and in Gods account, as any Diocæsan Bishop or Prelate whatsoever ;* That those Bishops who merge themselves in pleasures, idlenesse, or secular affairs, and do not diligently, faithfully, intirely give themselves to preach Gods word, instruct and teach the people, visit the Fatherlesse, imprisoned, sick, poor, widdows, and flocks committed to them ; (which few of our Prelates now deigne to do) are ‖ *in truth, in Gods, in Christs account, and in the Scriptures language, no Bishops at all, what ever they pretend ;* that the word Bishop is * *not a title of Dominion, Soveraignty, Jurisdiction, Glory, Power, Preheminency, Pomp, State, Authority and Command,* (as our Bishops pretend, who now presume to monopolize it to themselves alone, though common by Gods word and antient writers to every Minister,) *but of humility, office, service, labour, care, circumspection, watchfulnesse, meeknesse, tender-heartednesse, charity, familiarity, and brotherly kindnesse,* (which most Prelats have now quite shaken off) The Fathers stiling therefore of *Timothy, Bishop of Ephesus, or Titus Bishop of Crete,* or both of them Bishops, will neither prove them to be Diocæsan, or sole Bishops or Archb[ishop]s of those Churches, that they

---

*Bishop Jewel Defence of the Apology,* part 2. c. 3. Divif. 5 p. 107.
* *Marsilius Patavinus Defenf. Pacis* pars 2. c. 15, 16. *Richardus Armachanus Resp. ad Quaft. Armenorum* l 1. c. 1, to 8. *Fox Acts and Monuments,* p. 1009, 1116, 1465
‖ *Bishop Jewel Defence of the Apol.* part 2. c. 3. Divif. 7. part 111. *Thomas Beza on his Catechism.* Vol. 1. f. 499, 500. *Chrysost. Opus Imperf. in Mat. Hom.* 3. & 43 *Ambrof. de Dign. Sacerd.* c. 4.
* *Auguft. De Civ. Dei* l. 19. c. 19 *Hierom, Ambrose, Sedulius, Primasius, Haymo Rabanus, Maurus, Chrysost. in Theodoret, Theophilact, Oecumenius, Anselmus, Beda, in* 1 Tim. 2. 1, 2 *Bernard De Consid. ad Eugen.* 2. & 3.

they had a Superiority or Jurisdiction as they were Bishops over all other Ministers or Presbyters in those Churches; or that Archbishops or Bishops are *Jure divino* superior to, or different in order or degree from Presbyters, *who have the self-same Commission or Authority, given them by Christ, as they*; and so have equal authority, power, with them, and are as much Bishops every way by Gods Law, as they; even as every *High Commissioner* of the *Quorum*, is as much an High Commissioner as the Archbishop of *Canterbury* or *York*, and hath as much authority as an High Commissioner, as they; since they have all the self-same Commission, which gives no greater power to one of them than the other, but the same to both. Indeed had Christ given a different Commission to his Apostles and the seaventy Disciples; or unto *Timothy* and *Titus*, than to other Elders and Bishops of the Churches of *Ephesus* and *Crete*, or to Bishops, than he hath given to Presbyters and Ministers, there might have been some ground to have proved the 12. Apostles, *Timothy*, *Titus* and Bishops, greater in Jurisdiction, power, authority, and degree than the 70. Disciples, Presbyters, and other Ministers, by divine institution. But since it is apparant by * *the Scriptures*, that the 12. *Apostles* and 70. *Disciples* (what ever || *some men have rashly determined to the contrary*) *had but one and the self-same Commission given unto them by Christ*, *being sent out two and two in the same manner*, *the same condition*, *with the same Mandates*, *the same powers*, *the same promises*, *the same comminations against those who contemned their Doctrin*, without any discrimination at all between them, (as learned * *David Blundel'us* proves at large, refuting all authorities and allegations to the contrary,) That *Timothy*, *Titus*, Archbishops, Bishops, and other Prelates *have no other*, *no larger Patent, Commission or Authority granted unto them by Christ*, *then Presbyters and ordinary Ministers*, (as the book of *Ordination manifests: where the same words are used*, *the same Commission given from God to Ministers*, *at the ordination of every Minister*, *as there is to Bishops at the consecration of any Archbishop or Bishop*) since they are all joyned together in one and the self-same divine Char-

* *Mat.* 10. 1, to 16. *Mark* 6. 7, to 12 *Luke* 9. 1, to 6. compared with *Luk* 10. 1, to 21.
|| *Clemens Epist. apud Surium Tem.* 1. p. 141. and others, who have since followed his footsteps by h.
* *Apologia pro sententia Hieronymi* Sect 3. p. 99, to 130.

ter, and all claim by one and the self-same grant, ( as is evident by Matth. 28. 19, 20. Mark 6. 15, 16. John 20. 22, 23. Acts 1. 8. c. 10. 47. c. 20. 17, 28. Col. 4. 17. 1 Tim. 3. 1, to 7. c. 4, 12, 13. c. 5. 17, 18, 20, 21, 22. c. 6. 11, 12, 17, 18, 19, 20. 2 Tim. 2. 14, 15, 16. c. 4. 1, to 16. Tit. 1. 5, to 14. c. 2. 1, to 15. c. 3 1, 2, 8, 9, 10. 1 Pet. 5. 1, 2, 3, 4, 5. 2 Pet. 1. 12, 13. 1 Cor. 1, 12, 13, 17. c. 3. 4, 5, to 11, 21, 22. c. 4. 1, 6, 7, 17. c. 9. 16, 17. c. 13. 29, 30, 31, 32. Ephes. 4. 11, 12. with other Scriptures ) it is most apparant, and undeniable, that by Gods word and institution, *they are all equal, both in point of office, power, Jurisdiction, and authority, not one of them greater, higher or superiour than the other*, having the self-same divine ordination, commission, office, and charge.

\* *L. 3 c 4. Eccles. Hist.*

Finally, \* Eusebius records only, that Timothy IS REPORTED to be the First Bishop of *Ephesus*, and Titus of the Churches in Crete : So that all the Fathers Authorities,(who follow *Eusebius*,) as grounded only upon this bare report, not upon any certainty; therefore not to be granted or relyed on. The rather, ||*because there have been antienly in Crete no less than 4. Archbishops, and 21. Bishops, Suffraganes* : now is it very improbable that *Paul* would institute *Titus* Archbishop or Superintendent general of all *Crete*, it being so large a circuit, having so many Archbishops and Bishops Sees within it, and he so little resident in, so often absent from it, as I have manifested in the premises. From all these premises I presume, I may safely conclude this 2d question against the common received Error, *That Titus was never Bishop nor Archbishop of Crete*, whatever our Prelates and their favourites have written to the contrary: And so *Timothy* being neither a Diocæsan Bishop of *Ephesus*, nor *Titus* of Crete, the pretended Hierarchy of our Prelats *Jure Divino*, built only upon the\**sandy foundation* of these two supposed Bishops & their Bishopricks, must needs fall to ruine; and they being now lifted up so high above their fellow Brethren, their fall must certainly prove very great.

|| *See Mercators Atlas Minor. p. 812.*

\* *Mat. 7. 26, 27.*

Our Lordly Prelates have only one more *rotten prop* left them, to support their pretended *Divine Right* over other Ministers,

## The Un=bishoping of Timothy and Titus. III

Ministers, which having relation to *Timothy* and his Episcopacy, I shall briefly undermine, subvert, and turn upon them to their overthrow.

They pretend and contend with all their might, *That the Angel of the Church of Ephesus*, to whom St. *John* writ his Epistle, Rev. 2. 1, 2. was a *Bishop*, superior in power and Jurisdiction to other Ministers, by Divine Institution; because he writes only in the singular number to him, and stiles him the *Angel* (not *Angels*) of the Church of *Ephesus*; which implies a superiority of one single Minister over all other Elders or Ministers in this Church, to whom this Epistle is specially directed; as *a* Bishop *Hall*, *b* Bishop *Usher*, *c* Sir *Thomas Aston*, and *d* others confidently assert.

*Quest.* 3. Whether the Angel of the Church of *Ephesus* was a Diocæsan Bishop?

*a Episcopacy by Divine Right. An humble Remonstrance, p. 29. Defence of the Humble Remonstrance, p. 103. to 127. b The Judgement of Dr. Reynolds, &c. more largely confirmed out of Antiquity, by James Usher Bishop of Armagh. c Brief Relation of Episcopacy, Sect. 2. p 6,7. d William Bishop of Rochester, Sermon 1. at Hampton Court September 21.1606. George Downham his Sermon on Apoc. 1. 20. and Defence thereof. London 1611.*

To which I answer: First, that this word, *Angel*, is but a metaphorical Title, proper only to the heavenly Spirits in strictness of Speech, and in a large sense, as it signifies a * *Messenger*, or *Servant*, it may as aptly denote, a *Minister*, or *Presbyter*, as a *Bishop*. The Title therefore of it self, as it is used by S. *John*, makes nothing for Episcopacy, since ordinary *Presbyters* are in Scripture sometimes styled * *Angels*, but Bishops (distinct from Presbyters) are never so named therein.

Secondly, Our Bishops themselves if not the whole Church of *England* with our late famous King *James* in the Contents annexed by them to the Bibles of the last Translation, now only used and permitted in our Churches, in expresse terms, expound the Angels of the 7. Churches to be the *Ministers* of them, the Contents of the second Chapter of the Revelation running thus, *What is commanded to be written to the ANGELS, that is, the MINISTERS of the Churches of Ephesus, Smyrna, Pergamus, Thiatyra,&c.* Had

*\*Argelus nomen est Officii, non naturæ, &c. Angelus enim Greco vocabulo, Latine dicitur nuntius, si quæris nomen naturæ, spiritus est; si filium Angelus: ex eo quod subsistit spiritus est; ex eo quod mittitur Angelus Remigius Explan. in Epist. ad Hebræos, c. 1. † 1 Co. 11.10. Rev. 1.20.c.2. 1, 8, 12, 18. c. 3. 1, 7, 14.*

these

these Angels been such as you now call Bishops, you would have rendered the Contents thus, *What is written to the Angels*, that is, *to the Bishops of Ephesus, &c.* But since you expound *Angels* thus, to be the *Ministers of these Churches*, who in vulgar appellation and acceptation are distinct from Bishops, and as you hold inferiour to them; you must now either renounce your own and our Churches exposition, and your Episcopacy: For if the Angels of these Churches be the most Eminent persons and rulers in them, as you argue; and these, as the Contents testifie, be not Bishops, but Ministers; it follows infallibly, that Ordinary Ministers and Presbyters, are superiour to Bishops, not Bishops to them. And that these Angels were the Ministers of these Churches, is evident by the expresse resolution of St. *Augustin*, Ep. 132 & Hom. 2. in Apoc. *Gregorius Magnus. Moralium in Job. l. 34. c. 4. Quod dicit Angelo Thyatiræ, dicit Præpositis Ecclesiarum, Sæpe sacram Scripturam Prædicatores Ecclesiæ pro eo, quod Patris gloriam annunciant ANGELORUM nomine solere designare: quod Johannes in Apocalypsi septem Ecclesiis scribens, ANGELIS Ecclesiarum loquitur*, id est, *PRÆDICATORIBUS POPULORUM*; And by the judgement of our own learned *James Pilkington*, late Bishop of *Durham*, in his *Exposition upon the Prophet Aggeus, c. 1. v. 13. London*, 1552. where he writes thus, That more worshipfull names are given to the Preaching Minister, than to any sort of men. This name *Angel*, is given to the Preachers, for the heavenly comfort that they bring to man from God, whose Messengers they be. In the *Revelations* of St. *John*, he writes to the 7. Angels, *i. e.* to the 7. Ministers (not Bishops) of the 7. Congregations or Churches in *Asia*. By this Bishops resolution then, these 7. Angels are 7. Preaching Ministers, not Lordly Non-preaching Prelates. And Mr. *Fox* in his *Meditations on Apoc. c. 2. p. 27, 28*. concurres with him; averring, That by the seven Angels, is meant either the *Ministers* of the seven Churches, or the Churches themselves; which exposition is as antient as f *Aretas*, g *Primasius*, and h *Ambrosius Ausbertus*, who in their Commentaries on *Apocalypsis* write thus. 'Septem 'stellæ Angeli sunt septem Ecclesiarum. Nec putandum est quod

f *Lib. 1. c. 1, 2, 9, 10.*
g *In Apoc. c. 2. Bibl. Patrum, Tom. 6. pars 1. p. 523.*
h *Lib. 1. in Apoc.*

## The Un-bishoping of Timothy and Titus. 113

'quod hoc loco Angeli singuli singulis deputentur homi-
'nibus, quod incongrue ab aliquibus æstimatur, sed potius
'Angeli Ecclesiæ hic intelligendi sunt rectores populi, qui
'singulis Ecclesiis præsidentes, verbum vitæ cunctis annun-
'ciant. Nam & Angeli nomen, nuncius interpretatum
'dicitur. Et Angelo Ecclesiæ Ephesi scribe. Dativo hic
'casu Angelo posuit, non Genitivo. Ac si diceret, Scribe
'Angelo huic Ecclesiæ, ut non tam Angelum & Ecclesiam
'separatim videatur dixisse, quam quis Angelus exponere
'voluisset, unam videlicet faciens Angeli Ecclesiæque per-
'sonam. Quamvis enim Sacramenti dispensatione præpo-
'natur, compaginis tamen unitate connectitur. Nam hanc
'regulam a principio servans, non septem Angelis, sed sep-
'tem Ecclesiis scripsisset; Johannes inquiens, *Septem Eccle-*
'*siis quæ sunt in Asia*, & Dominus quem vidit; *Scribe*, inquit,
'*in libro quæ vidisti, & mitte septem Ecclesiis.* Postea tamen
'Angelis jubet scribi, ut ostenderet, unum esse. Sed etiam
'si qua singulis partiliter Ecclesiis prædicat, universam ge-
'neraliter convenire docetur Ecclesiam. Neque enim di-
'cit, Quid spiritus dicat Ecclesiæ, sed Ecclesiis. Angelum
'ergo Ecclesiam significans, duas in eo partes ostendit,
'dum & laudat & increpat. In consequentibus autem
'manifestatur non eandem increpare quam laudat, sic ut
'Dominus in Evangelio ome præpositorum corpus, *unum    * Luk 12. Mat.
'servum dixit beatum & nequam, quem veniens Domi-     24.
'nus ipse dividet, & non tantum servum sed partem, in-
'quit, ejus cum Hypocritis ponet: Yea, *Ludovicus ab Al-*
*cafar*, a late Jesuite, in his *Commentary on the Apocalyps.* Antu  † See Gersomus
1614. Proem, inc. 2. K. 3. Notatio. 1. p. 250, 251. writes, That  Bucerus de Gu-
*Andreas, Aretas, Ansbertus, Anselmus, Pererius, Victorinus,*  bern. Ecclesiæ p.
*Ticinius, Ambrosius, Haymo & Beda* are of this opinion. *Ange-*  205, 393,408,
*lorum & stellarum nomine designari Ecclesias ipsas: That by the*  419, 422,433.
*name of Angels the Churches themselves are signified;* not the  Smectymnuus,
Lordly Prelates in them, not one antient Commentator  Answer to an
on this Chapter that I find, and few modern expounding  Humble Re-
these Angels to be Diocæsan Bishops, as our Prelates, against  monstrance. p.
all sense, will make them; yea, *Andreas Cesariensis, Comment.*  52, to 59.
*in Joan.* Apoc. c. 3. p. 8. writes, *Probabile sit per 7. Angelos,*
R                              *totius*

*totius universi gubernationem, quæ in dextera Christi, sicut omnes quoque terræ fines, sita est, hoc loco significari.* Since then by *Angels* is here meant either the Ministers of the Church of *Ephesus*, or the whole Church it self, or Chrifts Government over the Universe, as these Authors averre; this Text makes nothing at all for our Lordly Prelates Hierarchy.

Thirdly, It is observable that Saint *John* neither in his Gospel nor Epistles, nor in his Book of the *Revelation*, doth so much as once use the name or word Bishop, but the name of *Elder*, or *Presbyter* very often, both in his *Epistles*, and in the *Apocalyps*. I then appeal to any reasonable Creature, whether it is not more probable, that Saint *John* by this word *Angel*, should rather mean the *Elders or Presbyters of those Churches*; ( a Title which he gives himself, 2 *John* 1. 3 *Iohn* 1.) and which Title and Office he so i frequently mentions in the 4, 5, 7. and other Chapters of the *Apocalyps* next ensuing, than the Lordly Bishops of those Churches superiour to, or distinct from Presbyters, whose office (for ought appears) he never knew, and whose Title he never useth in his writings?

Fourthly, it is remarkable, that St. *John* doth ever place the 24. *Elders sitting on so many seats, next unto the Throne of Christ himself*; and the Angels standing farther off from the Throne without the Elders. If then by the Elders ( as is generally agreed by all ) be meant the Presbyters or Ministers of the Church, and by Angels, as you pretend, be meant Bishops; then the Presbyters must needs be more honourable by divine institution than the Bishops, because they are next to the Throne of Christ, and *I sit on seats* or chairs, whiles the *Angels* m *stand about them*. Adde to this, that these Elders are still introduced by St. *Iohn* in this Book, n *Worshipping and adoring God and Christ, and giving thanks, honour, praise, and glory unto them*; That they only are said to *have* o *Crowns of Gold upon their heads*, ( the badge of Soveraignty and Superiority) *and* p *harps and golden Vials in their hands, full of Odours, which are the Prayers of Saints*; That they q *sing the new Song*; And among other

i *Rev.* 4. 10 c.
5. 5, 8, 11, 14.
c. 7. 11, 13. c
11. 16. c. 19. 4.
c 14 3.

k *Rev.* 4. 4. c.
11. 16.

l *Rev.* 4. 4. c.
11. 16.
m *Rev.* 7. 11.
n *Rev* 4. 10,
11. c. 5. 8, 9.
. 11. 16, 17,
18
o *Rev.* 4. 4, 10.
p *Rev.* 5 8, 9.
q *Rev.* 5. 9.

other passages prayse Christ for this in special manner, *Rev.* 5. 10. And *hast made US* ( not Bishops ) *unto our God KINGS and PRIESTS, and we shall reign on the Earth*. Therefore Presbyters doubtlesse are the chief and principal Ministers in the Church of Christ by divine institution; and being thus made *Kings* and *Priests*, and *adorned with Crowns*, to the end *that they may reign upon the Earth*; no Prelates or Lord Bishops ought to rule over them, or climb Paramount them, as they do. Besides, these Elders not Bishops informed St. *John* himself and instructed him in the things he doubted of, *Revel.* 5. 4, 5. c. 7. 13, 14, 15, 17. Therefore these Elders must certainly be the better, the most eminent Scient men, and so Paramount the Angel-Bishops.

Fifthly, though the *Angel* be here named in the singular number, yet the *Elders* are still mentioned in the Plural. And as for the Church of *Ephesus* in those dayes, it is most certain by Acts 20. 17, 28. 1 *Tim.* 5. 17. *Rom.* 1. 20. That there were divers Elders, of *equal authority ruling in it*, whom the Holy Ghost expresly not only called, but *made Bishops and Overseers of that Church, both to rule and Feed it*. To make therefore one Bishop and Superintendent in this Church, superiour to all the rest, and he only graced with the name of an *Angel*, is but a crazie conceipt of a proud Episcopal brain, contrary to apparent Texts.

Sixthly. This Angel is not said to have any Jurisdiction or Superiority over other Ministers or Presbyters in the Church of *Ephesus*, nor to be the supreme or general Superintendent Prelate of that Church, neither is there any thing spoken of him with reference to any other Minister of *Ephesus*. What then can this poor Title make for Episcopal Priority and Jurisdiction? The Spirit writes to the Angel of the Church of *Ephesus*; Ergo this Angel was a Bishop, and superiour to all other Ministers of *Ephesus*, is a strange *non-sequitur*, and yet this is all this Text affords our Bishops.

Seaventhly, Bishop *Hall* and other Contenders for Episcopacy, grant that there were divers particular Churches and Congregations in and about *Ephesus*, every one of which had its several Minister or Presbyter to instruct them; else they could prove no Episcopacy or Diocæsan Superintendency from one particular Congregation. This being granted by him and his party; Let them then tell me seriously, whether this Angel, which they will not have taken collectively and Plurally, for the whole Presbytery and Ministery of that Church, as many antient and *modern Commentators expound it, but individually for one particular Person) should not rather be one particular Pastor of one of the Churches of *Ephesus* only, who had lost his first love, and therefore was worthily reprehended, then a Diocæsan Bishop or Archbishop of that Church to whose Jurisdiction all other Presbyters and Bishops of that National Church were subordinate, for which there is no ground in Scripture.

*[marginal note:]* † *Smectymnuus Answer to Bishop Hall, Remonstrance, p. 52, to 59.*

Eighthly, our * Prelates all plead very hard, *That Timothy was ordained the first Bishop of Ephesus, and dyed Bishop of that See*; which if I admit (though I think untrue) then it is clear, that this *Angel of Ephesus, who lost his first Love*, was famous and zealous *Timothy*, not dead when this Epistle was written, as r *Pererius* and ſ *Alcazar*, both Jesuites, with *Lyra, Rytera*, t *P. Halloix* and others confesse. And who dares be so presumptuous as to think *Timothy*, a man so eminent, famous, zealous, and so much applauded in Scripture, would prove an Apostate or Backslider, and *lose his first love* ? Either therefore you must deny *Timothy*, or this Angel to be the Bishop of this Church.

*[marginal note:]* * *Downham, Hall, Usher, and others.* r *In Apoc c. 2. 2. Disp. 2.* ſ *Com. in Apoc. in. c. 2, 3. Notatio 1. p. 251. where he cites Lyra and Rybera to this effect.*

Ninthly, admit this Angel to be a Bishop, yet it was only such a Bishop as was all one and the same with Presbyters, and of which there were u *many in one Church*: nor one over many Churches) according to the Holy Ghosts and the Apostles own institution; as appears by *Acts* 20. 17, 28. *Phil.* 1. 1. *Tit.* 1. 5. 7. compared with the 1 *Pet.* 5. 2, 3. *Lam.* 5. 14. *Act.* 14. 23. 1 *Tim.* 5. 17. Therefore it maketh nothing for, but directly against that Episcopacy, you contend for.

*[marginal note:]* u *Centur. Magd. l. 1. 2. c. 10 col. 626 Niceph l. 3. c. 71. Vincentius, spec. Hist. l. 33. c. 10 Fasciculus Temporum.*

Tenthly, Grant him such a Bishop as you would make him; yet at the best he was an Apostate, who had fallen
*from,*

### The Un-bishoping of Timothy and Titus. 117

*from, and lost his first love*, by being made a Lord Bishop. And it will be but little credit for our Prelates, to found their Hiearchy upon an Apostate: Yea, if I conjecture not amisse, this may be one probable reason, why so many Ministers prove Turncoats, Apostates, losing their first love, zeal to God and diligence in Preaching, when they are made Lord Bishops, because they have an *Apostate Angel*, both for their foundation, and imitation; Happy men be their dole; let them make the best of this Apostate, I will not hinder but rather pitty them in this folly.

Eleventhly, it is very observable, that as *Angels being all ministring Spirits, sent forth to minister for them who shall be heirs of Salvation*, have little care, and no need at all of temporal Lordships, Mannors, or Possessions. So the *Angels* of the Church of God ( ‖ *whose conversations and affections ought wholy to be fixed on Heaven, and Heavenly things, not on Earth, or Earthly things*, and to make it their only employment to instruct and save the peoples souls committed to their charge, *Act*. 20. 2. to 30.) have little or no desire, use or need at all of *Lordly Palaces, Mannors, Lordships, Great temporal Possessions, Revenues*, or Pontifical *Miters, Crosiers, Rochets, Vestments*; and indeed the *Angels* of the Church of *Ephesus*, and the other Churches of *Asia*, for ought appears, had no such Palaces, Temporalties, Lands, or Pontifical Vestments belonging to them, as their Successors now claim, enjoy, use, and most eagerly contend for: neither had the Primitive best and holiest Bishops for above 300. years after Christ, any such Temporal Possessions or Accouterments. Yea a *Johannis Parisiensis*, b *Polychronicon*, c *Nauclerus*, d *Wicliffe*, the e Lord *Cobham*, f *John Frith* (both Martyrs for Religion) g Bishop *Jewel*, h *Thomas Beacon*, and the last Translators of the *English Bible*, in their Epistle prefixed thereunto, unanimously record, *That when the Emperor Constantine the great, endowed the Bishops and Church with temporal Lands and Posses-*

\* Heb. 1. 14.

‖ Col. 3. 1, 2, 3. Phil. 3. 8, 20, 21.

a *De Utraque Potestate* c. 21.
b *Hist. l.* 4. c. 26.
c *Chronicon in vita Sylvestri.*
d *Dialogorum l.* 4. c. 15, 16, 17, 26.

e Fox *Acts and Monuments*, p. 517, 522.   f *Answer to the Preface of Mr. Moores book.* p. 116.
g *Sermon on Hag.* 1. p. 175. *Defence of the Apologie*, part 6. c. 9. divis. 3.   h *Reports of certain men*, Vol. 3. p. 341.

*sions,*

fions, the voice of AN ANGEL *was heard in the air, crying out thus against it,* HODIE VENENUM INFUNDITUR IN ECCLESIAM; This day IS POYSON poured into *the Church of God: And from that time* (these Authors observe) *because of the great riches the Church and Bishops had, they were made the more Secular, and had more worldly business than spiritual Devotion, and more pomp and boast outward, then holinesse inward.* Whence grew this common Proverb, *Ecclesia peperit divitias, & filia devoravit matrem*, The Church hath begotten riches, and the daughter hath devoured the mother; there being usually the least real Piety and Religion in Churches and Churchmen, where there is greatest Wealth and Temporal Possessions. Upon which consideration our famous English Apostle *i John Wicliffe*, and his followers, together with our three Martyrs, k *William Swinderby, John Purvie*, and Sir *John Old-Castle*, publickly maintained; *That the King and Temporal Lords greviously sinned in endowing the Bishops with ample temporal Possessions; which had reversed Christs ordinances, and procreated Antichrist*: and THAT THEY WERE BOUND IN CONSCIENCE *to take away their Lands and Temporalties from them, which they had abused to pride, ambition, luxury, discord: And that the Commons ought not to be burdened with Taxes, as long as the Church had any Patrimony left, which was given only by way of almes, to relieve the people in their poverty.* Yea since these godly Martyrs *Hooper* Bishop of *Glocester*, (Martyred in Queen *Maries* reign) in his Commentary upon the 8. Commandement, p. 76. writes expresly, *The Primitive Church had no such Bishops as we, they had such Bishops as did preach many godly Sermons in lesse time then our Bishops horses be a brideling. The Magistrates that suffer the abuse of these goods, be guilty of the fault.* IF THE FOURTH PART OF THE BISHOPRICK REMAINED TO THE BISHOP IT WERE SUFFICIENT; *the third to scholmasters, the second to poor, and* SOULDIERS, WERE BETTER BESTOWED. *If any be offended with me for this my saying, he loveth not his own health, nor Gods Laws nor mans, out of which I am alwaies ready to prove the thing I have said to be true:* So this Martyred Bishop, whom

i *Dialogorum l. 4. c. 15, 16, 17, 18. 25 27. Walsingham H. St. Angl. p. 302. to 307. Henry de Knyghton de Eventibus Angl. l. 5.*

k *Fox Acts and Monuments. p. 398, 414 431, 434.*

whom *l* Mr. *Elmer* (afterwards Bishop of *London*) thus seconds. *Come off ye Bishops, away with your superfluities,* YIELD UP YOUR THOUSANDS, BE CONTENT WITH HUNDREDS, AS THEY BE IN OTHER REFORMED CHURCHES, *where there are as great learned men as you are.* LET YOUR PORTION BE PRIESTLIKE, NOT PRINCELIKE, LET THE QUEEN HAVE THE REST OF YOUR TEMPORALTIES TO MAINTAIN WARS (and why not the King and Kingdoms now?) *and to build Schols throughout the Realm, that every Parish Church may have its Preacher, every City her Superintendent, to live not Pompously,* WHICH WILL NEVER BE UNLESSE YOUR POSSESSIONS BE DISPOSED AND BESTOWED UPON MANY, WHICH NOW FEED AND FAT BUT ONE, &c. If any of our Prelates deem it Sacrilege for *Kings and People to make use of the Treasures, Lands and Revenues of the Church and Bishops in times of War,* let them peruse the 1 *Kings* 14. 26. 2 *Kings* 14. 8. *c.* 24. 13. 2 *Chron.* 12. 9. *c.* 25. 24. *c.* 36. 18. *Ezra* 1. 7, 8. and learned *Hugo Grotius* (whom *m Episcopal Divines* much admire as well as most Lawyers and Statesmen) *De Jure Belli,* l. 3. c. 5. & *Annotata,* where he proves at large by many Presidents; *that as Wars make all sacred things, yea Temples and Churches themselves and their ornaments prophane and common to the Conquerors, and wholy to be at their absolute disposal* as *Deut.* 7. 5,6. *c.* 12. 2,3, 30, 31. *Judg.* 2. 2. *Psal.* 79. 1. 2 *Chron.* 36. 18. *Psal.* 74. 7,8,9. *Psal.* 83. 12. compared with the forecited Texts, *Theodoret* Eccles. Hist. l. 5. c. 10, 11, 12. and all ages evidence; So, *Populus ipse mutata voluntate, potest ex sacro prophanum facere, and imploy those Lands and Treasures in the \* Wars which they had formerly consecrated unto God,* whereof we have many Presidents in our own and forein Histories. All which considered, if our Bishops will be like the *Angels* in these Primitive Churches of *Asia* and *Ephesus,* they must quit all their large Temporal Lands and Possessions to the King, from whom they received them, and who alwaies enjoyed them during the vacancies of their Sees in right of the Crown, from whom they were derived, to defray the publick expences of the Kingdom in these

*l Harbour for faithfull Subjects Printed at Strasburg*

*m Dr. Hamond in his Annotations on the New Testament.*

*\* Much more then in this late War, which some Bishops stiled* BELLUM EPISCOPALE

these times of need; And truly were all Appropriation, and Impropriations now belonging to Archbishops, Bishops Deans and Chapters (amounting at this day to above fifty thousand pounds a year) made presentable, and the Deans and Chapters Lands imployed in purchasing in all Impropriations belonging to Colledges, Hospitals, Freescholes, Corporations and Gentlemen, to make them presentable for the benefit of the peoples souls and bodies, according to their true original intention and donatior; The Clergy of *England* would enjoy a far better and properer Patrimony and Maintenance, equally distributed between them, than all their Temporalties and Spiritualties put together, do now amount unto, of which a few Lazie, non-preaching, or rare-preaching Prelates, Deans, and Prebends and their Farmers, now reap the greatest benefit. But of this, no more at present.

Finally, (Whatever (a) *Dionysius* and others fancy to the contrary, of the *different Orders and Degrees* among *Angels*) it is evident beyond contradiction, by all the Marginal (b) *Texts* of Scripture, that the *Angels of God* are all equal in order, power, dignity, office, degree, Ministry, none of them exercising any Dominion, Jurisdiction or Authority over another Angel, much lesse such Lordly power or authority, as our Archbishops and Bishops claim or use over other Ministers; And as that of Christ himself, *Lu.* 20.36. *Neither can they die any more,* for THEY ARE EQUAL UNTO THE ANGELS, *and are the children of God, and of the Resurrection*; proves an equality or parity among the *Angels* themselves; and between Saints and Angels after the Resurrection: so these words of the *Angel* himself to St. *John* (c) an ELDER) *when he fell down at his feet to worship him*; Rev. 19. 10. c. 20. 9: *see thou do it not, for I AM THY FELLOW-SERVANT, and of THY BRETHREN THE PROPHETS, worship God*, resolve; That *Angels* and *Elders* are *Fellow-Servants* and Equals, and therefore no ordination or worship is to be rendered by one of them to the other. Which compared with *Mat.* 18. 28, to 34. c. 24. 49. Col. 1. 7. c. 4. 7, 10. 2 Cor. 8. 29. Phil. 1. 23.

2 Thes.

*a De Cœlesti Hierarchia.*
*b Psf* 8. 5. *Psf* 9 1. 11. *Psf* 10;. 29. *Psf*. 104. 4. *Psf* 148. 1. *Mat* 4. 12. c. 13. 38, 49. c. 18. 10. c. 24. 30. c. 25. 35. *Mar.* 8. 38. *Lu.* 2. 15. c. 12. 18. *l.* 15. 10. c. 16. 21. c. 20. 36. *Rom.* 8. 38. 1 *Cor.* 4. 9. c. 20. 35. c. 6. 3 2 *Thes.* 1. 7. 1 *Tim.* 3. 16 c. 5. 21. *Heb.* 1. 4, 5, 7, 13, 14. c. 2. 2, 5, 15. c. 12. 22. 1 *Pet.* 1. 12. c 3. 22. 2 *Pet* 2. 11. *Jud.* 6. *Rev.* 5. 11. c. 3. 5. c 7. 21. c. 8. 2 c. 12. 3.
*c* 2 *John* 2. 3. *Jhn* 1.

## The Un=bishoping of Timothy and Titus.

2 Thes. 3. 2, 3. John 8. Rev. 6. 11. styling all *Evangelists, Ministers* and *Preachers of the Gospel, Fellow-Servants, Fellow-workers, Fellow-helpers, &c.* are an unanswerable evidence of the *Parity, Equality* of all *Angels, Elders, Ministers,* Bishops by Divine Institution; and utterly subverts the pretended Divine Lordly Hierarchy, Jurisdiction, and Superiority of Bishops over Ministers, from the Angels of the 7. Churches, founded in *Rev.* 1. 20. & c. 2. 1. As for the supposed Superiority and Authority of Bishops over other Elders and Ministers in the Primitive Church for 300. years or more after the Apostles, it was no other, no greater than the (d) Presidents in General, or National Councils, over the Councils themselves, and their respective Members, or of Prolocutors in our Convocations, of Speakers of the Lords or Commons Houses in Parliaments, of Chair-men in respective Committees, of Judges or Justices of Peace, who give the Charge or Judgement at Assises or Quarter Sessions, of Foremen of Grand-Juries, and Petty Juries, over the rest of the Convocations, Lords, Commons, Committees, Judges, Justices, and Jury-men; being nothing else but a priority of *order, session, place, nomination, or direction,* not of *Jurisdiction, Power* or *Degree,* for which there is no ground in Scripture or Antiquity.

Having thus through Gods assistance, briefly, clearly, and I hope irrefragably subverted the three main Pillars of our Lordly Bishops divine right of Superiority over other Ministers, and sole power of Ordination by Evangelical institution, (which * *Bishop Hall* asserts to be so inseparable to Episcopacy, that he would fain see where it can be shewed, That any *extremity of necessity was* ever acknowledged a *warrant sufficient to others to ordain*; ) I cannot but fore-see their near approaching downfall, unlesse they will henceforth renounce their pretended Papal claim of Episcopal Jurisdiction by a *Divine Title,* and betake themselves wholly and solely to the Kings Grace; deriving all their *superior Jurisdiction in and over all other Ecclesiastical persons and causes only from the Kings special Grants and Commissions,* and exercising it in his Royal name, style, right and authority, according

d *Quid est enim Episcopus nisi primus Presbyter? &c. Augustin, quæst. ex utroque Test. mixtim qu.* 100. *See Gersomus Bucerus de Gubernatione Ecclesiæ: David. Blondelli Apolog. pro sententia Hieronymi, de Episcopis & Presbyteris, Mr. Rutherfords due Right of Presbyteries, Centur. Magd.* 1, 2, 3, 4. ch. 6.
* *Episcopacy by Divine Right* part 2. p 91.

...ording to the Statutes of 26 H. 8. c. 1. 37 H. 8. c. 17. 1 Ed. 6. c. 2. 1 Eliz. c. 1. 5 Eliz. c. 1. 8 Eliz. c. 1. and abandon all their injurious incroachments upon our Kings Prerogative, the Ministers and Peoples just Privileges, Liberties, Consciences; the only means to allay and silence all future Controversies of this nature, and to establish Peace and Unity in our Church. And seeing many of them have long since dishonoured and forsaken God, given over or much neglected the constant *preaching of his Word, the chief part * of their Spiritual functions*, banded themselves against his truth, Ministers, people, and the preaching of his Gospel, which they suppress and put down in all places; yea such is their desperate impiety, that whereas in all former times of Plagues and Pestilence, (yea in ‖ 1 *Iacobi* & 1 *Caroli*) there hath been by publick authority a special day of fasting, prayer, preaching, and humiliation appointed every week, (especially in infected places) to divert Gods heavy judgements, as the *chief antidote against all Plagues and judgments*, a *prescribed by God himself*; yet now they are grown such open *Fighters against God*, Religion, the Spiritual, Temporal good and safety of the people, that to prevent the Plague, (as they pretend, but in truth to increase it more, and to suppress Preaching, Piety and Religion) they begin to put down all *weekday Lectures, and Lords day Sermons in the Afternoon*, (as if Gods publick Ordinances and Service, the best remedy against, were a means to increase and spread, not stay the Plague) yea they *debar* (*b*) *Ministers from using any Prayer at all after their Sermons, or any other Prayer before them, than what the* 55. *Canon prescribes*, in which there is not a word of prayer against the Plague, Drought, Famine, Sword or Pestilence. By means whereof, and by inhibiting Ministers to reprove the people for their sins, which provoke Gods wrath and judgements at this present, to bring them to repentance for them by their preaching; or to *pray against the Plague and other judgements of God, which now lye heavy upon the Kingdom*, and these sins have occasioned; by hindring that publick weekly fasting, preaching, prayer, which God by his

*judgements*

\* *The Instit. of a Christian manCh of Orders, and Thomas Beacons Catech. f.* 499, 500.
‖ *See the Fastbooks then printed.*
a *Joel* 2. 14, 19 20. 4. 2. 1, to 28. *Isay* 12. 12, 13, 14. 1 *Chron.* 6, 10 24, 30, 40. c. 7. 13, 14. 15. *Zeph.* 2. 1, 2, 3 *Jonah* 3. 5, 10 10 *Ezech.* 9. 4. *Mal.* 3. 16, 17 *Ezra* 9 & 10.
b *See Bishop Wrens Injunctions for Norwich, and his Visitation Articles, yet this Canon binds them not strictly to any form as the Words. Or to this effect, declare.*

Judgements (c) *now calls for at our hands; and* countenancing *all prophane Revels, Wakes, Churchales, Maygames, Dancing, Enterludes, Pastimes on the Lords day;* they have made not only the Kingdome, but themselves especially, ripe for ruine. And being now for these their atheisticall godless practises, their enmity to God, his truth, his faithfull Ministers and people, their Lordliness, tyranny, pride, oppression, worldlyness, prophaneness, and irreligion fallen under the very (d) *execration of God himself,* and (e) the curses of his People, who day and night cry for Vengeance against them, as Gods sworn and most professed open enemies, and having no divine foundation, prop, or Pillar now left, wherewith to support their tottering Thrones and Miters, needs must they shortly, like that (f) *High Priest Ely, fall from their high-towring Seats backward,* and so break their Necks, to the joy of all Gods people, whom they now by their persecutions and innovations so much oppress and offend; (g) *Even so let all thine enemies perish, O Lord; but let them that love thee, be as the Sun, when it goeth forth in his might.*

c *Jer.* 7. 16. c. 11. 14. c. 14. 11. c. 29. 7. c. 37. 3, 4. c 42. 2. 4, 40. *Joel.* 2. 17.
*Isay* 22. 12, 13.
\* See Canterburies Doom, p. 122, to 226, 504, 505, 506, 377, 378.
d *Psal.* 119. 21 *Judges* 5. 23. *Mal.* 2. 2. c. 3 9. 1 *Cor.* 16. 22.
e *Luke* 18. 3, to 30. *Rev.* 6. 9, 10. *Psal.* 28. 4, 5.
f 1 *Sam.* 4. 18.
g *Judges* 5. 31.

Bern. Homil. 1. *De laudibus Mariæ Virginis* (writ when he was \* *pressed to accept, and yet refused the Bishopricks of Genoa, and Millain*) Erubesce superbe cinis; Deus se humiliat, tu te exaltas? Deus se hominibus subdit, tu Dominari gestiens tuo te præponis authori. Quotiens, hominibus præ se desidero, totiens Deum meum præire contendo, & tunc quæ veré Dei sunt, non sapio.

\* *Cl. Espencæus Digres. in* 1 *Tim.* l. 3. c. 6.

# FI𝒩IS.

# ERRATA.

PRay correct thefe Miftakes at the Prefs, p. 6. l. 21. r. *Fathers*. p. 16. l. 17. r. *Title*. p. 17. l. 4. r. *Bifhop*. p 23. l. 13. *Paul*, r. *Timothy*. p. 32. l. 11. r. *Davidis*. p. 38. l. 29. *but*. p. 48. l. 18. *Sons*. p. 53. l. 1. ordinary, r. *ordaining*. l. 11. r. *conſtitutions*. l. 34. r. *fidem*. p. 55. l. 27. r. *Law*. l. 32. others, r. *the other*. p. 57. l. 6. r. *either*. *in* l. 12. they. p. 60. l. 13. r. *folemus*. p. 61. l. 15. *Act*. p. 64. l. 5. *diffonant*. l. 16. *Taborites*. p. 68. l. 30. r. 5, & 6 E. 6. c. 1. p. 72. l. 22. r. *Presbyters*. l. 38. endeavour. p 73. l. 36. dele *who*. p. 74. l. 25. r. *Laud*. p. 80. l. 35. deprived, r. derived. p. 91. l. 22. Scotland, r. *Ireland*. l. 28. *Juri*. p. 92. l. 17. *Monachorum*. l. 32. *inceſſu*. p. 93. l. 2. *deberent*. p. 93. l. 8. *Abbot*. p. 94. l. 12. *Wiclevists*. p. 101. l. 19. *Hæreſes*. p. 108. l. 2. dele *hath*, p. 110. l. 18. as, r. *are*.

Margin. p. 30. l. 6. *Hieronymi*, p. 49. l. 2. 1 E &c. r. 8 *Eliz*: p. 53. l. 1. codius. r. *codicis*. l. 18. r. *clementis octavi*. l. 22. r. *Presbyteri*. p. 81. l. 12: 7, r. 20. p. 85. l. 14. Minifter, r. *Munfters*. p. 92. l. 3. r. *Eremo*. l. 9. *Hieronymi*.

---

### Errata *in the Epiſtles*.

P. 6. l. 3. read *Spiers*. l. 28. *Eucherius*, p. 7. l. 3. dele *in*. l. 7. *Epifcopari*. l. 9. gave, r. *give*. l. 24. Semines, r. *Senus*. p. 10. l. 11. r. *Carnotenfis*, p. 23. l. 7. korols, r. *knols* p. 24. l. 9. r. *but he*.

*In the Margin*. P. 2. l. 18. defire, r. *deflier*. p. 7. l. 4. r. Edit. *Pamelii*. l. 11. Sonat. r. *Socrates*. l. 18. r. *Nicephorus*. p. 9. l. 18. *Cælacus*. p. 15. l. 3. Heromanum, r. *Hermannum*. p. 24. l. 11. part, r. *page*.

www.ingramcontent.com/pod-product-compliance
Lightning Source LLC
Chambersburg PA
CBHW030300170426
43202CB00009B/818